English Literature in History

Already published

1350–1400
Medieval Readers and Writers
Janet Coleman

1730–80
An Equal, Wide Survey
John Barrell

1780–1830
Pastoral and Politics
Roger Sales

In preparation

1580–1640
Margot Heinemann

English Literature in History

1780–1830
Pastoral and Politics

Roger Sales

Hutchinson

London Melbourne Sydney Auckland Johannesburg

Hutchinson & Co. (Publishers) Ltd

An imprint of the Hutchinson Publishing Group

17–21 Conway Street, London W1P 6JD

Hutchinson Group (Australia) Pty Ltd
30–32 Cremorne Street, Richmond South, Victoria 3121
PO Box 151, Broadway, New South Wales 2007

Hutchinson Group (NZ) Ltd
32–34 View Road, PO Box 40–086, Glenfield, Auckland 10

Hutchinson Group (SA) (Pty) Ltd
PO Box 337, Bergvlei 2012, South Africa

First published 1983

© Roger Sales 1983

Set in VIP Times Roman

Printed in Great Britain by the Anchor Press Ltd
and bound by Wm Brendon & Son Ltd
both of Tiptree, Essex

British Library Cataloguing in Publication Data
  Sales, Roger
    English literature in history 1780–1830
    1. English literature – History and criticism
    I. Title
    820'.9   PR83
ISBN 0 09 149830 9 cased
      0 09 149831 7 paper

For Bill and Katharine Sales,
great parents and scholars

Contents

Editor's introduction

'Literature' and 'history' are common names for two obviously related but apparently distinct bodies of human activity. By 'literature' we commonly mean certain kinds of writing, though at different times, and on different occasions, we often use the term variably, over a range from all printed writing, through printed writing of a certain quality, to the important specialized sense of a body of 'imaginative' writing. Further, because of this last sense, we often extend the term 'literature' to include 'imaginative' composition which was not primarily written to be printed but to be spoken or in some other immediate way performed. Thus 'literature' in the important but narrow sense of printed imaginative writing of a certain quality belongs, in fact, to a specific historical period, after the invention of printing, after further specializations, and before the invention of modern media of delivery and performance (especially radio and sound recording). At the same time, however, our thinking about literature, from the experience of that specific period, is commonly extended before and after it, to other related forms of composition.

These shifting meanings of 'literature' bear closely on the question of its actual and presumed relations with 'history'. Moreover, 'history' itself has a significant range of reference. At its broadest it indicates the sum and detail of all human actions. When this is so it must be held that it already includes the making of literature. In practice, however, 'history' is most commonly used to indicate general and specific accounts of such actions, grouped by period and by place. That is 'history' as an account, a narrative, and the writing of history, in this sense, is often reasonably seen as a form of 'literature'. Regularly, however, this element of account or narrative is overridden by the sense that the actions really occurred, at a level independent from their narration. Historical inquiry is often a continuous and detailed comparison of the received accounts or narratives and what can be shown, from other forms of evidence and record, to have actually taken place. Literature, in some respects, seems different from this process of historical inquiry, in that its works appear to have a relatively fixed form.

Any inquiry into the relations between 'literature' and 'history' has at some point, if it is to be adequate, to recognize these variable and shifting senses of the primary indicative terms. In recent years there has been widespread recognition of the inherent complexities of reference and evidence which these considerations emphasize. This is why there has been a move away from previous methods of inquiry, even when many of their results have been noted and respected. What is now felt as most difficult is the simple assumption that there is, on the one hand, a relatively unproblematic body of 'literature', with its own inherent and autonomous qualities, and on the other hand, a body of general and summary knowledge which is, correspondingly, 'history'. For if these two bodies existed, in simple ways, the study of 'literature and history' would be a matter of tracing and illustrating evident connections between them, in ways that illuminated both but altered neither. That assumption produced a good deal of interesting work, of two kinds. The possessors of 'history' illustrated aspects of their material from the literature of the time, going naturally to those works in which the connections were evident, and feeling no need to deal with those works in which such connections seemed to be absent. Meanwhile the possessors of 'literature' looked to history as a 'background', against which, in a foregrounded emphasis, works of literature occurred. It was then mainly when 'background' and 'foreground' evidently connected in discoverable and explicable ways, that history – parts of the history – became relevant.

Each of these methods was fundamentally selective and partial, and was at its best when this was recognized to be so. Yet paradoxically the confidence of the initial assumptions – the assumed possession of the bodies of 'literature' and 'history' – tended in practice to produce effects of completeness. The 'background' showed all the history that was relevant. The illustrative literature was all the writing of historical significance. Confident accounts of whole periods, extending in secondary work to fully reasoned catalogues of 'a period and its literature' or 'the literature of a period', had an intended and often achieved effect of completeness.

It is of course easier to criticize these conventional methods than to find better practical ways. Yet one result of this new sense of inherent difficulty has been a widespread retreat from the problems. This has been notably assisted by theoretical developments in which the significance of 'history' has been widely questioned and even denied. In some formalist and structuralist tendencies in literary studies the whole effort at correlation has been declared to be *a priori* irrelevant, and much has been made of the undoubted errors of externality and reduction which could be found in previous studies. Yet these errors cannot reasonably be used to justify the much more fundamental error of declaring an arbitrary distance between the acts of writing and other kinds of human action. It has been useful to define actual and variable distances, but to expand and stabilize them as an *a priori* refusal of relationships is merely evasive. However, it is in this more qualified and sceptical environment that new inquiries into such relationships have in practice to be undertaken.

The aim of the present series is to provide a place for essays of an open investigative kind, which do not have from the outset to be committed, or to pretend to be committed, to explanatory completeness. Its emphasis is on literature *in* history: the study of actual works, practices and conditions, in a particular place and period: some 'literary', some 'historical', but never assumed to belong, by definition, to pre-formed bodies of 'literature' and 'history'. Its authors were invited to choose a period of English life, typically but not exclusively of some fifty years, and then within that period (though looking before and after if it was necessary to clarify or complete an argument) to select two or three themes, in which the relations between actual writing and actual historical events and conditions seemed interesting and important. No author was asked to represent these themes as a whole account of the chosen period, though it is obvious that in choosing their themes authors have taken what they believe to be significant elements of that time. The method of inquiry and presentation then adopted has been the author's own choice of a method appropriate to the actual theme or themes.

It is hoped that as the series develops there will be a broad range of such themes and essays, over the whole run of English writing. It is possible that in particular periods there will be more than one book, representing different selections of themes. Moreover, several authors will have seen each other's work, and there will be cross-reference and discussion. A definite area and style of work

Part One
The politics of pastoral

1 The propaganda of the victors

Before nostalgia

A recent *Punch* cartoon shows a married couple watching television together. The husband asks his wife if she remembers the good old days before nostalgia. Pastoralism is nostalgia for the good old days. We are probably due for a nostalgic wallow in the 1960s fairly soon. Those of us who were shaken up during those stirring times may feel that they ought to be painted acne and all, yet we shall undoubtedly be asked to view them again through the softly out-of-focus colours of an aperitif commercial. The pastoral perspective takes the form of a blurred long-shot rather than a tight close-up. The couple in the cartoon may have been watching a period soap opera, but they could just as easily have been glued to the commercials, which represent the pastoral perspective in all its synthetic glory. No ghost is invited to these nostalgic celebrations of the good old days before mass advertising, where small is beautifully profitable and all times when old are good business. The pastoral perspective is also at work in most family photograph albums. Unpleasant faces and places have been edited out, as the family camera's eye is there to highlight the highlights. It does not move in for a close-up of the kitchen sink. Do you remember the good old days before colour photography? It was all so simple then.

Pastoralism is composed of the famous five Rs: refuge, reflection, rescue, requiem and reconstruction. Refuge represents the desire for escape, pure and simple. Although this may take the form of an escape from urban complexity to rural simplicity, this need not always be the case. Pastoral is the great escape from adult experience to childhood innocence. Small really was rather beautiful then. It is thus perfectly possible to have urban, and indeed suburban, versions of pastoral. Pastoral is an escape to another country where things are done differently as innocence and simplicity order the sunny days.

The mere juxtaposition of innocence and experience, simplicity and complexity is not a particularly challenging exercise. Yet pastoral is about distances as well as ultimate destinations. Distance can be used just to lend enchantment to the view, but it may also be used more strategically to reflect upon the relative merits of past and present. There may be carefully arranged freeze-frames of this other country, but they are usually accompanied by a voice-over narration that inevitably casts shadows over the picture. These shadows come from the knowledge that this other country can only be seen from a distance in the distance. It may even be a mirage or product of the distance. Thus reflection may not just take the form of thoughts on emotional, geographical and temporal distances. Pastoral may merely reflect or mirror the present in the past.

Pastoral's reflective rather than purely descriptive impulse can be seen in attempts to rescue certain values from the past. Reflection breeds selection. I know on reflection that the good old days can only provide a temporary refuge from pent-up environments and emotions, yet I still think that it is worth trying to import some of these simple values back into the modern world. I slap a preservation order on the past, but this is intended to stimulate the appreciation and collection of antique values. It certainly enhances their value. The pastoral poet loves to stuff his den with antiquity, yet uncultured historians prevent him from enjoying his collection by pointing out that it consists of craftily arty reproductions. These antiques merely reflect what the present feels the past ought to have been like. Values are rescued for purely personal reasons, but there are usually attempts at social rescue and restoration as well. The posture of contemporary society as a whole might be reformed if enough simple, solid oak furniture was imported from this other country.

The problem with social rescue is that values only tend to be defined as such because of their exclusive, limited appreciation. Requiem also complicates the transition from the personal to the social. The pastoral idiom affects a reflective melancholia at the transitory nature of life, but tries to locate and isolate still points of permanence. Arcadia can be hermetically sealed off so that death has no dominion there. We are more likely, however, to encounter the suggestion, made through the strategic devices of reflection and rescue, that though times unfortunately change, values do not. Pastoral may attempt to evade and elude mortality in this way, but it is also a celebration of death. This is the pastoral paradox. The values may only be values for the connoisseur, yet, at a much deeper level, they only become values when they are quite literally still or dead. This accounts for the circular nature of pastoral. The past is described and reflected upon. It is conceived, born again and nurtured in the poetic imagination, but its beginning must inevitably be its end as it is always doomed to be still-born. We cannot raise the dead and they are unable to rescue us. We can, however, praise and celebrate the dead.

Refuge, reflection, rescue and requiem all sustain the illusion that pastoral deals with universally acknowledged truths. It is, however, deceptive and prescriptive. It offers a political interpretation of both past and present. It is a propagandist reconstruction of history. It often employs what Dr Goebbels used to call the 'great lie' theory of propaganda.[1]* An audience is lulled into a false sense of empirical security by being told relatively unimportant things that are demonstrably true. Topographical details work well like this. Then the 'great lie' is smuggled in among such a collection of platitudes. The 'great lie' in pastoral concerns its presentation of change. Economic change in rural society is invariably presented as an external agency, despite the fact that rural society carried the seeds of its own destruction within itself. Capitalism was really quite at home in both the long and short grass of rural England. Late eighteenth- and early nineteenth-century pastoral was thus propaganda for the establishment in general and the aristocracy in particular. It conveniently ignored the fact that it was their stark economic addition which often caused cold comfort at the farm. Previous reflections on the nature of nature paraded a down-to-the-salt-of-the-earth populism and a prolier-than-thou egalitarianism. It would be fondly foolish to take all this at face value, for pastoral endorsed the essentially aristocratic codes of conspicuous consumption, idle ease and languid leisure. Oaten reeds merely disguised aristocratic deeds. It is customary to notice the domestication of these aristocratic codes in the transition from Renaissance through Neo-classical to Romantic idioms. Yet pastoral still provided sheep's clothing for aristocratic wolves, or indeed for anybody who was on the side of the victors in the civil war which was fought for control of rural society. Reconstruction is the most important of the famous five Rs. Economic distances are more important than geographical or temporal ones. Before you become too nostalgic about the merry old days of rural England, it is worth

* Superior figures refer to the Notes and references on pages 232–40.

thinking about which groups have a vested interest in such nostalgia.

Cooking the books

Robert Bloomfield was an agricultural labourer from Suffolk who reaped a bumper harvest in 1800 with a poem called *The Farmer's Boy*. It sold 26,000 copies and sped into seven editions within three years of publication. William Wordsworth was an also-ran by comparison, since *Lyrical Ballads* sold hundreds rather than thousands of copies. Bloomfield had worked down on the farm, but was forced to move to the big city in 1781 as he was unemployed. His two elder brothers, who had also been forced to migrate to London, eventually found him a job as a cobbler. He began to play back his impressions of country life when he was pent up in the city. He explained to his white-haired old mother how distance lent enchantment to the view:

though I am acquainted with the principle alterations and deaths and changes, children grown to men and women since aged, the first thought, I meen whenever I'm thinking of other things my mind returns to the country, for the first moment, it allways presents the old picture. I see my old master of the farm instead of my cousin, and can see in imagination my old neighbours and things just as they were . . . being allways shut up in a garrot I am debard from pleasures which I have so strong a relish . . . .[2]

Rural society provided a refuge from the outrageous misfortunes of metropolitan life. Bloomfield's reflections took the form of a freeze-frame in which rural and childhood innocence were inextricably connected. These were the values he wanted to rescue. Yet the picture is an old one, which depicts 'things just as they were'. Rescue itself becomes inextricably connected with requiem. The frame is frozen because a consideration of change and decay would shatter comforting illusions. One of the changes that would lend disenchantment to the view was the economic fact of rural life that farmers' boys had to migrate to London. The pastoral perspective may affect to present 'things just as they were', but it reconstructs the past to lighten the shadows of the present.

Bloomfield clung to this pastoral perspective even though he had had a close-up of the unacceptable face of rural society. His unpublished correspondence contains references to 'grinding' farmers and agrarian capitalism:

the shining part of the community – they go to market with the fruit of other people's labour, and then with a double chatter score it up to their own industry and hard striving . . . .[3]

His comments on poor law relief and the French Revolution indicate that he was a politically conscious artisan. Yet he was himself something of a double chatterer, since he preferred to split his personality between the farmer's boy and the artisan. He was conscious of this split, just as he was conscious of the way in which the pastoral perspective operated. He outlined a plan for a poetic come-back in 1814:

I sometimes dream that I shall one day venture again before the public, something in my old manner, some country tales, and spiced with love and courtship might yet please, for Rural life by the art of cooking may be made a relishing and high flavoured dish, whatever it may be in reality.[4]

Pastoralism cooks the economic books. There were personal and psychological reasons for this kind of culinary sleight-of-hand, as he himself indicated in his letter to his mother. There were also social pressures on any pastoral poet to serve up something to the taste of the reading public. Bloomfield was only just cobbling together a living when he wrote *The Farmer's Boy*. He appears to have been concerned to profit as well as to please. He therefore cut and edited the childhood images to please the reading public as well as himself. The unacceptable face of rural society had to remain on the cutting-room floor.

 The Farmer's Boy became a best-seller partly because Bloomfield was regarded as a curiosity. Like John Clare, he became something of a literary elephant man. There were also literary and political reasons for his popularity. *The Poetical Register, The Critical Review* and *The British Critic* all paid tribute to the way in which his version of pastoral was particular and detailed. It could be incorporated into arguments against Neo-classical idioms. Alexander Pope had argued in his 'A Discourse on Pastoral Poetry' (1709) that true pastoral had to be as untrue as possible, since it should be concerned with the ideal rather than the actual. It was a standard literary game in the eighteenth-century to juxtapose the ideal with the coarser English reality. This was part of the increasing tendency for pastoral to describe places like home. The reviewers made a little too much of Bloomfield's original contribution to this debate. William Hazlitt was right to point out in his *Lectures on the*

English Poets (1818) that in retrospect *The Farmer's Boy* was a remarkably conventional poem. He suggested that Bloomfield's literary and social insecurity had led to heavy reliance on familiar eighteenth-century models. He also felt that in adapting such models for his own purposes Bloomfield had missed the main point of them:

> Bloomfield never gets beyond his own experience; and that is somewhat confined. He gives the simple appearance of nature, but he gives it naked, shivering, and unclothed with the drapery of a moral imagination. (p. 188)

The reviewers did manage to incorporate Bloomfield's homely rather than heroic version of pastoral into debates about the nature of nature, but Hazlitt's criticism of the poem suggests that there might have been more important reasons for its popularity.

It soon becomes apparent from a study of contemporary reviews and correspondence that this literary debate was part of a wider political one. Bloomfield's sense of place was being defined in political as well as literary terms. He was successful because he knew that the reading public expected farmers' boys to show that they were blissfully contented with their place in society. Literary criticism, then as now, was merely a peg on which various social prejudices were hung. Bloomfield's reception may be related to that of James Woodhouse, who was also a cobbler who cobbled together verse in his spare time. Woodhouse and his aged parents were invited in 1767 to stay with Edward Montagu, who fancied himself as a literary patron. Montagu later described the effect that this visit had had on him to his blue-stocking wife, Elizabeth:

> all this honest heartfelt happiness below darted many rays of joy up into my dressing room. There is something so angelick in Paternal tenderness and filial piety that I shared inexpressible delight in this happy assembly. I left them all, begging old Mr. Woodhouse to stay at Sandleford to ye end of next week that I might have ye pleasure of thinking they were all happy.[5]

Ye Woodhouse clan proved that paternalism was alive and well. 'Upstairs' could rest assured that all was well with the world since 'downstairs' really knew and loved their place. Those who could not afford to give old man Woodhouse the run of his teeth in the servants' quarters bought pastoral poetry instead. The effect was more or less the same. Bloomfield was popular because he too managed to dart 'rays of joy' into thousands of dressing rooms. If he knew his place, then perhaps the other labourers and artisans did as well. Joy was a valuable commodity in 1800, after a decade of political and social tension. As Bloomfield endorsed the pastoral belief in a responsible paternalism, or welfare estate, he provided the ideal antidote to a political shoemaker called Thomas Hardy, who had been the first Secretary of the London Corresponding Society. Pastoralism became an essential part of the counter-revolution. The pastoral idiom had always tended to endorse the *status quo*. Its political statements became shriller and more explicit during the period of the agricultural revolution and the Napoleonic wars.

Bloomfield was marketed to the reading public as a paragon of British virtues. He was, apparently, a great believer in passive domesticity. Quiet neighbour Bloomfield would give you no trouble. It was argued in a parliamentary debate in 1802 on bull-baiting that his passive pursuits were much safer and sounder than such rowdy sports. This was going a little too far for great traditionalists like William Windham. He felt that Bloomfield might actually represent the thin end of the Jacobin wedge. Those who had been 'bred to a useful trade' ought not to desert their station in life. Who would plough the fields and mend the shoes, if labourers became poets? Any degree of literacy amongst the people meant potential recruits for the infernal Corresponding Societies, while

out of the whole number of the disaffected, he questioned if a single bull-baiter could be found, or if a single sportsman had distinguished himself in the Corresponding Society.

The 'jolly bull-baiting peasant' was always going to be a patriotic member of the local militia, while a literate one was going to be a troublesome barrack-room lawyer at best.[6] Windham's hostility towards Bloomfield may have had something to do with the fact that *The Farmer's Boy* was associated with a leading patrician radical named Capell Lofft. His prefaces to Bloomfield's poems did have a radical edge to them, although they were essentially concerned with preaching a message of unity and community. Political rivalry may well have conditioned Windham's extreme reaction against Bloomfield. This provides an excellent example of the way in which literary criticism was merely a peg on which various political and social prejudices were hung. The fact that pastoral poetry was discussed in the House of Commons confirms the interpretation that a version of pastoral was judged as a statement of political creed. Like Clare, Bloomfield moved from the shadows of obscurity to the sunshine of popularity because, despite certain differences of opinion, it was felt that his life and poetry supported the *status quo*. Oaten reeds had always endorsed aristocratic deeds, but it was important in this particular period that the reed should be played by a real farmer's boy. The Duke of Grafton, who was the local landowner partially responsible for the fact that the Bloomfield brothers had been forced to uproot themselves, invited the poet to pay a visit to his estate in Suffolk. Bloomfield had an uncomfortable time since he was made to feel that he did not really belong downstairs any more. The Duke did not notice this unease as he was much too busy basking in 'rays of joy' upstairs. Bloomfield's reconstruction of rural society was very comforting. He made sure that his book was popular by cooking the economic books.

Pie in the sky

William Cobbett stopped to ask directions from a little girl when he rode through West Stratton on 17 November 1822. He noticed that she was carrying a religious tract in her hand. His description of the incident in *Rural Rides* (1830) shows that this acted like a red rag to a John Bull:

It *must* create hypocrites, and hypocrisy is the great sin of the age. Society is in a *queer* state when the rich think, that they must *educate* the poor in order to insure their *own safety*: for this, at bottom, is the great motive now at work in pushing on the education scheme, though in this particular case, perhaps, there may be a little enthusiasm at work. (p. 72)

Evangelical christianity was aiding and abetting the counter-revolution. Cobbett believed that these tracts were no substitute for proper wages and working conditions. A pig in the sty was much better than a counter-revolutionary poke in the eye. The rich started to educate the poor with a vengeance in the 1790s to try to ensure that the country was safe from the threat of revolution. The British inquisition attempted to track down republicans and levellers and then stop them from talking sedition by stuffing tracts down their throats. Francis Place recorded how John Reeves and the other vigilantes succeeded in sweeping 'gross publications' off the streets:

The association printed a large number of what they called loyal songs, and gave them to ballad singers; if anyone was found singing any but loyal songs, he or she was carried before a magistrate who admonished . . . him or her, they were then told that they might have loyal songs for nothing . . . .[7]

They presumably had to pay a fine if they refused this generous offer. The authors of these 'loyal songs' and tracts felt that they were in the front line of a psychological war in which the spoils would go to the simplest. William Jones stated in his *A Letter to John Bull . . .* (1793) that

Common understandings having been deceived, were to be addressed in a common way, and argued with from plain principles of common sense. (p. 4)

The common people must be made to listen to common sense, for it was so much more sensible and British than all those complicated foreign notions about equality. It became impossible to argue with facts like these.

Religion was the most important ingredient in this plain, bland counter-revolutionary cooking. Yet these recipes for peace in our time had a distinctly country flavour to them as well. Hannah More's tracts were full of homespun, parish-pump conservatism. From her twee little cottage, Cowslip Green, she attempted to pump the parishes of England full of common sense. She scripted dialogues between working men that make third-rate chat shows seem positively Socratic. *Village Politics* (1793) takes the form of a dialogue between Jack Anvil the blacksmith and Tom Hod the mason. Jack is the conservative lad, who has a good line in pastoral platitudes:

My cottage is my castle; I sit down in it at night in peace and thankfulness, and 'no man maketh me afraid'. Instead of indulging discontent, because another is richer than I in this world (for envy is at bottom of your equality works), I read my Bible, go to church, and look forward to a treasure in heaven. (p. 17)

The pastoral emphasis on the cottage as castle is part and parcel of the counter-revolutionary emphasis on the lie that there will be cottage pie in the sky when you die. The Reverend Legh Richmond's *Annals of the Poor* (1826) also explicitly brought pastoralism to the aid of the counter-revolutionary party. He gave his unfortunate readers a description of the 'pastoral scene' in a story about 'The Young Cottager':

The shepherd, tending his flock on the side of some spacious hill, or in the hollow of a sequestered valley; folding them at night, and guarding them against all danger; leading them from one pasture to another, for refreshment to the cooling waters – these objects have met and gratified our eyes, as we travelled through the fields, and sought out creation's God amidst creation's beauties. (pp. 14–15)

The order and hierarchy of the pastoral scene is used to argue in favour of the existing social structure. Creation's God, like creation's beauties, are, however, very much in the eye of the beholder. God turns out to bear a striking resemblance to a paternalistic, counter-revolutionary clergyman. The labourers must have had difficulty distinguishing between God's and sod's law. If the pastoral activities of good shepherds do not quite convince you that you owe a passive obedience to Legh Richmond and perhaps even to his God, then just consider the flowers of the field. We are all growing in the same good earth:

like the flowers also, some Christians may be said to grow on the mountain tops, some in valleys, some in the waters, and others in dry ground. Different colours, forms, and sizes distinguish them from each other, and produce a diversity of character and appearance, which affords a delightful variety, both for the purposes of use and beauty. Yet is that variety perfectly consistent with the essential unity of nature in the vegetable kingdom, to which they all equally belong. (pp. 69–70)

Poverty is natural, so there is no point in trying to change the garden of the commonwealth. Some flowers may be more equal than others, but they all wither and die anyway:

The capacious mansion of a rich neighbour appeared on the right hand, as I walked: on my left were the cottages of the poor. The church spire pointing to heaven a little beyond, seemed to say to both the rich and the poor, 'set your affections on things above, not on things on the earth'. (p. 60)

One of the many problems with this argument is that, if you waited to get to heaven and then found it was just like early nineteenth-century England, you might start kicking yourself even before they started kicking you.

These tracts aimed to police society. Hannah More's were sold to the rich by the yard and then distributed among the poor and needy. Most of the evidence suggests that, although the paper often came in useful, the views expressed on it were not heeded. Yet village politics could be mighty unpleasant in practice, if you lived on the wrong side of the tracts; the hamlets contained too many princes and paupers. Parishes had all the restrictive drawbacks of prisons, public schools, and provincial universities. We should consider village politics in Nayland, deep in the heart of the Constable country, rather than the flowers of the field:

The vestry is, to all intents and purposes, a Parochial oligarchy, promoting self-interest or gratifying personal feelings at pleasure; individuals are obliged to submit to the most grievous oppressions because there is no remedy but by an expensive Appeal.[8]

God's pastoral laws begin to look even more like sod's laws when it is remembered that labourers in Nayland did not even have the option of uprooting themselves, for Laws of Settlement could not be ignored quite as easily as a fistful of tracts. The labourer's cottage was his castle dungeon. The church spire pointing up to heaven had one message for Legh Richmond and another for the labourers. Joseph Arch recorded what it was like for those whose place was not Cowslip Green:

First, up walked the squire to the communion rails; the farmers went up next; then up went the tradesmen, the shopkeepers, the wheelwright, and the blacksmith; and then, the very last of all, went the poor agricultural labourers in their smock frocks. They walked up by themselves; nobody else knelt with them; it was as if they were unclean . . . .[9]

Variety is the spite of life. John Clare often felt himself trapped out in the flatlands of East Anglia. His cottage became his lunatic asylum:

I live here among the ignorant like a lost man in fact like one whom the rest seem careless of having anything to do with – they hardly dare talk in my company for fear I shoud mention them in my writings & I find more pleasure in wandering the fields then in mixing among my silent neighbours who are insensible of everything but toiling & talking of it & that to no purpose.[10]

He felt that education was needed to spark these villagers into life, but he did not have in mind the kind of education which merely tried to ensure the safety of Cowslip Green. Familiarity had a habit of breeding contempt rather than content. The English have always tried to construct villages in which neighbours can keep a watchful eye on each other. We have a moveable village fête mentality which travels everywhere with us. London is made into a series of twee villages and, after the global village, we shall probably all find ourselves living in the galactic one. Heaven is probably just a hellish village in which everybody knows their place. That's the humble pie in the sky.

The radicals challenged the pastoralism of the tract-mongers. Thomas Spence took the parish as his social unit in *The Restorer of Society to its Natural State* (1807), but that was where the similarities with More and Richmond began and ended. Spence believed that all landed property, far from being divinely ordained and sanctioned by that landowner in the sky, was created by naked aggression and theft. The land should be the people's farm, but it had become a field of blood. Anybody with a few pieces of silver could cheat the people of their natural rights. All private ownership was unnatural, for

pride accompanies land to such a degree that the smallest freeholder is possessed with all the aristocratic haughtiness and contempt for his fellow creatures of the highest duke, and is much more insufferable on account of his greater ignorance. (p. 49)

Spence rejected Wordsworthian equations between independence and virtue. He wanted all land taken into public ownership by the parishes and then reallocated to individuals, who were to have an interest, but not a vested one, in the cultivation of the soil. Tom Paine's *Agrarian Justice* (1797) was a lot more cautious. He started from the same natural right premises as Spence:

There could be no such things as landed property originally. Man did not make the earth, and though he had a natural right to *occupy* it, he had no right to *locate as his property* in perpetuity any part of it; neither did the Creator of the earth open a land-office, from whence the first title deeds should issue. (p. 6)

Paine was concerned, however, to safeguard property rights. The present owners could keep their land, if they agreed to hand over a sum equivalent to its original, uncultivated value. This was rather laboriously calculated at one tenth of its present value. The money would then be put into a land fund, which would be used to get small proprietors digging and delving. This was also the main object of Feargus O'Connor's Chartist Land Plan in the 1840s. The 'fustian jackets, unshorn chins and blistered hands' were invited to buy shares in a land company. There was then a ballot to decide on the lucky few to take up the two-, three- or four-acre holdings on the Chartist estates. O'Connor presented the Land Plan as the jewel in the Chartist crown. His opponents pointed out that he wanted to wear this crown himself. They called him Fingers O'Connor when certain financial improprieties came to light. They felt that this back-to-the-land movement was a betrayal of progressive radical principles, yet King Feargus still managed to hold out a dream of independence, which was not to be found in the nightmares of Hannah More or Legh Richmond.

Like the counter-revolutionary tracts, radical pamphlets about the land must be seen as being inextricably connected with political action. Thomas Spence was usually rather vague about exactly how England was going to be transformed into a federation of parishes. He believed that if one parish took the land into communal ownership, the others might follow suit. His followers were not so naive. They grafted onto the original plan a theory of revolutionary change, which they became increasingly anxious to try out in practice. The Spenceans almost certainly kept the flame of advanced radicalism flickering underground during the early years of the century. It is likely that their views on the necessity for violent means to achieve their ends were influenced by direct involvement in the Luddite riots of 1812. It is certainly true that when they re-emerged after the end of the Napoleonic wars there was a pronounced emphasis on violence. The Home Office spies reported on their various schemes to overthrow Hannah More's conception of village politics. Dr Watson, the leader of the land reformers after Spence's death in 1814, told a large public meeting at Spa Fields on 2 December 1816 that the

earth is capable of affording us all the means of allaying our wants and of placing man in a comfortable situation – if a man has but a spade a hoe and a rake and turns up his mother Earth – He will be sure to find the means of averting starvation.[11]

Dr Watson's elementary plan to avoid starvation ran into one major problem: Mother Earth was possessed by others. It was therefore necessary to dispossess them. Lord Liverpool told the landowners in Parliament that Spence's Land Plan represented the end of civilization. Secret committees were thus hastily convened to try to find out what these dangerous men were up to. The Spenceans still continued to haunt the Government, even after the rest of the radical movement had been contained by counter-revolutionary legislation. Arthur Thistlewood, the leader of the Cato Street conspirators who attempted a *coup d'état* in 1820, was an active land reformer.

Pastoral poetry should not be seen in terms of an elegant literary game. It was a statement of political creed. Similarly, inelegant tracts always need to be related to political action. Most versions of pastoral could be extremely unpleasant in practice. Harsh vestries and militant churches illustrate the sharp end of the creed, as indeed do the executions after the East Anglian bread or blood riots of 1816 and the Swing riots of 1830. Radicals such as the Spenceans were also quite prepared to take up arms as well as pens to defend their beliefs about the land. Raymond Williams has suggested the need to study drama in performance. It is also essential to see pastoral in performance or action. Members of Parliament debated the merits of a particular pastoral poet and the overseers at Nayland turned cottages into prisons.

Them and us

Like Hannah More, Mary Mitford believed that the small and parochial were positively beautiful to behold. She asserted during her famous description of the village cricket match in *Our Village* (1824–32) that

to be a voter, or a voter's wife, comes nothing near the genuine and hearty sympathy of belonging to a parish, breathing the same air, looking at the same trees, listening to the same nightingales! Talk of a patriotic elector! – Give me a parochial patriot, a man who loves his parish! (I, p. 154)

She is reassured by a double sense of place and firmly believes that familiarity breeds content. As these statements were intended for a middle- rather than a working-class audience, there might be a tendency to ignore their status as propaganda. Yet the pastoral perspective itself is, as already suggested, a propagandist one. It cooks the economic books. Mary Mitford may not have been engaged in street warfare with the members of the British inquisition, but nevertheless she was involved in maintaining morale on the home front. She was aiming at the dressing-rooms of the middle and upper classes, whereas Hannah More was aiming her tracts, almost literally, at the distressing rooms of the poor. Mary Mitford was concerned to present her readers with the acceptable face of rural society. She too was writing propaganda for the victors in the rural war.

This did not mean actually ignoring events such as the Swing riots, which might appear to undermine her cosy world of parochial patriotism. It meant reconstructing these events to make them more acceptable and understandable to those of the pastoral persuasion. 'The Incendiary: A Country Tale' describes how the Swing rioters used to appear like thieves, or poachers, in the night:

The stilly gatherings of the misguided peasantry amongst the wild hills, partly heath and partly woodland, of which so much of the northern part of Hampshire is composed, – dropping in one by one, and two by two, in the gloom of evening, or the dim twilight of a November morning . . . .

The Hampshire downs are transformed into 'wild hills' to lend even more power to the propaganda image of wolves bearing down upon the fold. Mary Mitford tried to suggest that the parochial patriots were forced to join these wild men of the hills:

the open and noisy meetings of determined men at noontide in the streets and greens of our Berkshire villages, and even sometimes in the very churchyards, sallying forth in small but resolute numbers to collect money or destroy machinery, and compelling or persuading their fellow-labourers to join them at every farm they visited . . . .

The Swing riots are a conspiracy against both church and state. A small group of outsiders persuade our villagers to listen to them rather than to the nightingales. Pastoral's enemies are invariably outsiders. The grievances of the rioters are displaced by the suggestion that a mercenary concern for collecting cash by threats is first and foremost in their minds. Mary Mitford's use of military metaphors may be seen as a justification for the eventual savage repression of the riots:

their day-light marches on the high road, regular and orderly as those of an army, or their midnight visits to lonely houses, lawless and terrific as the descent of pirates, or the incursions of banditti; – all brought close to us a state of things which we never thought to have witnessed in peaceful and happy England. (v, pp. 5–6)

Those that live by the sword deserve to perish by it. An army marching around the countryside suggests organization and this in turn suggests outside influences. The alien nature of the riots is further strengthened by the description of those involved as 'banditti'. The village cricket match is used to provide a comforting pastoral image of community and unity. This can only be sustained by reconstructing rural society. Our village remains our village only because disruptive elements are kicked out of it. Agricultural labourers with genuine grievances against early nineteenth-century village politics are transformed into wild men of the hills. Our village is not, when it comes to the crunch, their village.

It is Mary Mitford herself who, at the very beginning of *Our Village*, suggests the comparison with Jane Austen. She indicates that they are both involved in making the small seem beautiful:

nothing is so delightful as to sit down in a country village in one of Miss Austen's delicious novels, quite sure before we leave it to become intimate with every spot and every person it contains . . . . (I, p. 2)

Austen was not, however, on 'intimate' or familiar terms with 'every person' in a 'country village'. That would have been a little too vulgar. She described in the famous letter to aspiring novelist, Anna Austen, how '3 or 4 Families in a Country Village is the very thing to work on – '.[12] It was for blunter pens to dwell on the lives of those who dwelt outside the first society of a particular neighbourhood. Such persons would, after all, represent spots on the delicate face of rural society. Jane Austen therefore erects wittily barbed fences to prevent familiarity from breeding a contempt for breeding. It is still quite common for critics to accept such lethally elegant boundaries. Perhaps they vainly hope that, if they do not make too much noise, they might themselves be able to walk through that creaking door into the world of the rural gentry. Aesthetic necessity, rather than political prejudice, is usually found to be both present and correct. Such a fawning approach is harder to take now that Jane Austen's novels have been clearly located within a tradition of anti-Jacobin polemic and propaganda. Universally acknowledged truths turn out to be political prejudices.

Edward Ferrars tries to oppose Marianne Dashwood's passion for the picturesque in *Sense and Sensibility* (1811). He prefers a neat, orderly and productive landscape to all those ruggedly useless ruins:

I do not like crooked, twisted, blasted trees. I admire them much more if they are tall, straight and flourishing. I do not like ruined, tattered cottages. I am not fond of nettles, or thistles, or heath blossoms. I have more pleasure in a snug farm-house than a watch-tower – and a troop of tidy, happy villagers please me better than the finest banditti in the world. (I, p. 228)

Picturesque 'banditti' are as alien to a truly English landscape as are the wild 'banditti' of Mary Mitford's Hampshire. A cosmopolitan sensibility is being contrasted with sound English sense. Yet this aesthetic argument provides a vehicle for a wider political one. The imagery is, for instance, in the conventions of 'the garden of the commonwealth'. England, untainted by the dangerous political notions of the Jacobins, is like a 'tall, straight and flourishing' tree, probably an oak. Reform will leave it 'crooked, twisted, blasted'. The garden of the commonwealth, or what might be more appropriately called the realm of the estate, is a recurrent theme in Jane Austen's novels. The debates in *Mansfield Park* (1814) about the pros and cons of landscape improvement need to be seen in terms of the state as well as the particular estate. Edmund Burke was not the only anti-Jacobin propagandist who insisted that the country, like the estates of which it was composed, ought to be handed on intact to the next generation. Henry Crawford and Mr Rushworth offend against such conservatism by their insistence that it is the right of one generation to alter radically and transform one's inheritance. The estate for them is something to be dressed up to play the particular part they want it to. This may include making sure that 'snug' buildings do not intrude between the sensibility of the observer and the landscape. Such improvement was too dramatic for the good of the estate.

If universal truths are merely political prejudices, then it should be possible to be more perceptive about Jane Austen's wittily barbed fences. When Anne Elliott is forced to move from Kellynch Hall to the village of Uppercross in *Persuasion* (1818), she realizes that she will have to adapt consciously to village life:

Anne had not wanted this visit to Uppercross, to learn that a removal from one set of people to another, though at a distance of only three miles, will often include a total change of conversation, opinion and idea . . . . She acknowledged it to be very fitting, that every little social commonwealth should dictate its own matters of discourse; and hoped, ere long, to become a not unworthy member of the one she was now transplanted into . . . . (I, pp. 94–6)

Outsiders need to learn the rules of the social game, something which Mrs Elton conspicuously fails to do in *Emma* (1816). The 'little social commonwealth' which is being referred to is made up of a handful of families. They regulate dinner and card-table conversation and lay down the rules about what pastimes are permissible. The Musgroves apparently spend a lot of time guarding and destroying the fowls of the air. Jane Austen has few pastoral illusions about this way of life. The 'social commonwealth' belies such a description by actually dictating 'its own matters of discourse'. It is a piece of irony which touches a raw nerve. Yet the real irony in this particular description is the way in which Anne Elliot goes through the motions of being an outsider, when she quite patently is not one. She is a prominent member of the rural gentry and thus has a membership card for any 'little social commonwealth'. These commonwealths of three or four families tended to dictate the political and economic discourse of the community as a whole.

Unlike Mary Mitford, Jane Austen does not include the labourers and others within her village commonwealth and then boot them out when they start breaking the rules and regulations. She excluded them from the start in favour of the dictators, or victors, in the rural war. She does not even allow a 'troop of tidy, happy villagers' to trample across her pages. Indeed, we are much more likely to hear about unhappy villagers. For, as objects of charity, to appropriate an obscene expression from the period, they have a part to play in the evaluation of moral worth. Jane Austen could tell all she needed to know about a person by glancing at their trees, library and bank account. If any doubts remain, these could be resolved by some quick questions on landscape improvement, the theatre and London barbers. Attitudes towards charity provide a similar kind of social touchstone. Henry Crawford tries to impress Fanny Price by playing the part of a benevolent landowner. He makes a long overdue visit to his very flat acres in Norfolk:

He had introduced himself to some tenants, whom he had never seen before, he had begun making acquaintance with cottages whose very existence, though on his own estate, had been hitherto unknown to him. This was aimed, and well aimed, at Fanny. It was pleasing to hear him speak so properly; here, he had been acting as he ought to do. (III, p. 205)

Yet Henry was 'acting' all the time. He enjoyed watching himself perform the part and hankered after Fanny's adulation and applause. As befitted a superficial man of property, he made the acquaintance of cottages as well as cottagers. Fanny's brand of charity, by contrast, is presented as being much less ostentatiously self-gratifying and self-seeking. She has the discreet calm of the bourgeoisie. Like Henry Crawford, Lady Catherine de Bourgh drops points in *Pride and Prejudice* (1813) through her indiscreetly autocratic relationship with the village:

Elizabeth soon perceived that though this great lady was not in the commission of the peace for the county, she was a most active magistrate in her own parish, the minutest concerns of which were carried to her by Mr. Collins; and whenever any of the cottagers were disposed to be quarrelsome, discontented or too poor, she sallied forth into the village to settle their differences, silence their complaints, and scold them into harmony and plenty. (II, pp. 79–80)

The passage crackles and pops with a snappy irony, which is aimed at this lady of the manor who does not have the discreet manner. Young Master Darcy did not need to indulge in such theatrical histrionics at Pemberley, since he had patiently forged a sound and sensible working relationship with the members of the community. Sir Walter Elliot, that marvellous embodiment of what Matthew Arnold described as a barbarian spirit, is another character who is tried by his attitude towards rural society as a whole and found wanting. His obsession with outward appearances means that he has rehearsed 'condescending bows for all the afflicted tenantry and cottagers who might have had a hint to shew themselves' (I, p. 80) when he ostentatiously takes his leave of Kellynch.

Henry Crawford, Lady Catherine and Sir Walter all represent an essentially old-fashioned gentry manner of behaving on their manor. Fanny Price and Mr Darcy represent newer and more acceptable codes of conduct. Emma Woodhouse's charitable disposition is also commented favourably upon. She and Harriet Smith go to visit some of the poor who, significantly, live 'a little way out of Highbury' (I, p. 175):

Emma was very compassionate; and the distresses of the poor were as sure of relief from her personal attention and kindness, her counsel and her patience, as from her purse. She understood their ways, could allow for their ignorance and their temptations, had no romantic expectations of extraordinary virtue from those, for whom education had done so little; entered into their troubles with ready sympathy, and always gave her assistance with as much intelligence as good-will. (I, p. 183)

Although this description is only faintly brushed with irony, it is rather knowingly undercut by the way in which Emma, despite her own protestations to the contrary, is more interested in making suitable matches than cottagers tolerably happy. Emma's heart overrules her head but there is always a Mr Knightley in every country town to save nice girls from themselves. Knightley is good sense and unimpeachable integrity personified, yet these moral characteristics are linked very explicitly with his social and economic position. He owns the Donwell Abbey estate, to which almost all of Highbury itself belongs. He manages the affairs of the parish of Donwell and is a local magistrate. If the gypsies, who committed the heinous crime of frightening Harriet Smith and Miss Bickerton, had stayed on the outskirts of Highbury, we might have found out what kind of a magistrate he was. He is also heavily committed to agricultural improvement. He speaks to brother John about his agrarian schemes, as well as asking him for clarification on points of law. He studies his farm accounts and has a good working relationship with his tenants. He is not a mere *rentier* like Henry Crawford. One of these tenants, Robert Martin, has followed in his master's footsteps by making a heavy commitment to agricultural improvement. He mugs up the latest agricultural reports and is thus able to produce the best wool in the country. Emma has no 'romantic expectations' about either farmers or the poor. As far as she is concerned, Robert Martin is just a yeoman farmer. She is a thoroughly modern miss, who does not believe all that silly stuff and nonsense about yeomen being the backbone of England. Yet Mr Knightley is forced to point out that she has missed the point, for Robert Martin is an 'intelligent gentleman-farmer' (I, p. 129). He is, in other words, one of the new breed of breeders.

The comparison with Mary Mitford is therefore a very dangerous one, for Jane Austen is definitely not beautifying the small and static. She is endorsing agrarian capitalism. Mrs Elton's *cottage ornée* pastoralism receives very short shrift from Mr Knightley, the working gentleman farmer. Jane Austen's novels are about the marriage of ideas as well as people. She succeeds here in uniting the conservatism of the rural gentry with the ethics of capitalist production. Such a union strengthened the former by removing potentially disruptive elements and helped the latter to acquire a sense of direction and continuity. United they could stand firm against Jacobinism, whereas divided the whole social structure might fall. Jane Austen looks at the books rather than cooking them. She has no reason to disguise the fact that Mansfield Park is financed through money from a Huntingdon lawyer and the profits from West Indian slave plantations. This is all grist to her reconciling mill. She watches the inhabitants of her 'little social commonwealths' looking over the barbed fence at the rest of the rural community and judges them by what she sees, but prefers to stay behind the barricades of her propaganda. *Emma* was published in the same year as the East Anglian bread or blood riots. Mr Knightley was certainly the bright sun in the reordered social firmament, but how oppressive was he? Realists, like pastoralists, tended to see other forms of life sternly and see them wholly from a partial point of view.

2 George Crabbe's reverence for realism

Matters factual

Historians, travailing helpfully on official sources, tend to arrive at the 'shocking realism' fallacy. These sources reflect a perspective from above, in which the agricultural labourer is not a person but a problem that needs solving. The full horror of the problem may be shockingly exposed, but it is fallacious to take this approach as the realistic one. It is also dangerous to assume that a poet who shares this *de haut en bas* perspective is more realistic than one who does not. William Hazlitt provides an important warning against the easy equation of shocking fact with realism in his *Lectures on the English Poets*. He rightly saw that Crabbe was often as official and officious as rubber stamps, or rubber bullets:

He describes the interior of a cottage like a person sent there to distrain for rent. He has an eye to the number of arms in an old worm-eaten chair, and takes care to inform himself and the reader whether a joint-stool stands upon three legs or upon four . . . . If Bloomfield is too much of the Farmer's Boy, Crabbe is too much of the parish beadle, an overseer of the country poor. He has no delight beyond the walls of a workhouse, and his officious zeal would convert the world into a vast infirmary. He is the kind of Ordinary, not of Newgate, but of nature. His poetical morality is taken from Burn's Justice, or the Statutes against Vagrants. (pp. 190–2)

Richard Burn's *The Justice of the Peace and Parish Officer* (1755) gave beaky magistrates an A to Z of whom to send down, together with a fistful of heavy hints about how to do it. He knew how to deal with idle apprentices, blasphemers, buggers, dissenters, poachers, Roman Catholics, servants and vagrants. He also cast a stern glance at the poor in general. Hazlitt very rarely missed his target, particularly if it was a ponderous, slow-moving one like Crabbe. He appears to be referring specifically to the inventory which Crabbe laboriously draws up towards the end of his letter on 'The Poor and

Their Dwellings' in *The Borough* (1810). Such inventories certainly give the appearance of realistic documentary as they deal with matters factual. Yet Crabbe is playing one of the oldest tricks in the empiricist's cooked book. He tells us whether a stool has three legs or four. We feel unable to argue with facts like these. By the time that Crabbe has measured everything from side to side, we may well be too tired to distinguish between fact and opinion. Crabbe collects facts because he is 'an overseer of the country poor'. Empiricism itself is not a neutral position. It needs, as Hazlitt suggests, to be associated with beadles, gaolers, magistrates and all those set in authority over us. The collection of facts must not be divorced from their abuse.

Historians, then, tend to mistake *an* official version of rural England for *the* official, or accurate, account. This is probably why they often quote Crabbe's famous description of the workhouse in Book One of *The Village* (1783) as an example of what conditions were really like. This description may tell us what 'overseers' like Crabbe felt about workhouses, but it does not provide evidence about what conditions were really like for the overseen or observed. Clare, like Hazlitt, felt that Crabbe should not be allowed to fool most of the people for most of the time into believing that his descriptions were documentary or realistic ones:

Crabbe writes about the peasantry as much like the Magistrate as the Poet. He is determined to show you their worst side: and as to their simple pleasures and pastoral feelings, he knows little or nothing about them . . . .[1]

Clare's idea of hell on earth was to be shut up for a week with Crabbe and to have to listen to him moralizing about the poor. It must have been like wading through crude oil trying to talk to Crabbe. His poetry, as Clare suggests, is at best one-sided and highly selective. Mrs Gaskell, who was disposed to be more charitable towards him, also felt that he was unable to perceive that life need not necessarily always be 'solitary, poor, nasty, brutish and short'. His concentration on the 'worst side' of rural society does provide information about and insights into the bureaucratic mind. The full horror may be exposed, but this is not necessarily the full story. There are a number of pictures of country life in the late eighteenth and early nineteenth centuries. Crabbe's is just one of them. They have all been shot from different angles, and the camera's eye altering, alters all. Crabbe's obsession with the 'worst side' of rural society was just as selective, polemical and distorting as, say, what John Constable used to refer to as opera-house pastoral. Like Clare, D. H. Lawrence resented the way in which the overseers palmed off opinions as facts. He took the French artist Jules Bastien Lepage to task for failing to appreciate that a realistic portrayal of rural society did not necessarily have to be stern and grim:

> Grey pictures of French peasant life – not one gleam, not one glimmer of sunshine – that is speaking literally – the paint is grey, grey-green, and brown. The peasant woman is magnificent – above all things, capable: to work, to suffer, to endure, to love – not, oh Bastien Lepage, oh Wells! Oh the God that there isn't – to enjoy. . . . Surely, surely Bastien Lepage and Wells are not the Truth, the whole Truth, and Nothing but the Truth.[2]

Parson Crabbe saw life as an assault course or endurance test. The thought for the day from the pulpit at the beginning of *The Borough* is that endurance and submission should be the order of the day. That was an order. As Hazlitt noticed, he had all the subtlety of an elephant's foot. His grim picture should never be taken for the whole truth. The very notion of the whole truth is itself a legal fiction, which is used by magistrates when sending the buggers and the gypsies down.

Reading the register

Crabbe maintained in his Preface to 'The Parish Register' (1807) that his picture of rural society was a balanced one, yet it has all the balanced arrogance and bias of a school report. Crabbe's theme is one that still continues to fall on the stony floors of the school assembly room:

> How pass'd the youthful, how the old their days;
> Who sank in sloth, and who aspired to praise;
> Their tempers, manners, morals, customs, arts;
> What parts they had, and how they 'mploy'd their parts;
> By what elated, soothed, seduced, depress'd,
> Full well I know – these records give the rest. (I, 9–14)[3]

He took care to point out that only those who conformed to his image of the deserving poor would be receiving prizes on speechday:

> Toil, care, and patience bless th' abstemious few,
> Fear, shame, and want the thoughtless herd pursue. (I, 29–30)

This pupil will go far, perhaps even as far as me, if he tries to be exactly like me. If he refuses to conform, then the further away he goes from me the better for all concerned. There are a limited number of teacher's pets, but the vast majority are merely a herd of real swine. They do not even deserve sham pearls of wisdom. Crabbe's poetry, like the school report, is a peg on which a number of prejudices are hung. He certainly believed that there was considerable room for improvement as far as the majority of the rural poor was concerned. There were extreme cases, however, when even his own brilliant teaching could not make any impression. He hoped that the ground would cover these rogues. He liked what he knew or understood. Despite the illusion of balance and objectivity, his reports on rural England were reports on his own schoolmasterly prejudices, which were written for the parent rather than the pupil. After a description of the undeserving poor which makes Victorian temperance tracts appear restrained, he comments:

Ye who have power, these thoughtless people part,
Nor let the ear be first to taint the heart! (I, 210–11)

'The Parish Register' was written by one who had power for others in the same fortunate position. It appeals to 'the true physician' to walk 'the foulest ward' (I, 213). It urges the schoolmaster to be abroad:

Whence all these woes? – From want of virtuous will,
Of honest shame, of time-improving skill;
From want of care t' employ the vacant hour,
And want of ev'ry kind but want of power. (I, 226–9)

An hour a day keeps the devil at bay. It is no accident that the village 'schoolmarm' is singled out for particular praise. She adopts an orphan and sets the child exactly the right example:

Then I behold her at her cottage-door,
Frugal of light, – her Bible laid before,
When on her double duty she proceeds,
Of time as frugal, knitting as she reads.
Her idle neighbours, who approach to tell
Some trifling tale, her serious looks compel
To hear reluctant – while the lads who pass,
In pure respect walk silent on the grass.

Then sinks the day; but not to rest she goes,
Till solemn prayers the daily duties close. (I, 599–608)

The moral of Crabbe's story is that frugality and piety are virtues
which society ought to be taught to respect.

Crabbe attempts to authenticate his descriptions in two ways.
First, he can personally and knowingly vouch 'full well' for their
accuracy. Second, if anybody should doubt the validity of his
personal experience, 'these records give the rest'. The argument is,
of course, dangerously circular. If you object to the prejudices in the
school report, then the mark book is produced with a flourish. You
are told that you are unable to object to facts or 'records'. Yet these
'records' enshrine the same prejudices as the reports. When a
historian wants to reconstruct the history of a particular parish, he
certainly has to rely quite heavily on the damp or dusty registers of
births, marriages and deaths. The Annalistes and the demographers
have shown that, if questions are asked and assumptions and
classifications challenged, these 'records' are of historical rather
than purely antiquarian interest. If Wordsworth often writes about
rural society like a fussy folklorist, Crabbe exhibits all the faults of
the fusty antiquarian. This does not just mean that, as Hazlitt
noticed, he accumulated detail. It also means that he tended to
accept existing classifications. His society is divided into God's
poor, the Devil's poor and the poor devils. He always found it
difficult to unbuckle the bible belt.

Crabbe suggests that he offers us a realistic description of 'the
simple annals of my parish poor' (I, 2) in 'The Parish Register'. He
makes the same claim at the end of the poem as well:

Thus, as the months succeed, shall infants take
Their names; thus parents shall the child forsake;
Thus brides again and bridegrooms blithe shall kneel,
By love or law compell'd their vows to seal,
Ere I again, or one like me, explore
These simple annals of the VILLAGE POOR. (III, 965–70)

It is true that he does offer some individual portraits of the
agricultural labourer. Isaac Ashford is presented as 'a wise good
man, contented to be poor' (III, 307). He is an instructive example
of what God's, and therefore Parson Crabbe's, poor ought to be
like. Even his criticism of parish relief has its place in Crabbe's neat
and orderly scheme of things. It is cautiously advanced and meant to

suggest that those 'who have power' ought to put their various workhouses in order. Crabbe, the sternest of markers, gives full marks to Reuben and Rachel for prudently postponing their marriage until they could actually afford to live together. The Devil's poor are also referred to. The 'rustic infidel' is as black as Ashford is white:

But he, triumphant spirit! all things dared,
He poach'd the wood, and on the warren snared;
'Twas his, at cards, each novice to trepan,
And call the wants of rogues the rights of man;
Wild as the winds, he let his offspring rove,
And deem'd the marriage-bond the bane of love. (I, 812–7)

Like Hannah More, Crabbe did not draw shades of grey. The labourers were either 'noble', or else they were gamblers, infidels, poachers and radicals to a devil. Crabbe's society is not just a black and white one, it is also a static one. Samuel Smiles might have presented Richard Monday, the workhouse orphan who makes good, as an encouraging example for all those on the self-help ladder. Yet Crabbe is concerned to show that Monday only makes his way in the world through low cunning and obsessive selfishness. The virtues of patience, perseverance and frugality, which Smiles offered as social passports to the mid Victorian artisans, were used by Parson Crabbe to make the labourers content with their station in life. If Isaac Ashford made the mistake of trying to quit both social and geographical place, he would realize pretty soon that we are all poor devils. The rich have their trials and tribulations as well. There is, as Crabbe put it in 'The Parish Register', 'one fate' (I, 508), which catches up with the rich as well as the poor. This was also a constant theme in his sermons.

'The Parish Register' gives rise to two expectations, neither of which is fulfilled. First, despite the way in which the 'records' are referred to, the labourers are presented as stereotypes. They would not have been out of place in counter-revolutionary tracts. Second, despite the emphasis on the fact that this is a poem about the poor, it is by no means concerned exclusively with them. It deals extensively with farmers and tradesmen. Crabbe was a better observer of the rural professional and commercial classes than he was of the poor. This may have been because the Crabbe family had always been, according to his son, only 'somewhat above the mass in point of situation'.[4] George Crabbe therefore found it psychologically essential to continually assert and affirm his own distance from this 'mass'. His obsession with 'records' may be seen as part of this distancing process. He had been forced to work as a labourer on Slaughden Quay, near Aldeburgh, for a few months in 1767. He did not want to repeat or remember the experience. This was his blacking factory. He therefore attempted to keep the labourers at arm's length by hiding their individuality behind a series of rigid classifications and pious homilies. He was, however, in something of a social no-man's-land himself. He became a respectable pillar of society, in other words a clerical magistrate and a pluralist. Yet he had his fingers trodden on as he ascended his own self-help ladder. This was particularly true of the period when he was the Duke of Rutland's domestic chaplain. Crabbe remained at Belvoir, even though most of the household had followed the Duke to Ireland on his appointment as Lord Lieutenant. Those that stayed amused themselves at the expense of the self-made, self-important chaplain. Crabbe was partially to reopen the wounds inflicted by the patronage system when he came to write 'The Patron' for his *Tales* (1812). It was inevitable that he should have felt, and been made to feel, insecure when he was attached to one of the great aristocratic families. The values of Estate entailed a rigid sense of place. Crabbe experienced the same insecurities and tensions, in less dramatic forms, throughout his life. This made him prone to satire, but seemed to restrict his subject matter to the group into which he had risen. He wrote about the labourers like a magistrate, but was able to point out the private vices that lurked behind the public virtues of the magistrates themseves.

'The Dumb Orators' in *Tales* illustrates both the strengths and weaknesses of Crabbe's social vision. It deals with the rivalry between Justice Bolt and a radical orator named Hammond. Although Bolt is a true blue church-and-king Tory, he is also presented as being a somewhat overpowering one. The causes he championed were close to Crabbe's pocket, but the way he did so left a certain amount to be desired. He is both proud and vindictive. While he is touring the Midlands, he drops into a debating club. It is there that he is forced to listen to Hammond's radical polemic against church and state. Although he is a bully-boy in his own backyard, his courage fails him when it comes to playing his part in foreign parts. The roles are, however, reversed a few years later. Hammond is forced to endure Bolt's heady rhetoric and extravagant gestures. He is taunted into trying to make a reply:

By desperation urged, he now began:
'I seek no favour – I – the Rights of Man!
Claim; and I – nay! – but give me leave – and I
Insist – a man – that is – and in reply,
I speak'. – Alas! each new attempt was vain:
Confused he stood, he sate, he rose again;
At length he growl'd defiance, sought the door,
Cursed the whole synod, and was seen no more. (454–61)

Bolt basks in the glory of his triumph. It is a hollow one, since all that has been proved is that radical orators are also unable to preach to the unconverted. Crabbe's apologists might claim that such poetic narratives should not be interpreted ideologically. This particular one is a satire on the presentation of ideologies of both right and left. It points to universal human failings, which lie behind the accidents of social position. That is certainly Crabbe's theory, but in practice the dice are loaded against Hammond. He is used primarily as a foil to probe and expose Justice Bolt's double standards. Crabbe writes about other magistrates satirically, but treats the labourers and their representatives like a magistrate. He registers their presence, but is quite willing to throw the book at them if they start being naughty behind his back.

Officious documentary

Jessica Mitford described in *The Making of a Muckraker* (1979) how honourable rebels ought to treat noble causes, when she outlined the way in which she approached an investigation of the American deep south. She regarded it as essential to

> slide into the daily lives of people, to soak up their ordinary conversation, to savor their manner and manners, to achieve an oblique rather than a direct look was my plan. Slightly easier said than done, I found; people are always shoving you off to talk to community leaders or to meetings where the Problem is under discussion. (p. 61)

This technique may be described as radical documentary. It is crucial to bypass official versions of events. The direct highway, the straight and narrow path, is always going to be blocked by people who want to hit you over the head with rubber stamps, rubber truncheons or some other version of the reality principle. They are the real problem. It is therefore essential to take the eyes and ears into the byways to record impressions about 'the daily lives of people'. These impressions should not be presented in the form of a voice-of-God narration, but rather as your own personal assessment. The documentary ought, in other words, to be signed. Official documentary is much safer and more predictable. You do not waste time, nervous energy and expensive footage attempting to discover something as elusive and abusive as the voice of the people. It is much better to arrange a series of interviews with the great and the good. They will then suggest whom you ought to interview. You then present your conclusions in a form appropriate to the whole truth.

Crabbe does take to the byways in *The Borough*, but only after an exhaustive and often exhausting plod around the corridors of power. It is only after he has been shown representatives of 'The Poor and Their Dwellings' that he decides it is time to extend the official guided tour:

Farewell to these; but all our poor to know,
Let's seek the winding lane, the narrow row – (242–3)

Crabbe is too professional a reporter merely to report verbatim what the spokesmen say, but he usually likes to call on them first. His approach is essentially institutional and bureaucratic. The borough is broken down into its constituent parts relatively easily: the church, the professions, the trades, the hospital, the schools, the prison, the almshouse and so on. The poem does encroach upon the guide-book's privilege. It is, however, also concerned with probing the weaknesses of such official positions and statements.

Crabbe was too busy proving that he had slid out of the 'daily lives of the people' to want to slide back. One of the ways in which he attempted to confirm his laboriously acquired professional status was by reminding such as cared to attend that ethics should never be dropped. Converts are usually a little too zealous about principles and standards. Crabbe attacked contemporary lawyers for preying on the community like the spider on the fly. He felt that quack doctors, who gambled on the people's gullibility, were letting the professional side down. His satire on the professions is lame and tame when compared with those of William Hogarth and Thomas Rowlandson. Yet it still has to be seen as the focal point of the poem. It serves two functions. First, as suggested, it is meant to keep the professionals on their toes. Second, it is used to support the 'one fate' argument and thus to argue in favour of the *status quo*. The 'weary rustic' is moved along with all the firmness of a local policeman when he begins to question his station of life in Letter IX:

Ah! go in peace, good fellow, to thine home,
Nor fancy these escape the general doom;
Gay as they seem, be sure with them are hearts
With sorrow tried; there's sadness in their parts.
If thou couldst see them when they think alone,
Mirth, music, friends, and these amusements gone;
Couldst thou discover every secret ill
That pains their spirit, or resists their will;
Couldst thou behold forsaken Love's distress,
Or Envy's pang at glory and success,
Or Beauty, conscious of the spoils of Time,
Or Guilt, alarm'd when Memory shows the crime –
All that gives sorrow, terror, grief, and gloom:
Content would cheer thee, trudging to thine home. (179–92)

The labourer ought to be whistling all the way to his hovel, since there is always bound to be somebody worse off than him. Material wealth brings its own trials and tribulations. Crabbe may try to suggest that *The Borough* is a slice of documentary realism, yet the social doctor is dishing out the prescriptions. The labourers ought to be content with the simple life because they do not have to be concerned with the doubts and difficulties that apparently lie in wait for those with large bank accounts. The 'one fate' argument sounds plausible enough in theory, but in practice there appears to be one fate for the poor and another one for the rich. Crabbe sets out an official code of conduct for the rich in general and the professions in particular, but sternly reminds the labourer that, as few can really live up to these ethical standards, they are bound to suffer pangs of remorse and guilt. If the labourer actually follows the equally rigid social code which is prescribed for him, then he really will be better off.

Crabbe's reputation as a realistic poet of the poor is an unrealistic one. 'Peter Grimes' is one of sketches of 'The Poor of the Borough'. It is, thanks in part to Benjamin Britten's adaptation of it, perhaps Crabbe's best known piece. As many approach it through anthologies, it is worth stressing that 'The Poor of the Borough' only make their appearance at the end of the poem itself. Official documentary always starts at the top. Like so many of Crabbe's other characters, Grimes is no stranger to the bureaucratic machinery of local government. Indeed, Crabbe's treatment of this particular story ought to confirm his reputation as the official poet of officialdom, the poet laureate of red-tape. Grimes's father 'seem'd that life laborious to enjoy' (3). He knew when he was well off. Grimes himself does not accept this social prescription. He rejects his father's authority and inevitably that of the paternalist society as well:

With greedy eye he look'd on all he saw,
He knew not justice, and he laugh'd at law;
On all he mark'd he stretch'd his ready hand;
He fish'd by water, and he filch'd by land:
Oft in the night has Peter dropp'd his oar,
Fled from his boat and sought for prey on shore; (40–5)

Slaughden Quay was threatening to destroy Crabbe's professional world. It was being allowed to do this as local government turned a blind eye to the dangers of social anarchy. The local community do not pay any attention to Grime's use and abuse of his first apprentice:

But none inquired how Peter used the rope,
Or what the bruise, that made the stripling stoop;
None could the ridges on his back behold,
None sought him shiv'ring in the winter's cold;
None put the question, – 'Peter, dost thou give
The boy his food? – What, man! the lad must live:
Consider, Peter, let the child have bread,
He'll serve thee better if he's stroked and fed.'
None reason'd thus and some, on hearing cries,
Said calmly, 'Grimes is at his exercise.' (69–78)

Crabbe's approach is similar to that adopted by the great American journalist Lincoln Steffens in his *The Shame of the Cities* (1904). Steffens argued that the investigative journalist ought to try to make his readers aware of two related facts. First of all, that a 'shock, horror, probe' exposure of corruption in high places is too easy. It is also bad journalism, since it usually displaces the blame from the community as a whole. The people are seldom as pure and innocent as they pretend to be. Thus, secondly, the real story ought always to be how much corruption they actually accept as part and parcel of everyday life. The inhabitants of Crabbe's Borough accept the ill-treatment of apprentices as a fact of life.

The local community is unable to police itself, so magistrates like Crabbe have a crucial part to play in the maintenance of law and order. There is an inquest after the death of the second apprentice. Although the jury suspected Grimes of foul play, they were prepared to give him the benefit of the doubt. The moral of Crabbe's story is that wet liberalism causes more problems that it solves. You have to be stern to be kind. It is only after the third apprentice has met a sticky end that local government finally begins to flex its legal muscles. Grimes is summoned to the Moot Hall to 'tell his tale before the burghers all' (156). Mr Mayor forbids him to have any more apprentices and warns him that he will feel the full weight of the law if he disobeys this command. Such chastisement is too little and too late. Crabbe believed that an abuse of, or a loophole in, any part of the professional structure of local government was bound to diminish its effectiveness and credibility. Grimes is able to get the apprentices in the first place because the workhouses in London do not maintain high administrative and professional standards. He is able to exploit these apprentices because magistrates and burghers reflect rather than set standards. Slaughden Quay can only be controlled and repressed through ruthless attention to professional codes and conduct.[5] Crabbe listened to official spokesmen, but was often rather impatient with them. He saw himself as the true spokesman for the magistrate, the doctor, the priest and the rural professions generally. His poetry, far from being a realistic treatment of the rural poor, is a polemic for officialdom, as it ought to be rather than as it was.

Village fates

Crabbe suffered from many ailments. The physician attempted to heal himself by taking doses of opium. Stiff or pastoral neck was the least of his problems, for he was not given to gazing back at the good old days of rural England. His dog collar was a little too new and tight for this kind of backward glancing. He did uphold the old-fashioned virtues of plain speaking and honest dealing against the modern vices of ostentatious wheeling and devious dealing when he dealt with the professions, in *The Borough* and elsewhere. Yet such pastoralism was not as explicit in his presentation of rural society. It is Benbow, rather than Crabbe himself, who indulges in the traditional lament for the good old ways of rural England in *The Borough*. Benbow dwells fondly on the memory of Asgill, an eighteenth-century wenching and trenching squire, but Crabbe implies that such nostalgic reflections ought to be treated more soberly than Benbow himself is ever capable of doing. *The Village* also takes a sober look at pastoral refreshment. Crabbe suggests that rural society represents economic pain rather than emotional or aesthetic pleasure for the vast majority of its inhabitants:

I grant indeed that fields and flocks have charms
For him that grazes or for him that farms;
But, when amid such pleasing scenes I trace
The poor laborious natives of the place,
And see the mid-day sun, with fervid ray,
On their bare heads and dewy temples play;
While some, with feebler hands and fainter hearts,
Deplore their fortune, yet sustain their parts:
Then shall I dare these real ills to hide
In tinsel trappings of poetic pride? (I, 39–48)

Pastoral needs to be countered by the exposure of 'real ills'. The tight close-up on real people and real places should replace blurred shots of imaginary landscapes. Crabbe's rural wasteland has few saving rustic graces. The village green is as bare and barren of people as it is of vegetation. Smuggling is the only sport the 'wild amphibious race' (I, p. 85) are interested in. The young men have become smugglers and poachers every one. Crabbe's later poetry may smack of antiquarianism, but in Book One of *The Village* his perspective appears to be closer to that of the social anthropologist. He explores relationships between the bleak environment and the 'race' who are doomed to inhabit it. This perspective is still that of an 'overseer', but it seems to be a more sensitive one than that of the stern magistrate. It appears to support an environmental interpretation of poverty. Like Gilbert White and a whole host of late eighteenth- and early nineteenth-century parsons, Crabbe was an accomplished natural historian. He includes the rural labourers in his natural history of an English village. He uses the techniques of the natural historian as another way of distancing himself from his subject matter.

Crabbe's satire on pastoral perspectives is certainly sharp and to the point, yet, as in his later poetry, his main concern seems to be that 'those that have power' should exercise it according to the rules and regulations. Quack doctors and negligent priests make the labourer's stern existence even worse than it should be. The quack is actually protected by the very people who have the power to expose him:

A potent quack, long versed in human ills,
Who first insults the victim whom he kills;
Whose murd'rous hand a drowsy Bench protect,
And whose most tender mercy is neglect. (I, 282–5)

The magistrates are also indirectly responsible for the sour charity which is doled out grudgingly in the workhouse. The priest adds the final insult to the injury of a labourer's life and death:

The busy priest, detain'd by weightier care,
Defers his duty till the day of prayer;
And, waiting long, the crowd retire distress'd,
To think a poor man's bones should lie unbless'd. (I, 343–6)

This priest prefers his pack of hounds to his flock of sheep. Crabbe certainly lays on the detail about the misery of agricultural life as thickly as possible, but it would be wrong to assume that he is arguing in favour of a fundamental change in the economic relationships of rural society. The poem is addressed to the leaders of this society. Its language of 'them and us' is very explicit. Crabbe appears to be accumulating the counter-pastoral detail as a way of trying to shock magistrates, priests and doctors back into an awareness that they have duties and responsibilities as well as privileges.

If this is so, then it may be possible to challenge the view that *The Village* contains two distinct and very different poems. It is often maintained that Book One offers realistic counter-pastoral, while Book Two reverts to more familiar pastoral idioms. First of all, as already suggested, *de haut en bas* counter-pastoral should never be regarded as realistic. Second, the two parts of the poem are linked by the controlling perspective of the overseer. Crabbe can certainly be accused of licking the hand which fed him when he came to write the panegyric to Rutland's brother, Lord Manners. The parson does indeed know enough who knows a Duke. Although Crabbe could not accept the back-handers of aristocratic patronage fast enough, such grovelling may not have caused quite such a rupture in the poem's message as has often been assumed. He continues to explore the same themes in Book Two. He describes rural slums and suggests that the labourer's brutish existence needs to be related to the breakdown of responsible authority. The justice of the peace who finally puts down the drunken riot on the village green is yet another local official who wants privilege without responsibility. He uses the law to cow the local inhabitants and does not practise what he preaches. He takes a stern line with the 'country copulatives', but enjoys seducing country girls himself. This justice likes his piece on the side. Crabbe follows this description of the breakdown of law and order with the 'one fate' argument:

So shall the man of power and pleasure see
In his own slave as vile a wretch as he;
In his luxurious lord the servant find
His own low pleasures and degenerate mind:
And each in all the kindred vices trace
Of a poor, blind, bewilder'd, erring race;
Who, a short time in varied fortune past,
Die, and are equal in the dust at last. (II, 93–100)

Such pessimistic theorizing should not disguise the fact that in practice Crabbe prescribes two fates. The labourer must reconcile himself to the fact that life is an endurance test. If he complains, then he ought to be made to realize that everybody else, regardless of their social position, is having their dismal score totted up by that stern marker in the sky. Those higher up the social scale might score very badly, since they are required to discharge certain social functions. As they are only human, their performance is always bound to fall short of the desired effect. The labourer's fate is to endure passively. Such endurance ought to be supported by the activity of the professional classes in providing a responsible paternalism.

Crabbe uses the examples of Manners's devotion to duty at the end of Book Two to encourage all local officials to play their bureaucratic parts. Manners is the solution to the local corruption which Crabbe exposes in Book One. He uses the oak tree to symbolize the potential power and authority of the territorial aristocracy:

As the tall oak, whose vigorous branches form
An ample shade and brave the wildest storm,
High o'er the subject wood is seen to grow,
The guard and glory of the trees below; (II, 119–22)

Manners may also be seen as the solution to the problems that the labourers have in suffering and being still. Their lives are symbolized by blighted or withered trees. The re-establishment of responsible paternalism will get the sap rising again. The stables of corruption will be cleansed and the tall oak will protect the smaller trees from blight. Although there are tensions and inconsistencies between the two books of *The Village*, it is important to remember that Crabbe is always the 'overseer of the country poor'. It is then perhaps inevitable that the poem should end with a tribute to the aristocracy as the natural overseers of the overseers. This is part of Crabbe's polemic for officialdom as it ought to be rather than as it was.

3 William Wordsworth and the real estate

Unworthy purposes

Wordsworth toadied the counter-revolutionary line with the worst of them towards the end of his career. He was forever moaning away about the way in which social edifices were crumbling because tried and tested props and buttresses had not been repaired. He also lamented the lack of 'moral cement'[1] to bind the whole structure together. He felt, somewhat predictably, that self-interest was shaking the very foundations. His breathtakingly unoriginal solution was to try to persuade everybody to support their local landed aristocrat. He showed them the conservative way when he lent his support to the Lowthers in the 1818 election. Self-interest was apparently destroying civilization. Now the Lowthers had used their substantial influence to secure Wordsworth's appointment as distributor of stamps for Westmorland in 1813. Although minor bureaucrats were not supposed to be actively involved in electioneering, Wordsworth nevertheless inflicted two almost unreadable election addresses on the unfortunate freeholders of Westmorland in 1818. It would appear that self-interest and civilization were not exactly incompatible. Civilization was, according to this very civil servant, a large landed estate:

As far as it concerns the general well-being of the Kingdom, it would be easy to shew, that if the democratic activities of the great Towns and of the manufacturing Districts, were not counteracted by the sedentary power of large estates, continued from generation to generation in particular families, it would be scarcely possible that the Laws and Constitution of the Country could sustain the shocks which they would be subject to. And as to our own County, *that* man must be strangely prejudiced, who does not perceive how desirable it is, that some powerful Individual should be attached to it; who, by his influence with Government, may facilitate the execution of any plan tending, with due concern for the *general* welfare, to the especial benefit of Westmorland. The influence of the House of

Lowther is, we acknowledge, great; but has a case been made out, that this influence has been abused?[2]

It presumably depended on whether the Lowthers used their influence wisely on your behalf, or abused it by taking action against you. Henry Brougham, who entered the electoral lists against such 'sedentary power' certainly felt that he could rest his case on the fact that the family had a whole county, not to mention a hack writer, in their political pocket. Wordsworth's election addresses ought to have sent the freeholders scampering over to Brougham, but the Lowther boys did in fact romp home. Wordsworth was entitled to vote in the election himself as Lord Lowther had helped him to buy a freehold in Westmorland in 1806. No wonder he was strangely prejudiced in favour of the landed aristocracy. They helped William to pay the bills with a handful of silver.

Angry young men become more aristocratic than the aristocracy with monotonous regularity. Wordsworth made surprisingly few twists and turns on his journey down this well-trodden path. There is only really a difference of emphasis between the 1818 election addresses and poems such as 'Michael'. Wordsworth wrote to Charles James Fox in 1801 to try to interest him in the plight of small farmers in the Lake District:

In the two Poems, 'The Brothers' and 'Michael', I have attempted to draw a picture of the domestic affections, as I know they exist amongst a class of men who are now almost confined to the North of England. They are small independent *proprietors* of land here called statesmen, men of respectable education who daily labour on their own little properties. The domestic affections will always be strong amongst men who live in a country not crowded with population, if these men are placed above poverty. But if they are proprietors of small estates, which have descended to them from their ancestors, the power which these affections will acquire amongst such men is inconceivable to those who have only an opportunity of observing hired labourers, farmers, and the manufacturing Poor. Their little tract of land serves as a kind of permanent rallying point for their domestic feelings, as a tablet upon which they are written which makes them objects of memory in a thousand instances when they would otherwise be forgotten.[3]

The increasing belief that small was inefficient was, according to Wordsworth, leading to the virtual genocide of this race of small proprietors and all that they stood for. These 'statesmen', like the Lowthers, handed down their estates from father to son. In this, and other respects, they merely illustrated that the great and small were inextricably connected. If these small estates were allowed to be broken up, then it was only a matter of time before the aristocratic estates and the realm of the state itself crumbled away. 'Domestic affections' and a sense of place and pride would, presumably, be replaced by mere self-interest. The argument is essentially the same whether you work downwards from the large estate, or upwards from the small one. 'Michael' and the 1818 election addresses only differ in emphasis.

'Michael' appears to be concerned with refuge.[4] It is necessary to leave 'the public way' in order to reach the 'straggling heap of unhewn stones', which, like the bones of a dead sheep, are strewn over a particular part of the landscape. This 'public way' represents orthodox interpretations of historical progress. Wordsworth establishes a contrast between such official, linear versions of history and a more private version. Michael's story is significantly 'ungarnish'd with events', in other words with what historians classify as important events. It is 'a history' or a story, rather than history. Wordsworth is not, however, just taking refuge in early eighteenth-century rural society. He is trying to suggest that the lessons which may be drawn from this simple story of farming folk might offer a more acceptable social foundation. He draws out these lessons or worthy purposes by reflecting on the relative merits of past and present. His emphasis is reflective rather than purely descriptive. He implies that the virtues of thrift, frugality, patience and perseverance, all of which he claims to have found in this early eighteenth-century society, could put the country back on the right road. Reflection has led to thoughts of rescue. His initial suggestion is that such rescue will be on a fairly limited scale:

Therefore, although it be a history
Homely and rude, I will relate the same
For the delight of a few natural hearts,
And with yet fonder feeling, for the sake
Of youthful Poets, who among these Hills
Will be my second self when I am gone.

Pastoral is an underground literature in which stories are passed on and kept alive by the faithful few. Yet the unfinished sheep-fold provides a warning for the present. You may not need cement to build with dry-stone, but you must have 'moral cement' in order to achieve anything permanent in both private and public life. If public life is based on 'domestic affections', then there may be a chance of rescuing it from the error of its ways. Public figures like Charles James Fox were invited to read the poem and then act upon it. Such attempts at social rescue are severely compromised by strains of requiem. The farmhouse needs to be approached with due religious care and attention. The brook may be 'boisterous', but the atmosphere at this shrine is dominated by 'an utter solitude'. The clipping tree represents a spire and the heap of stones a bare, ruined choir. Wordsworth has come both to praise and bury Michael. The poem has come full circle. We start by leaving 'the public way' to find these stones and we finish up there as well:

The Cottage which was nam'd The Evening Star
Is gone, the ploughshare has been through the ground
On which it stood; great changes have been wrought
In all the neighbourhood, yet the Oak is left
That grew beside their Door; and the remains
Of the unfinished Sheep-fold may be seen
Beside the boisterous brook of Green-head Gill.

Our beginning is also our end. This circular movement, and the requiem which accompanies it, rules out any chance of effective social rescue.

Wordsworth's vision of rural society is mediated and controlled by refuge, reflection, rescue and requiem, yet the most significant aspect of 'Michael' is the way in which it reconstructs the past. The plough that broke this plain style of living was not actually driven by anybody. This provides a good example of the way in which Wordsworth is unwilling to commit himself even to general propositions about economic agency in relation to the internal structure of rural society. The nearest he comes to it is when he raises the issue of land tenure, which was very much the grievance of grievances as far as the Lakeland farmers were concerned:

These fields were burthen'd when they came to me;
'Till I was forty years of age, not more
Than half of my inheritance was mine.

Yet fields do not burthen themselves, just as ploughs do not drive themselves. Wordsworth is deliberately vague about economic agency because he is trying to play the oldest trick in the crooked pastoralist's cooked book. He wants to suggest that early eighteenth-century rural society was a pre-capitalist utopia.

Michael and his wife, Isabel, are, apparently, able to take such a pride in their work because it is their work. There is no division of labour. Cottage industry appears to take place in a vacuum:

She was a woman of a stirring life
Whose heart was in her house: two wheels she had
Of antique form, this large for spinning wool,
That small for flax, and if one wheel had rest,
It was because the other was at work.

The cottage was a veritable hive of 'eager industry'. If this was taken away, it too would become merely a heap of useless stones. Property and possessions provided a vitalizing eagerness, or what Wordsworth referred to in 'The Old Cumberland Beggar' as 'vital anxiousness'. Adam Smith and the political economists would have agreed with this equation between economic vitality and 'anxiousness'. Yet Michael and his ilk might well have been a great deal more anxious than Wordsworth implies, for cottage industry was not carried out in such splendid isolation. All the evidence, including Wordsworth's own prose works, suggests that there was an economic market-place in the Lake District itself. The products of cottage industry were bought and sold. Any mention of this in the poem would have raised questions about economic agency, so Wordsworth reconstructs the past by presenting us with a self-sufficient family unit, who are hermetically sealed off from the outside world. Their cottage stands 'single' and they too stand aloof from any economic community. It is therefore impossible for them to be attacked and destroyed by economic agents from within Lake District society itself. We learn that Michael has agreed to stand surety for his nephew. We do not learn, incidentally, whether this nephew actually lives and works in the Lake District. The implication is that he does not, for 'unforeseen misfortunes suddenly/Had press'd upon him'. This sounds like the supposedly alien commercial world with its booms and slumps rather than the natural rhythms and patterns of farming life. Michael decides to try to pay off this forfeiture by sending his son, Luke, off to work in the 'dissolute' city with another member of the family. This means that the small estate does not have to be broken up and sold off. It also means that son will be able to inherit from father. Luke leaves the cottage and begins his journey along 'the public way'. He fails to remember the virtues of the face-to-face, shoulder-to-shoulder world he has left behind. He forgets that pride and dignity in labour cement a family together. It is, then, an ill-defined and significantly distanced commercial ethos which destroys Michael's estate. This presumably drives the plough by remote control. The land is, incidentally, not bought up by a member of the Lakeland community. A stranger, who may well have made his money in the 'dissolute city', finally gets possession of the estate. As suggested, Wordsworth can only achieve this distance between commerce and the farming community by a process of reconstruction. We do, it is true, learn about other members of the family and some of the neighbours are allowed walk-on parts. Yet the overall impression conveyed by the poem is that Michael, Isabel and Luke are an island entire unto themselves. Robert Burns shows in 'The Cottar's Saturday Night' that it is perfectly possible to evoke this sense of splendid isolation without necessarily reconstructing the entire agricultural community. Saturday night is an island in a sea of commercialized agriculture. The family make a special point of returning from their various scattered occupations for this particular evening. One of the many problems with 'Michael' is that every night is Saturday night.

It is easy enough to think of products which are advertised as being both natural and historically authentic. If the advertising boys wanted us to wear old-fashioned, hand-knitted socks, they would probably show us a farmer's wife, all wrinkles, white hair and toothless smile, cheerfully at work on an antique spinning-wheel. We would probably realize, instanter if not sooner, that the natural setting and the antique, or historical, props were being used by them as hidden persuaders. Similarly, if they tried to persuade us to drink pints and pints of 'old familiar' by showing us a venerable old shepherd having a quick one as the sun went down over the clipping tree, we would probably be able to read the image without too much difficulty. What is Wordsworth trying to peddle in 'Michael'? It is substantially the same product as he was trying to sell to the freeholders of Westmorland in 1818, for he is primarily concerned to divorce real estate, or economics, from concepts of estate. He does this, as suggested, by ignoring or evading questions of economic agency. Farmers' wives do not go to market. Ploughs drive themselves and fields are mysteriously burdened with debts. Strangers snap up property and an alien commercial system casts dark shadows over the landscape. Such an image must be seen as propaganda for the local gentry and aristocracy, as it conveniently ignores even the possibility that they might have been Michael's real enemies. The historical evidence, particularly with regard to land tenure, suggests that this was more of a probability than a possibility. John Bailey described in his *General View of the Agriculture of the County of Cumberland* (1794) how the large landowners were able to extract feudal obligations from the statesmen:

There are probably few counties, where *property in land* is divided into such small parcels as in Cumberland; and those small properties so universally occupied by the owners; by far the greatest part of which are held under the lords of the manors, by that species of vassalage, called *customary tenure*; subject to the payment of fines and heriots, on alienation, death of the Lord, or death of tenant, and the payment of certain annual rents, and performance of various services, called *Boon-days* such as getting and leading the lord's peats, plowing and harrowing his land, reaping his corn, haymaking, carrying letters, &c, &c whenever summoned by the lord. (p. 11)

Bailey estimated that two-thirds of the county was held under the feudal sway of customary tenure. Those who leased their property were even worse off, since the aristocracy and gentry of Cumberland rarely signed any binding documents or let out their property for longer than nine years at a stretch. A. Pringle's *General View of the Agriculture of the County of Westmorland* (1794) made the same complaints against customary tenure. Statesmen in the Lake District also had the lords of the manor on their backs for tithes since most of these were owned by lay impropriators.

Unlike the election addresses, 'Michael' should be seen as implicit rather than explicit propaganda for the Lowther family, since relationships between the Wordsworths and the Lowthers were cool to freezing when the poem was actually written. Wordsworth's father had acted as a political agent for the Lowthers, which ought to make us cynical of the attempts in Book Nine of *The Prelude* and elsewhere to pretend that the Lake District had once been an egalitarian republic. It was in reality more like an extensive pocket borough. The community as a whole had never been Hawkshead writ large. After his father's death, Wordsworth and the other members of the family were involved in a long wrangle to try to get the Lowthers to pay up for the services which had been rendered. This dispute was not settled until 1802. Although 'Michael' was not written specifically for the Lowthers, there was nothing in it which they, or their rivals such as the Curwens, could object to, for their role as economic agents in the community is not even hinted at. Luke is not packed off to a local town such as Whitehaven, from which the Lowthers controlled their extensive coal and tobacco empires. He is sent to an unnamed city. Thus the message that the estate is being swamped by an alien commercial spirit is not compromised by the recognition that the large estates of the Lowthers and the Curwens were built on the foundations of capitalist enterprises. If Luke had gone to Whitehaven, he might have noticed that a lot of small statesmen had been cleared off the land so that they would not impede the production and transportation of coal. Statesmen were also cleared off to make way for agrarian as well as industrial capitalism. Like most other rural areas in this period, the Lake District was subjected to a double standard. Those at the bottom of the scale were hemmed in with paternalistic, in this particular case almost feudalistic, restrictions. They also had to put up with the disadvantages of capitalism just for good measure. Those at the top of the scale were able to exploit both paternalism and capitalism to the full.[5] Wordsworth tries to peddle us an image in which paternalism is presented as individualism and capitalism as totally alien. He is thus writing propaganda for the victors.

Wordsworth told Fox that both 'Michael' and 'The Brothers' were 'faithful copies from nature'.[6] They were, of course, nothing of the kind. There may appear to be a contradiction between this assertion of authenticity and the fact that 'Michael', like other lyrical ballads, is subtitled 'A Pastoral Poem'. Yet this subtitle probably needs to be taken ironically. It is clearly stated in the 1800 Preface to *Lyrical Ballads* that conventional literary expectations are going to be turned upside down:

It is supposed, that by the act of writing in verse an Author makes a formal engagement that he will gratify certain known habits of association, that he not only thus apprizes the Reader that certain classes of ideas and expressions will be found in his book, but that others will be carefully excluded. (p. ix)

Wordsworth and Coleridge tried iconoclastically to smash such formal engagements. As far as 'Michael' is concerned, Wordsworth assumes that the reader, like the tourist, has certain preconceived ideas about pastoral. These need to be confronted by the realities of rural life. Wordsworth's brisk, guidebook tone at the beginning of the poem needs to be seen as pastiche. The description of 'The pastoral Mountains' probably needs to be taken ironically as well, for, as a general but by no means infallible rule, Wordsworth does not describe mountains in the Lake District as being pastoral. The farms around Tintern Abbey, the downs around Salisbury Plain and the valleys around Goslar in Switzerland are described as being pastoral, but this is almost to differentiate these landscapes from the mountains, if not the valleys, of the Lake District. Wordsworth claims in Book Eight of *The Prelude* that he has always been fascinated by real rather than imaginary shepherds. Classical and Renaissance pastoral fictions were no substitute for the real thing. Although Wordsworth does claim, rather interestingly, that there were jolly English peasants who danced around maypoles, such creatures played no part in his childhood:

... the times had scattered all
These lighter graces, and the rural custom
And manners which it was my chance to see
In childhood were severe and unadorned,
The unluxuriant produce of a life
Intent on little but substantial needs,
Yet beautiful, and beauty that was felt. (204–10)[7]

Wordsworth's emphasis on the 'severe and unadorned' may be seen as part of a general attempt to convince us that his descriptions of Lakeland society really are faithfully copied from nature. Yet particular shepherds are so inextricably connected with the geographical and emotional landscape of childhood that the equation between 'severe' and 'faithful' or realistic, which is a shaky one at the best of times, does not hold. They emerge from the mountain mists like giants and disappear into the setting sun. A love of nature leads to a love of mankind simply because, as far as these shepherds are concerned, it is difficult to work out what the difference is. They thus become an integral part of Wordsworth's pastoral perspective. 'Michael' follows the same pattern as Book Eight of *The Prelude*. There is an attempt to juxtapose pastoral conventions with the 'severe and unadorned'. Wordsworth uses a number of devices to try to achieve this kind of authenticity. He pointed out that the poem was a true story as it was based on

a family to whom had belonged, many years before, the house we lived in at Town-End, along with some fields and woodlands on the eastern shore of Grasmere.[8]

He tells us, in the poem itself, that the story was one he had heard in his youth. Topographical details help to sustain this illusion of authenticity. The stones are also important in this attempt to move from pastoral fictions to historical facts. If these stones actually exist, then the implication is that the story associated with them is, if not quite so tangible, then certainly real. Like Oscar Wilde, we should be suspicious of these and other documentary strategies. Vivian in 'The Decay of Lying' notices that Wordsworth has a habit of finding 'in stones the sermons he had already hidden there'.[9] We should always be on our guard against interpretative sleights-of-hand, particularly when they may be hidden behind supposedly realistic trappings. Wordsworth may not present us with a world of jolly good shepherds fleecing their flocks, but his pastoralism hides a world in which such members of rural society are fleeced by their local overseers.

Circus turns

If all the young men like Luke have gone to become just another face in another crowd, then the writing is well and truly on the cottage wall. Wordsworth maintains, in 'Michael' and elsewhere, that the days of 'domestic affections' have been numbered. Although he does in fact try to convince Charles James Fox that these values were still just about alive and well in 1801, poems such as 'The Female Vagrant' present a rather different picture.[10] 'Domestic affections' are only kept alive by outcasts and solitaries. The vagrant's troubles are brought about by gentrification:

... Then rose a stately hall our woods among,
And cottage after cottage owned its sway.
No joy to see a neighbouring house, or stray
Through pastures not his own, the master took;
My Father dared his greedy wish gainsay;
He loved his old hereditary nook,
And ill could I the thought of such sad parting brook.

Wordsworth is again deliberately vague about economic agency. Halls do not build themselves, just as ploughs do not drive themselves. We are also not told whether the new master is a native of the Lake District or an outsider. All the indications are that he is a stranger. So, once again, there is no consideration of the internal economic structure of the community. This new master attempts to buy out the vagrant's father. He may have suggested that a few 'domestic affections' might accidentally get broken, if the old man continued to block his view. The father is certainly 'Sore traversed in whate'er he bought and sold' and so has to leave this particular cottage. Economic sharp practice is being associated with outsiders. The family manage to set themselves up in another cottage, so father is at least able to die happy. He may not have 'One field, a flock, and what the neighbouring flood/Supplied' any more, but there was a good old cottage roof over his head. He is thus able to retain illusions about the permanence of this way of life:

. . . My happy father died
When sad distress reduced the childrens' meal:
Thrice happy! that from him the grave did hide
The empty loom, cold earth, and silent wheel,
And tears that flowed for ills which patience could not heal.

The vagrant and her husband are forced to leave the Lake District and follow like dogs at the 'heels of war'. Tragedy strikes yet again:

. . . All perished – all, in one remorseless year,
Husband and children! one by one, by sword
And ravenous plague, all perished: every tear
Dried up, despairing, desolate, on board
A British ship I waked, as from a trance restored.

She responds in true Wordsworthian fashion to the calming influence of nature, in this case represented by the sea, but is finally turned adrift. When she reaches dry land she is eventually taken to a hospital, since she does not speak 'the beggar's language' and is thus unable to support herself. She becomes more in tune with this language later on:

My heart is touched to think that men like these,
The rude earth's tenants, were my first relief:
How kindly did they paint their vagrant ease!
And their long holiday that feared not grief,
For all belonged to all, and each was chief.
No plough their sinews strained; on grating road
No wain they drove, and yet, the yellow sheaf
In every vale for their delight was stowed:
For them, in nature's meads, the milky udder flowed.

These vagrants are nature's statesmen because, against all the odds, they manage to cling to the simple virtues. Wordsworth is suggesting that, when both local and national communities are dislocated, only those who remain on the margins can keep these crucial values alive. The vagrant finally realizes that she must to her own self be true:

. . . But, what afflicts my peace with keenest ruth
Is, that I have my inner self abused,
Foregone the home delight of constant truth,
And clear and open soul, so prized in fearless youth.

Times may change, but values should remain the same.

It is sometimes suggested that this particular poem offers a savage critique of unjust wars on both the home and foreign fronts, but Wordsworth's treatment of the internal structure of rural society is, once again, evasive. Indeed, it has many similarities with 'Michael' in this respect. Michael may have been splendidly isolated, but at least he was able to die on his own estate. He was probably even buried in the 'family mold', yet, if the plough had ripped up the ground immediately after Luke's fall from Wordsworthian grace, then Michael too might have been forced onto the roads and margins of rural society. His 'domestic affections', instead of being fixed and tangibly located in a particular place, would have become completely internalized. The hum of contented industry was in fact replaced by an 'utter solitude' after his death. The solitaries and outcasts keep alive the values which would otherwise have died with Michael and been buried forever in the 'family mold'. Dorothy Wordsworth recorded in her *Journal* for 2 June 1802 one of the many visits to their backdoor by beggars:

Yesterday an old man called, a grey-headed man, above 70 years of age. He said he had been a soldier, that his wife and children had died in Jamaica. He had a Beggar's wallet over his shoulders, a coat of shreds and patches altogether of a drab colour – he was tall, and though his body was bent he had the look of one used to have been upright.[11]

The vagrant's father had a 'bending body' and the leech gatherer, in 'Resolution and Independence', is 'bent-double'. Those who manage against all the odds to keep 'upright', like the discharged soldier in Book Four of *The Prelude*, are still arrestingly abnormal. Wordsworth's travelling circus of freakish outcasts may appear to offer a critique of the unacceptable face of rural society, yet they merely endorse the same propagandist interpretation of social change as 'Michael' tries to sell us. We are certainly presented with a rural wasteland. The last of the human flock meagrely shuffle about trying to remember what the good old days were really like. The brothers Ewbank are described as 'the last of all their race' in 'The Brothers'. It is almost as if a nuclear bomb has been dropped on the landscape. This is precisely the problem. Wordsworth is so busy depicting the effects of such bombs, that he can conveniently ignore the explosion taking place within rural society itself. The landscape and its inhabitants are attacked from the outside by bombs such as commerce, gentrification, 'dissolute cities' and even the Napoleonic wars. Yet there was an economic bomb, which was being exploded right under his nose. As it was being detonated by the local aristocracy and gentry, we do not hear a great deal about it.

It is also worth stressing that, like Michael, these solitaries and outcasts were only expected to be independent in carefully prescribed dependent situations. Dorothy's description in her *Journal* for 22 December 1801 of an encounter with yet another beggar illustrates how these outcasts were expected to conform:

As we came up the White Moss we met an old man, who I saw was a beggar by his two bags hanging over his shoulder, but from a half laziness, half indifference, and a wanting to *try* him if he would speak I let him pass. He said nothing, and my heart smote me. I turned back and said You are begging? 'Ay', says he. I gave him a halfpenny. William, judging from his appearance joined in I suppose you were a sailor? 'Ay,' he replied, 'I have been 57 years at sea, 12 of them on board a man-of-war under Sir Hugh Palmer.' Why have you not a pension? 'I have no pension, but I could have got into Greenwich hospital but all my officers are dead.'[12]

This game of beggarman's bluff represents a means test, in every sense of the word. Dorothy felt not only willing but able to '*try*' this particular beggar. He should, after all, have put himself in a dependent position straight away. That was the rule of the social game. The beggar, who had probably heard that the Wordsworths usually liked their money's worth as well, decided it was not worth making a pitch. As far as Dorothy was concerned, this represented a defiant and independent gesture. Her heart may have been smitten by compassion, but she wanted to control this compassion on her own terms. So she immediately forced the discharged seaman into the obligatory subservient role. Once money had actually been told into his hand, he was under an obligation to tell William about his life and hard times. William, at first anyway, treated him as any overseer of the country poor would have done. There is, incidentally, no evidence to suggest that this particular beggar had any connection with small statesmen living or dead, but his treatment may still be related to Wordsworth's prescriptive attitude towards Michael and his kind. The poems themselves contain evidence of this attitude. Michael knows his place. He also knows a great deal about patience, perseverance and frugality. If external evidence is required, then examples of pastoralism in performance, like the drama which took place at Moss Side on 22 December 1801, ought to be considered. Wordsworth's pastoralism is riddled with paradoxes: the independent are expected to be dependent and the outcasts are expected to conform.

Face-to-face

The real problem with Wordsworth's representation of rural society is that the poachers are transformed into the gamekeepers. The Lowthers and their kind are either explicitly or implicitly held up as shining examples to all other gamekeepers, yet they were not averse to economic poaching expeditions. The 1818 election addresses show Wordsworth at his most explictly conservative, although *Lyrical Ballads, The Prelude*, and indeed most of the poems on which his inflated poetic reputation is based, carry at least the seeds of this conservatism within them. Hannah More, Legh Richmond and Mary Mitford all sang the praises of the small, face-to-face community. Wordsworth chimed in with them. He found, rather surprisingly, welcoming faces at Cambridge, but failed miserably to respond to London street theatre. He describes his bumpkin's progress in Book Seven of *The Prelude*:

Here there and everywhere a weary throng,
The comers and the goers face to face,
Face after face; the string of dazzling wares,
Shop after shop, with symbols, blazoned names,
And all the tradesman's honours overhead: (171–5)

It was the London Corresponding Sociey which threatened to replace 'face to face' with 'members unlimited', or 'face after face'. Wordsworth is lost in the streets of London town because the good old days when everybody knew each other and their place appear to have gone forever:

How often, in the overflowing streets,
Have I gone forwards with the crowd, and said

Unto myself, 'The face of every one
That passes by me is a mystery!'
Thus have I looked, nor ceased to look, oppressed
By thoughts of what and whither, when and how,
Until the shapes before my eyes became
A second-sight procession, such as glides
Over still mountains, or appears in dreams;
And all the ballast of familiar life,
The present, and the past; hope, fear; all stays,
All laws of acting, thinking, speaking man
Went from me, neither knowing me, nor known. (594–606)

The city is 'dissolute' because it dissolves personal identity. Wordsworth is swept into the ebbing and flowing tide of street life against his will. He is carried along by the crowd and feels as if he is drowning. His identity and will are being submerged. He is being literally reduced to a part of the mainstream. This passage is often interpreted as a great poet's affirmation of individual, nay human, values, which is both of its time and for all time. Wordsworth is all for reason when he stands there feeling 'oppressed' in those city streets. Such interpretations accept Wordsworthian propaganda as the whole truth. They firmly believe, for instance, that familiarity does not breed contempt. They do not question assumptions that villages and policemen are good things. Like the village bobby, Wordsworth only feels at home when he knows all the faces on his patch or manor. He can then successfully interrogate them with 'thoughts of what and whither, when and how' as they pass by. This rescues him from drowning, but it means that most other people are swamped by a parochial paternalism. George Canning, the Tory politician, struck a Wordsworthian note when he defended the counter-revolutionary legislation which had been passed in the wake of Peterloo during the 1820 election campaign:

Ancient habits, which the reformers would call prejudices; preconceived attachments, which they would call corruption; that mutual respect which makes the eye of a neighbour a security for each man's good conduct, but which the reformers would stigmatize as a confederacy among the few for the dominion over their fellows – all these things make men difficult to be moved on the sudden to any extravagant and violent enterprise. But bring together a multitude of individuals having no permanent relation to each other, no common tie, but what arises from their concurrences as members of that meeting, a tie dissolved as soon as the meeting is at an end; – in such an aggregation of individuals there is no such mutual respect, no such check upon the proceedings of each man from the awe of his neighbour's disapprobation . . . .[13]

Political meetings ought to be put down because they were not ballasted up with the familiar. Pastoral suggests that all communities, including the political one, are made up of friends and neighbours. They are face-to-face societies, which are based on a 'common tie' and a 'mutual respect'. Yet our village was not really their village. Similarly, for all his parade of homely, folksie togetherness, Canning was in fact trying to justify some ruthlessly paternalistic legislation. The implementation of the Six Acts against the radical movement is another example of pastoralism in performance.

Wordsworth retreats from the 'overflowing streets' of the big city to the safe, secure and predictable community of the Lake District. He is not oppressed by the 'little Family of Men', who gather under Helvellyn's watchful eye for a country fair. He sets the contrasting scene at the beginning of Book Eight of *The Prelude*:

Booths are there none; a stall or two is here;
A lame man or a blind, the one to beg,
The other to make music; hither, too,
From far, with basket, slung upon her arm,
Of hawker's wares – books, pictures, combs and pins –
Some aged woman finds her way again,
Year after year a punctual visitant!
The showman with his freight upon his back,
And once, perchance, in lapse of many years
Prouder itinerant, mountebank, or he
Whose wonders in a covered wain lie hid. (25–35)

The 'Ancient habits' and 'preconceived attachments' that have been built up 'year after year' provide the perfect antidote to the sea of metropolitan faces. Friends and neighbours have been looking forward to the event all year. The fair is given an economic dimension. A heifer gets a new master and some sheep are put in a pen and sold. A 'sweet lass of the Valley' rather shyly tries her hand at flogging some apples and pears. Yet country fairs, in the Lake District and elsewhere, were also places where the 'little Family of Men' bought and sold each other. Wordsworth was obviously feeling far too fragile after being oppressed up in London to want to deal with economic oppression. Perhaps the mountain mists actually obscured all but the quaint and folksie from neighbour Wordsworth's eye.

The 1800 Preface to *Lyrical Ballads* may be related to the ruthlessly folksie conservatism which controls Books Seven and Eight of *The Prelude*. The poetic soul is, once again, in full flight from the city. We are pompously informed that 'the great national events which are daily taking place, and the encreasing accumulation of men in cities' is reducing the mind 'to a state of almost savage torpor' (p. xviii). This was to be Mary Mitford's line thirty years later as well. Parochial patriotism was much safer than an interest and involvement in national and international issues. An hour a day listening to the nightingales keeps Tom Paine at bay. As the city apparently corrupts language and literature by producing a craving for sensationalism, Wordsworth retreats back to the land. The cottage becomes a linguistic and philosophical castle:

Low and rustic life was generally chosen because in that situation the essential passions of the heart find a better soil in which they can attain their maturity, are less under restraint, and speak a plainer and more emphatic language; because in that situation our elementary feelings exist in a state of greater simplicity and consequently may be more accurately contemplated and more forcibly communicated; because the manners of rural life germinate from those elementary feelings; and from the necessary character of rural occupations are more easily comprehended; and are more durable; and lastly, because in that situation the passions of men are incorporated with the beautiful and permanent forms of nature. (p. xi)

The low life may really be the high life. The rustics are at least rooted in the good earth like the flowers of the field. This earth does not move in a sensationally extravagant fashion, so there is permanence and continuity. A virtue can be made out of any necessity. Rural occupations are not hard work, but the best possible linguistic and philosophical training ground. A face-to-face community should never be regarded as constricting, since it provides nature's statesmen and scholars with all the opportunities they need to hone up their discourse:

from their rank in society and the sameness and narrow circle of their intercourse, being less under the action of social vanity they convey their feelings and notions in simple and unelaborated expressions. (p. xii)

Joseph Arch and John Clare might have had a few 'simple and

unelaborated expressions' to vent against this kind of patronizing nonsense about the closed university of life. The Preface is certainly riddled with contradictions. Is this philosophical language the product of all rustic life, or does it just occur in specific areas like the Lake District? Pastoral poets may well have put their own words into the mouths of their jolly shepherds, but isn't neighbour Wordsworth doing exactly the same by refusing to recognize that rustics have an unfortunate habit of speaking in dialect? He has obviously written the sermons himself, before hiding them behind the stones. The most interesting contradiction concerns the way in which the Preface argues against previous versions of pastoral only to conclude that peasants are philosophers. Wordsworth's clothing may be 'severe and unadorned', but it is sheep's clothing none the less. As such, it provided excellent cover for aristocratic wolves. Pastoral platitudes about the 'sedentary power' of aristocratic estates being the bulwark of poor old Michael's small estate disguised the sharp practices of real estate.

4 The unacceptable face of rural society

Playing the game

William Cobbett often appears to be endorsing rather uncritically the values of the welfare estate in his *Rural Rides* (1830). He suggested in his description of the Duke of Richmond's estates that the aristocracy might well provide the best umpires for village politics and village cricket:

This is a series of villages all belong to *the Duke of Richmond,* the outskirts of whose park and woods come up to these farming lands, *all of which belong to him*; and, I suppose, that every inch of land, that I came through this morning, belongs either to the Duke of Richmond, or to Lord Egremont. No *harm* in that, mind, if those who till the land have *fair play*; and I should act unjustly towards these noblemen, if I insinuated that the husbandmen have not fair play, as far as the landlords are concerned; for everybody speaks well of them. (p. 73)

Cobbett is dealing with the present here, yet the implication is that this is an isolated example of the kind of '*fair play*' which had once made the whole of England so merry. Samuel Bamford's lament for the social relationships of the Lancashire of his childhood suggests that the aristocracy and gentry played fair by being there. He recorded in *Early Days* (1849) how there were

no grinding bailiffs and land-stewards in those days, to stand betwixt the gentleman and his labourer, or his tenant; to screw up rents, to screw down livings, and to invent and transact all little meanesses for so much per annum. Mercenaries of this description were not then prevalent on our Lancashire estates. The gentleman transacted his own business; he met his farmer, or his labourer, face to face. (p. 19)

The engraver Thomas Bewick also fondly recalled alliances between the cottage and the big house in the Geordieland of his childhood. Cobbett, Bamford and Bewick had no quarrel with property rights as such. They believed that if the aristocracy and gentry actively and personally discharged their responsibilities, then everybody's property would be safe and sure.

This belief meant that the main thrust of Cobbett's conservative-radical bludgeon was directed against 'mercenaries' and other new men. The main purpose behind his 1823 Norfolk Petition was to show how certain new families had profiteered during the Napoleonic wars and thus been able to buy their way into positions of power and influence. They were the grievance of grievances. The false and the fraudulent succeeded at the local as well as the national level. Gentrification was a desolating abomination. Cobbett caught a *nouveau riche* squire called Charington in the sights of his old blunderbuss as he rode through Reigate on 20 October 1825. Charington's farm was up for sale. It was a sign of the gentrified times:

There appeared to have been hardly any *family* in that house, where formerly there were, in all probability, from ten to fifteen men, boys, and maids: and, which was the worst of all, there was a *parlour*! Aye, and a *carpet* and *bell-pull* too! One end of the front of this once plain and substantial house had been moulded into a 'parlour'; and there was the mahogany table, and the fine chairs, and the fine glass, and all as bare-faced upstart as any stock-jobber in the kingdom can boast of. And, there were the decanters, the glasses, the 'dinner-set' of crockery ware, and all just in the true stock-jobber style. And I dare say it has been '*Squire* Charington and the *Miss* Charingtons; and not plain Master Charington, and his son Hodge, and his daughter Betty Charington, all of whom this accursed system has, in all likelihood, transmuted into a species of mock gentlefolks, while it has ground the labourers down into real slaves. (pp. 241–2)

This particular squire's poisonous taste in fixtures and fittings damages the health of the labourers, for, instead of providing them with board and lodging, Charington has booted them out of his prissy, cissy home. If they do not know what a fish fork looks like, then it would be embarrassing for all concerned to eat around the same table. Cobbett has Charington in his sights but he does not blast away at him, except perhaps for an angry whiff of grapeshot now and then. It is, according to Cobbett, 'this accursed system' which is the real target. Charington is just another one of its victims. The poor man has to be so appallingly tasteless just to try to keep up the low standards of the *nouveaux riches*. It is they, rather than poor Charington, who are grinding the labourers down into 'real slaves'.

They start off by encouraging these honest farmers to live beyond their means, and then try to wrest these very means from them by a monstrously unfair system of taxation. These stock-jobbers have no manners or morals. They might even commit the ultimate sacrilege of buying the old oak table from the farm. Cobbett has a moment of sheer panic. Perhaps this symbol of the good life will be treated as a joke:

I could not quit this farmhouse without reflecting on the thousands of scores of bacon and thousands of bushels of bread that had been eaten from the long oak-table which, I said to myself, is now perhaps, going, at last, to the bottom of a bridge that some stock-jobber will stick up over an artificial river in his cockney garden. '*By — it shant*', said I, almost in a real passion: and so I requested a friend to buy it for me; and if he do so, I will take it to Kensington, or to Fleet-street, and keep it for the good it has done in the world. (p. 245)

This is pastoral rescue at its purest and simplest. The description of the farm sale as a whole is also pastoral in the sense that rural society is not allowed to carry the seeds of its own destruction within itself. Its enemies are outsiders. Cobbett also appears to be reconstructing rural society by refusing to talk about economic relationships. Commerce is sighted and cited as the enemy. Cobbett obviously felt personally involved in this sale of the Reigate farm. He had himself been declared bankrupt in 1820 and forced to sell up what remained of his once extensive estates around Botley. Although he and Charington were poles apart, their enemies were apparently the same.

This particular description, like the one of the Duke of Richmond's estates, is inherently conservative. Yet they formed the basis for some of Cobbett's radical attacks on early nineteenth-century society. Pastoralism could be a vehicle for social protest as well as a method of containing and controlling this very social protest. When rain stops play in important cricket matches, the radio commentators start to play with pastoralism. We hear a lot about the good old days of true sportsmanship. It is maintained that poor, but well-groomed and greased, heroes of yesteryear could teach the rich modern professional a thing or two. I doubt whether any of the commentators really want to return to those good old days when, before lunch anyway, you could always tell the difference between a gentleman and a player at twenty-two paces. They are merely using these casual corinthians, who did not have to be paid up before they played up, as a way of making certain criticisms of the modern game. Their acceptance of pastoralism is, in other words, essentially rhetorical. It is a means to a particular end. This was often the case with Cobbett's pastoralism. Did he really want the labourers to go back to being dependent upon the Duke of Richmond and Master Charington? I doubt it, even though he could be rather an autocratic employer himself. It was, however, the forelock-tugging Wordsworth rather than Cobbett who actually threw his lot in with 'the sedentary power of large estates'. Cobbett preferred to throw the theory of 'sedentary power' at his enemies. Every stick was needed to beat these mongrels and curs with. He held up the Duke of Richmond as a shining example, but, rather ironically, by the time that *Rural Rides* was published in book form he had lost any faith he might have had in the ability of an aristocracy to set the standards. They were, more often than not, the villains of his journalistic pieces on the Swing riots. Hazlitt was right to notice that contradiction was Cobbett's strength as well as his weakness. It would therefore be silly to try to explain away these contradictions. He used Squire Charington to try to illustrate the fact that the labourers were worse off than before, yet, at the same time, he was offering them a degree of political and social independence which would have caused old Master Charington to turn in his oak coffin in the family mold. His acceptance of pastoralism was rhetorical, but not entirely so.

Raymond Williams has suggested that all nostalgic descriptions of the good old ways of rural England should not be taken literally. If we take a ride on his historical escalator, we will notice fairly quickly that such laments were hardly invented by Cobbett. We can, for instance, stop off at the eighteenth-century floor of the historical department store and listen to Daniel Defoe haranguing the new squires of Essex in his *A Tour Thro' the Whole Island of Great Britain* (1724–7). An oddment which caught my eye recently, tucked away on the seventeenth-century floor, was the petition of 'The Diggers of Warwickshire to all Other Diggers'. This was written during the Midland revolt of 1607. England was obviously none too merry then. The diggers were worried, to put it mildly, by the way in which encroaching tyrants were destroying the patterns of communal life. Sheep had been allowed to become more important than men. Sir Thomas More was, of course, making exactly the same point almost a century before. We do not need to travel any further, for we have already arrived at the conclusion that every generation writes its own history in terms of a fall from economic and social grace. The pastoral lament is the hardiest of perennials. Even Saint Frederick Engels, much to the dismay of the faithful, casts rather a Wordsworthian shadow over the economic life of the eighteenth-century independent cultivator and domestic out-worker in the Introduction to *The Condition of the Working Class in England* (1844). They may have been bone from the neck up, but they were apparently pretty contented chaps. Yet Saint Freddy, even more so than Cobbett, had no desire to return to these good old days. He merely uses them as a means to another end. Such a rhetorical acceptance of pastoralism meant that nostalgia could become a vehicle for social protest, as well as the means of containing and controlling such protest. Cobbett's pastoralism did have its conventional side, yet within these very conventions he managed to produce his own individual brand of social protest. The fact that his acceptance of the conventions might have been rhetorical is not so important as the rhetoric he actually used to convey this protest, for the idiosyncratically independent tone and style of *Rural Rides* provide the best arguments against the dependent paternalism of merry old England.

Fat cats

The good old vicar, like the good old farmer, was a conventional enough pastoral character. Cobbett used him to open up the vexed question of tithes. He noted in his *Legacy to Parsons* (1835) how the Napoleonic wars had been capitalized upon by the establishment. Anybody who dared to criticize tithes was none other than a Jacobin. He might even start trying to undermine bull-baiting next. Pluralism was thus allowed to become rampant. As Cobbett argued in *The Doom of Tithes* (1836), the lay impropriators of tithes were even more to blame than the church rampant, as they were merely using and abusing them to feather their own already well-lined nests. The grotesqueness of the situation was highlighted in 1818 when the Government decided it was necessary to supplement the incomes of the poorest clergy. If tithes were used properly, the clergy would be able to look after themselves and their parishioners as well. The poor but honest vicar, who practised as well as preached charity, became an important part of this argument against modern abuses. Cobbett even left the merry England of the eighteenth-century to go back to late medieval times in his *History of the Protestant Reformation in England and Ireland* (1830). The good old monks could teach the modern church a thing or two about the pastoral care of the people. Like Thomas Carlyle, Protestant Bill Cobbett had no real love for the doctrines of the Roman Catholic Church. It merely provided a thundering good debating point. These points may have been somewhat conventional, yet the point of the debate as a whole needs to be related to specific developments within the period.

Cobbett's version of pastoral, with its plain speaking and dealing farmers and vicars, was bound to have an emotional appeal for those who had seen the unacceptable face of rural society. During the East Anglian bread or blood riots of 1816, the Reverend Vachell's vicarage at Littleport was attacked by an army of agricultural labourers. The jolly peasant was in reality a landless labourer, who baited vicars rather than bulls. Vachell was a clerical magistrate. He was also, in the contemporary jargon, a 'squarson', or a parson who had more in common with the squires than the people. He was thus closely associated with attempts to confine the labourer to both his locality and station in life. His farming techniques tended to confine the labourer to the verge of poverty. He was to claim that over £700 worth of damage had been done by vicar-baiters, although even sympathetic accounts suggest that this estimate contained a certain amount of clerical licence. Even allowing for this, Vachell could not be said to have led a particularly plain life. Isaac Harley, who led the looters, pillagers and villagers against the reverend magistrate, was one of the five labourers hanged at Ely after the riots had been put down.[1] Now there have always been, and probably always will be, odious clergymen like Vachell. If a militant church is established, it is going to ally itself with the establishment. We might therefore worry about whether Cobbett's version of pastoral had an objective as well as a subjective reality. I do not suppose that Isaac Harley did.

The Reverend Fairfax Francklin, the Rector of Attleborough, was also a target of the vicar-baiters during the Swing agricultural riots of 1830. He described in a 'yours, outraged of Attleborough' letter to the Home Office how

about 150 persons chiefly labourers, assembled together armed with large sticks and proceeded from place to place breaking drill and chaff cutting machines.

This mob lurched to the Rectory by about three o'clock in the morning. It was, perhaps ironically, a Sunday. Francklin was suffering from gout at the time and so felt unable to give these disobedient children a dose of Legh Richmond or Hannah More. Two friends of his manfully stepped into the breach and managed to preserve both civilization and machinery:

after parleying with them for more than an hour, prevailed upon them to go away without breaking a chaff cutting machine, by promising that it should not be removed till Monday – on Monday morning at 10 o'clock a vestry meeting took place which was attended by most of the occupiers & a large body of labourers in all at least 300 armed as before . . . .

Francklin had recovered by this time and went to meet his congregation. They demanded that he should reduce his tithes by half. He did not seem short of money. It was, however, the principle which worried the Rector. If God has joined something together, like a parson and his tithes, then it would be sacrilege even to consider putting them asunder. We all know what happens to those who break God's commandments. The labourers responded by breaking the Rector's precious chaff-cutting machine. They kept him cornered in the vestry in the hope that they might eventually break his principles. The cavalry arrived from Wymondham in the nick of time and dispersed the labourers. They did not immediately go off and listen to the nightingales. Francklin's beady eye spotted some strange things that Monday night:

a tricolor flag was hoisted and the language of the rioters was of the most violent & inflammatory description.

The pompous fraud was trying to suggest that Jacobins were leading the jolly bull-baiting peasants astray. There was nothing fundamentally wrong with the structure of rural society itself. There could not be, since it was ordained by God himself. All the problems were caused by an alien, urban radicalism. At its simplest level, this belief that the enemy is never within is similar to Cobbett's special pleading for Squire Charington. Yet the same pastoral foundation could produce very different buildings; Francklin's was frankly counter-revolutionary, while Cobbett's provided shelter for these very urban radicals.[2]

The church took quite a battering in Norfolk throughout the autumn of 1830. There was trouble at the mill pond in Ellingham. The local incumbent, one Reverend Colby, was baptized in it by his congregation. Such incidents provide the raw material for one of the most disturbing scenes in Edward Bond's play about John Clare,

The Fool: Scenes of Bread and Love, which was first performed at
the Royal Court on 18 November 1975. Parson Twice, like Vachell
and Francklin, is heavily committed to agricultural improvement.
His glebe lands profiteth him much. He therefore decided to hide in
the forest as he is likely to be a prime target for the rampaging
villagers. Parochial patriotism is, alas, no more:

And after this terrible night? – When I ride down a lane and meet a labourer
can we look each other in the face? I baptized him and we can't give each
other a decent good morning. They'll raise their hats like an insult . . . . We'll
be reduced to relying on anger or strength or our wits – master *and* servant.
And then what are we? – animals trying to live in houses. For one night's
violence and a handful of silver to spend on drink! (Scene 3)

The villagers discover him while he is mouthing these sort of
pastoral platitudes. They start to strip him. They rather timidly take
away his gold and silver knick-knacks. Deference begins to give way
to defiance. They grab his pearly shirt buttons and then his shirt
itself. The crescendo is reached when finally he stands naked before
them. They grab at his skin. It is soft 'like silk lace' rather than hard
and horny. They are surprised and then outraged that the fine
clothes can cover such a multitude of fine skin. This fat cat is almost
literally torn to pieces in the forest, but Bond is concerned to show
that the labourers, against all the odds, manage to retain their
humanity. Parson Twice is eventually covered with the
blood-stained garments of one of the wounded labourers. Like
Francklin, he is finally rescued by the forces of law and order. Like
Harley, Darkie, the prime mover in this attack on the squarson, is
executed for attempting to undermine his particular village's
politics.

Bond suggests, both here and throughout the play, that early
nineteenth-century rural society needs to be seen in terms of the
survival of the fittest and slickest. Pastoralism covers a multitude of
economic sins. Literary criticism ought, therefore, to take the form
of a brutal strip-tease. Pastoralism should be divested of its
silver-tongued language and myths of the golden age. The shirt
should be taken off its back. It is only when teasingly superficial
frills such as refuge, reflection and requiem have been removed,
that reconstruction, deception and prescription appear in their full
naked horror. Pastoral may be charmingly circular, but Bond
suggests that we can break its spell by reminding ourselves of the
vicious economic circles which trapped John Clare and the other

labourers. Bond is also quite right, at a more specific level, to stress that the established church represented the unacceptable face of rural England. Political and religious dissent went together as far as Joseph Arch was concerned. Even if the clergyman no longer owned his tithes, he was likely to own enough land to put him on the winning side. Jane Austen's father was one of many parsons who were involved in agricultural improvement. There were French agricultural prints in the best bedroom at Steventon Rectory. Mr Knightley really was a father-figure. Vachell, Francklin, Richmond and pluralists like the Reverend George Crabbe had sermons full of solutions to rural problems. They were themselves, however, one of the most pressing and oppressing problems.

Swings and roundabouts

Wars do not generally begin until the harvest has been safely gathered in. The Swing agricultural disturbances of 1830 are no exception to this general historical rule. The beginning of an autumn and winter of discontent was marked by the destruction of threshing machines near Canterbury on 28 August 1830. Machine breaking and more generalized acts of arson quickly established themselves as the disorder of both day and night throughout Kent and neighbouring Sussex. This epidemic of violent protest had spread to other Home counties, as well as Midlands and East Anglian ones, by November. Threshing machines certainly provided a focal point for the rioters in many of these counties, since they threatened to take away what little winter work there was left. Hampshire and Wiltshire were particularly badly infected by machine breaking, yet local conditions tended to produce variations on the general theme of discontent. The Swing rioters had grievances against fat cats like Francklin and Poor Law overseers. They were also concerned with fair trading and so tradesmen lived in fear of the threatening Swing letter, or the even more threatening Swing mob. Indeed, it was precisely because their grievances were essentially local, or perhaps even parochial, that the Swing rioters never posed a really serious threat to the new Whig administration. Although the system of law and order was often very precarious out in the loamy shires, it is generally true that, when the rioters did not disband once their local objectives had been achieved, they were no match for the local yeomanry and militia troops. Retribution was exceeding swift and exceeding sure. Nearly 2000 jolly peasants were put on trial. Some were tried at the local assizes and quarter sessions. Others found themselves face-to-face with a Special Commission. The Government had been concerned by rumours that local juries in Hampshire, Wiltshire, Berkshire, Dorset and Buckinghamshire might be a little too lenient. Swing might just set fire to their property if they were courageous in their convictions. So the Special Commission toured these particular counties meting out justice without any fear of local reprisals, or any knowledge of local conditions. There were 252 death sentences handed out nationwide. The howls of anguished liberal consciences managed to reduce this number to a mere nineteen. Nearly 500 people were, however, kicked 'down and under' and transported to Australia. 600 more were imprisoned in merry old England. If you strip down pastoralism, this is what you find underneath. I almost forgot to mention that nearly 400 threshing machines were destroyed.[3]

The Swing riots took place largely in the corn-belt of England. Cereal farming had always traditionally employed fewer labourers than dairy farming. Cobbett recalled the good old days when all the workers lived in or around the farm. They were in fact farm servants, who were usually hired by the year at the various country fairs. There was always bound to be enough annual work on any reasonably large farm, even a cereal one, to ensure the continued existence of a limited number of these servants.

The great change that took place in the corn-belt in the decades before the Swing riots was the substitution of seasonal employment for guaranteed fixed term contracts. Labourers were only deemed worthy of being hired at certain times of the year. They had to be content with seasonal employment for which they were usually contracted by the day, or during the harvest, by the week. The increasingly prevalent system of paying piece-rate, in other words the contract was for a particular job rather than for a specific length of time, made life even more precarious. The fact that more and more marginal land was taken into cultivation during the Napoleonic wars to increase cereal production meant that there was more work available, but the steady increase in the rural population created a labour surplus. This surplus was exploited by the farmers. They were in a buyer's market and they knew it.

The labourers might have been able to handle the fluctuations of seasonal employment in a surplus labour market, if there had been other means of subsistence to fall back on. Yet such self-help remedies diminished during the early years of the century. Gilbert

White noted in his *The Natural History and Antiquities of Selborne* (1779) how, during what he referred to as the 'dead months' of the agricultural year, it had been customary for the industrious housewives of Hampshire to support themselves

greatly by spinning wool, for making *barragons,* a genteel corded stuff, much in vogue at that time for summer wear; and chiefly manufactured at Alton, a neighbouring town, by some of the people called Quakers: but from circumstances this trade is at an end. (p. 14)

There was, apparently, a brief revival in this particular cottage industry, although in the long term its days were numbered. The inhabitants of Selborne, unlike those of Wordsworth's imagination, were part of an economic chain. The decline of cottage industry in Selborne was fairly typical of what was happening throughout the southern, eastern and central counties of England, to judge by the *Answers to Rural Queries* which were published by the Poor Law Commissioners in 1834. When Cobbett rode through the corn-belt of England, he was appalled by the poverty there:

Invariably have I observed, that the richer the soil, and the more destitute of woods; that is to say, the more purely a corn country, the more miserable the labourers. (*Rural Rides*, p. 207)

This poverty was caused by the decline of legitimate self-help remedies and the mixed household economy, as well as by the introduction of seasonal employment on a large scale. The threshing machine became such a powerful symbol of degradation and exploitation because it conjured up visions of a long, hard, unemployed winter.

The change that was taking place in rural society needs to be seen in terms of the introduction of improved, essentially capitalist, business methods on a large scale. The real revolution was in organization and method. The introduction of new machinery and enclosure itself need to be seen as perhaps the most dramatic, but not necessarily the most far-reaching, results of this attempt to apply the clipboard and stopwatch mentality to agriculture. Nathaniel Kent had urged the Government in his *Hints to Gentlemen of Landed Property* (1776) to help adventurous agricultural speculators to step up the rate of agrarian productivity. Such patriotic chaps should not be hemmed in by almost feudal land laws, which prevented them from fighting the good fight on the commons and other marginal land. War provided the rural adventurers with the opportunities they were looking for. Enclosure had been a fact of rural life for centuries. It was also endemic to rural society rather than something that was imposed from outside, so pastoral laments need to be handled with a certain amount of historical care. Yet there can be no doubt that the rate of enclosure increased during the Napoleonic wars, according to some calculations by almost 50 per cent. The General Enclosure Act of 1801 made it easier for the adventurers to fight Napoleon in the ditches and hedgerows of the countryside. Literary treatments of enclosure tend to give the impression that it was a dramatic, almost over-night, process of transformation. One day there was Eden, and the next there was nineteenth-century England. The process could, however, be spun out over a number of years. This meant that surveyors, lawyers, land agents and others were often able to reap bumper financial harvests. Although it is often difficult to estimate exactly how hard the smallholders or labourers were hit in the short term by enclosure, it is easy enough to see who benefited from it. Social historians such as the Hammonds may well have exaggerated the importance of enclosures as nails in the labourers' coffins. They might have taken away the possibility of crucial self-help, self-sufficiency remedies, but they could provide more work. Such qualifications should not, however, lead to optimistic interpretations. Enclosure itself may well have been over-emphasized, but it was a part of the capitalistic package which seriously damaged the health and wealth of the labourers.

The operation of the Poor Law in the years before the Swing riots indicates that rural society as a whole was subjected to the same double standard as the Lake District. The clip-board and stopwatch mentality sat, cheek by jowl, with more traditional forms of control and containment. The labourers were expected to sow the seeds for agrarian capitalism, but reap none of the benefits for themselves. A group of Berkshire magistrates met in May 1795 at the Pelican Inn, Speenhamland, aptly named no doubt because of its long bill. Their purpose was to try to cut down on their own bills as far as wages and poor rates were concerned. They decided to make economic necessity a virtue by agreeing to a plan for supplementing low wages out of the rates. They rejected plans for a basic minimum wage by introducing a sliding scale which depended on the price of bread and the number of children in a particular family. Their solution represented a licence for farmers, particularly large ones, to make the proverbial financial stack, since they could be sure that the paltry pittance they doled out would be rounded up by the parish to an existing wage. Farmers were, of course, assessed for rates, but they knew a thing or two about spreading the load of their personal responsibility over the rural community as a whole. They played rural roulette. The object of this game was to try to get the community to pay for the labourers you hired. If you fired them almost before you hired them, your own wage bill could lie virtually fallow. Speenhamland was originally intended as a stop-gap measure, but it was adopted in various shapes and forms throughout most of the corn-belt. It made very good sense in times of surplus labour – good sense, that is, if you happened to own the fence you sat on.

It was estimated that there were seventy labourers in Yardley Hastings in Northamptonshire whose services were surplus to requirements. There was work for about half of these during harvest time, but they all had to be supported by the parish during the winter or 'dead' months. Those who were in work were not in luck:

An Allowance is made from the Poor Rate of 10s a week to families having four children under ten years of age, and 11s 6d a week when there are five under ten, provided the head of a family cannot earn that sum . . . . Relief is usually given according to a Scale, varying with the price of bread, about the price of 1½ lb per day to each individual.[4]

The average weekly wage, not taking harvest time into consideration, was just under 10s. for a labourer in constant employment. Thus the parish often had to come to the aid of those who had the moral fibre to hold down a job, as well as to those who were too spineless to work. The Speenhamland system probably did encourage some labourers to let procreation thrive, since more apparently meant more. This was happening at the same time as Parson Malthus was warning all and sundry against the evils of overpopulation. The Overseers in Nayland would not even offer the time of day until a family had reached a certain size:

Ten out of 44 able-bodied Labourers receive allowance weekly from the Parish, on account of their families, their wages not being considered sufficient . . . . Parish allowance begins, to an able-bodied Labourer, when his Family exceeds 3 children; the allowance to the whole Family being such as to make their whole income equal to half a stone of the best flour, and 6d to each individual.[5]

The labourers in East Anglia had no alternative but to accept dependence on this system of bread without sympathy, since the workhouse had a nasty habit of claiming all who were not instantly satisfied with outdoor relief. Unemployment was also a fact of life in Blything Hundred in Suffolk. There was no fixed scale of relief, but

the overseer, who makes the best bargain he can with the poor, under the threat of placing them in the Poorhouse, if they do not accept the terms offered: Single Man, 2s 6d a week; Married Man, 6s a week, with an allowance of about 8d or 9d for each child.[6]

This could be entered for the 'most one-sided bargain in history competition' as the local workhouse was the infamous one at Bulchamp, where 130 people died after an outbreak of fever in 1781. The labourers in Blything Hundred only had the devil's alternative. It was absurd to pretend that they had any bargaining power. The overseer talked a commercial language of bargains and competitive price fixing, yet in practice the system was a paternalistic one. The labourers lost on the capitalist swings as well as the paternalistic roundabouts. Anger should not be wasted on the disappearance of the good old days of cottage industry, when it is needed for the Tolpuddle martyrs. Although the Combination Acts were repealed in 1824, the Tolpuddle Friendly Society of Agricultural Labourers was still deemed to be illegal. This was because counter-revolutionary legislation conveniently remained in force. George Loveless and the other labourers were convicted under the 1797 Mutiny Act, which had been passed originally to put down the floating republicans at Spithead and the Nore. Loveless's ostensible crime was having feloniously administered an oath. He was sentenced to seven years transportation on 19 March 1834. His real crime was that in trying to organize a trade union he was refusing to accept the prevailing double standard. It was a Catch-34 situation. Whose village was Tolpuddle?

The administration of the Poor Law in rural society was one of the great scandals of a scandalous age. The overseers at Yardley Hastings came up with one solution, almost the final solution, to the problem of surplus labour. They decided to auction off all those whom they did not want to support any more. On one particular occasion a job lot of ten labourers was knocked down to a farmer for 5s. I expect he thought he had got a real bargain. This kind of flesh market appears to have been quite widespread in Northamptonshire:

In some instances, instead of taking the supposed surplus of men into the service of the parish at once, they are put up to auction at the vestries. At Sulgrave, where this practice prevails, according to the overseer's account, only with regard to the old and infirm labourers, they are sold at the monthly meeting to the best bidder . . . some pains are taken to conceal from the men how they are disposed of.[7]

Overseers, like fat clerical cats, represent the unacceptable face of rural society. If you were riding through early nineteenth-century England, you were just as likely to hear an auctioneer's hammer coming down as the sound of rustics playing cricket on the village green. If you suddenly heard a thunderous rattle behind you, this would almost certainly have been a cartload of paupers being rushed over the parish line so that any sort of responsibility for them could be avoided. If you heard a volcanic eruption behind you, that would be Cobbett commenting on these scandals. I wonder exactly what pains were taken at Sulgrave to prevent the labourers from finding out that village fates could be almost worse than death. I wonder whether the farmers operated a ring among themselves so that they could get some real 'bargains'. I do not wonder, however, why nobody asks us to be nostalgic about this side of rural society. Do you remember the good old days when you could pick up a labourer for sixpence? It does not sound quite right.

The landed interest was, in theory anyway, supposed to consist of all those who had any connection with the land. The labourer did not need the vote because his interests were taken care of by those nice landowners in Parliament. The interests of one were the interests of all. We all row together, old Etonians and old Sulgravians, in the same jolly boat. Byron warns us to be scornful of such bogus Wordsworthian nonsense. Self-interest, he suggests, should always be substituted for interest. He was certainly right as far as the various Corn Laws were concerned. Legislation to protect home-grown corn should, in theory, have benefited all those connected with the land, yet, in practice, the profits from such protectionism usually found their way into the back pockets of the large landowners. These 'uncountry gentlemen', as Byron called them in *The Age of Bronze* (1823), were merely interested in trying to keep rents at the same high levels as had operated during the Napoleonic wars. Like all *rentiers*, they tended to squander this money rather than ploughing it back into the land. The labourers could wave farewell to the corn because it was alien, or alienated, from them. They were hard-shouldered onto the verges of rural society. The tillers of the soil were often fingered off it.

Legislation to preserve game also preserved economic and social hierarchy. Like some of the other nails which were hammered into the labourer's coffin, this one was not particularly new. The Waltham Black Act of 1722 was one of the most brutal pieces of legislation in a brutal age. It was originally designed to make the protection of deer in royal forests more efficient, but the principle was extended to include game as well. Anybody who was either armed or disguised and not 100 miles away from fur and feather was deemed to be a poacher. A blackened face counted as disguise. It was almost like arresting people for being in possession of working-class accents. The Black Act, like the numerous Game Laws which followed it, operated in the same way that 'sus' laws do today. Suspicion could be ten-tenths of the law. Cobbett noticed in his *Rural Rides* the irony of a sign of the times which read 'PARADISE PLACE: *spring guns and steel traps are set here*' (p. 209). The rural paradise, where the interests of one were supposed to be the interests of all, had steel traps lurking in the long grass. Thomas Love Peacock offers a marvellous satire on the landowners who trapped their labourers in *Crotchet Castle* (1831). Lady Clarinda describes Sir Simon Steeltrap, the Member of Parliament for Crouching-Curtown, as

a great preserver of game and public morals. By administering the laws which he assists in making, he disposes, at his pleasure, of the land and its live stock, including all the two-legged varieties, with and without feathers, in a circumference of several miles round Steeltrap Lodge. He has enclosed commons and woodlands; abolished cottage-gardens; taken the village cricket-ground into his own park, out of pure regard to the sanctity of Sunday; shut up footpaths and alehouses, (all but those which belong to his electioneering friend, Mr. Quassia, the brewer;) put down fairs and fiddlers; committed many poachers; shot a few; convicted one third of the peasantry; suspected the rest; and passed nearly the whole of them through a wholesome course of prison discipline, which has finished their education at the expense of the county. (pp. 92–3)

Peacock's satire works on at least two levels here. He appears to be sending up down-home, folksie perceptions of the countryside, which are all twee gardens, cricket matches and country fairs. Steeltrap threatens this paradise by taking a pot at every peasant. His is not, however, the cross, rubicund face of the traditional rural gentry. He is a new man with new money. Perhaps this also represents a conscious satire on *cottage ornée* pastoralism. Steeltrap votes in favour of legislation like the Game Laws to preserve his own self-interest. The foul of the earth protected themselves as well as the fowls of the air. This was how the game was played.

According to my version of events, rural society can be divided into two teams. The labourers were playing the rest in a game that was definitely not cricket. Historians would be right to insist on some qualifications. The Game Laws were a bone of contention for tenant farmers as well as labourers. It was not until 1881 that a tenant farmer could destroy game on his land without asking the landowner's permission first. The intensification of agrarian capitalism tended to drive a wedge between large farmers, who could afford improvements, and smaller ones, who were unable to. Indeed, one of the most interesting aspects of the Swing riots was the alliance between small farmers and labourers against those who could actually afford to hire threshing machines. These small farmers rightly felt expensive machinery would mean that their occupations would be gone as well. Tithes were a grievance to all cats who did not get so much as a sniff at the cream. It was an army of occupiers and labourers which threatened the gouty Francklin. Such alliances also went into battle against the Poor Law overseers. John Clare told his publisher in 1826 what it was actually like to live and work in rural society:

I do assure you that I live as near as ever I can & tho I did not tell you I have been out to hard labour most part of this summer on purpose to help out my matters but the price of labour is so low here that it is little better than parish relief to the poor man who where there is a large family is litterally pining I know not what will be the end of these times for half the Farmers here will be broken again this dry summer & I think that low rents & no taxes is the only way to recall a portion of their former prosperity . . . .[8]

He describes what Speenhamland looked like to the overseen, but is concerned not to lay too much blame for rural distress on the farmers. He suggests that there is an identity of interests between farmers and labourers. The prosperity of the former guaranteed the prosperity of the latter. Clare's enemies are broadly similar to Cobbett's. Rural society is being destroyed by high taxation and the rampant commercialism of the *rentiers*. This analysis points in the direction of populist radicalism. The two teams battling it out on the village green are the people against a fraudulent commercial establishment. Clare did not, however, advance such an interpretation consistently. His other letters indicate that he was cynical about the way in which an identity of interests theory was actually translated into practice. Although he favoured a repeal of the Corn Laws, he pointed out in his 'Apology for the Poor' that the labourers would feel cold winds from any economic change:

I am sure that the poor man will be no better off in such a matter – he will only be 'burning his fingers' and not filling his belly by harbouring any notions of benefit from that quarter for he is so many degrees lower in the Thremometer of distress that such benefits to others will not reach him and tho the Farmers should again be in their summer splendour of 'high prices' and 'better markets' as they phrase it the poor man would still be found very little above freezing point – at least I very much fear so for I speak from experience and not from hearsay and hopes as some do.[9]

The voice of experience should always be listened to. As it turned out, Clare was a little too pessimistic about the effects of the repeal of the Corn Law on the labourers. Such pessimism was the inevitable product of a life spent being cheated on the capitalist swings as well as the paternalist roundabouts.

5 John Clare and the politics of pastoral

Friends and neighbours

Edward Drury, an ambitious young bookseller, used some pretty fast footwork when it came to capitalizing on his main chance. He described how a routine visit to a bookshop in 1819 led to his discovery of a 'peasant poet' called John Clare:

Thompson of Stamford, whom I succeeded, was in altercation with a man about some books that he had bound for Clare; and during the wrangling I observed a piece of dirty paper, that had enveloped the letter brought by the man, had writing like verse on it, and picking it up found the sonnet of the setting sun signed J. C. – learning that it was probably written by Clare, as his love of '*Song writing*' was common talk and fun to the village. I paid the 15/- in dispute & sent home the books.[1]

Drury went to Helpston two days later to see whether this money could be regarded as an investment. He found the village itself particularly unattractive. Although he was just a provincial wide-boy, he did have a sharp elbow for business. He met Clare and realized that with a bit of luck and a great deal of hard work a star might be born. He felt that the poet could become the 'common talk and fun' of another village community, namely the London literary establishment. He thus bought up the copyright to Clare's poems, successfully elbowing other interested parties aside. Clare did not get a good deal. Drury then enlisted the services of his cousin, John Taylor, who had a small but flourishing London publishing house.

Coleridge complained in 1820, after Clare's first volume had been published, of being pestered by

Letters from Lords & Ladies urging me to write reviews & puffs of heaven-born Geniuses, whose whole merit consists in their being Ploughmen or Shoemakers.[2]

Persons with poor flocks of poor poets should not be allowed to disturb a real genius like this. Untalent probably is best left untapped. Drury and Taylor did not, however, just market Clare as a farmer's boy, who could string a few words together. They realized that the reading public would only patronize a poet like Clare, if his politics could be shown to be meritorious as well. Indeed, they thought long and hard about the most effective way of launching the product. Their correspondence ought to be required reading for all aspiring, conspiring advertising executives and pop group managers. Their problem was that Clare did not conform completely to the high standards of low life, which clerical magistrates were bound to demand. Drury was particularly worried by the poet's relish for the bad life of wine and women. The justices of the peace wanted songs of praise. Clare was not content to be content. He wanted to 'spend, spend, spend':

Though his day-dreams picture the most exaggerated success, & though his hopes are preposterous to excess, I do not fear with careful management his pride & ambition will be checked & that his understanding as it gains strength from refinement will teach him to love virtue.[3]

Drury appears to be trying to convince himself as well as Taylor here. This course of 'careful management' included introducing Clare into the high society of Stamford in the hope that rough edges would be smoothed down. It also meant advising the poet to make 'industrious efforts to polish and refine your writings'.[4] Even rough diamonds need to be polished before they are sold. It was suggested that Clare should try to keep references to his condition as an agricultural labourer down to a minimum. The best place for controversy was in the woodshed. Clare had flirted with religious dissent, but Drury, tactful as ever, managed to smooth this over with one local worthy:

I mentioned to him that you were certainly undecided in your religious opinions though by no means as bad as he had heard. By his recommendation I beg you will accept 'Law's Serious Call' which will lead you to a more comfortable chain of reflections . . . .[5]

Drury realized that success would depend on an ability to induce among the rich 'a more comfortable chain of reflections' about the poor. Conformity, passivity, gratitude and contentment had to be the order of the day, if Clare was really going to dart rays of joy up into the dressing rooms of the rich.

The poet's introduction to Stamford society was a dummy run for the really crucial interviews he was to have after the publication of *Poems Descriptive of Rural Life and Scenery. by John Clare. A Northamptonshire Peasant* in January 1820. He was invited to Milton Hall on Sunday, 5 February. He met Lady Milton and various members of the family and was then put to his sternest test so far:

Lord Milton then came out of his dressingroom, & in his slow sententious manner questioned Clare, but very kindly, & gentle speeches prefaced a present of a *ten pound* note from his Lord[sp].

Earl Fitzwilliam also gave him some money, but warned him never to 'leave off labour'. He wrote to Taylor afterwards to find out whether Clare was to receive any formal education. These interviews suggested the existence of a genuine face-to-face community, which was morally cemented together by a common purpose. Lady Milton introduced Clare to the family as 'our neighbour the poet'.[6] It was very Mary Mitford, very *Our Village*. Milton and Fitzwilliam were obviously pleased to find a parochial patriot in the backyard of their own manor. Fitzwilliam had, incidentally, just been replaced as Lord Lieutenant of the West Riding of Yorkshire for attacking the Government's role in the Peterloo massacre of August 1819. A parochial patriot was obviously a comforting chap to have about in such troubled times.

This neighbourly little scene was in fact very carefully stage-managed by Drury and Taylor. Drury fussed about to make sure that Clare actually looked like a jolly independent peasant:

Let me recommend you not to wait on his Lordship in your 'Sunday Clothes' – which are more suitable to a 'Squire of high degree' than humble John Clare. The dress you wear at Stamford with clear clean shirt, clean stockings & shoes will occasion the Lord Milton to judge more favourably of you. I send you one of my shirts which you will perhaps be disposed to make use of – tucking in the frippery of the frill under your clean waistcoat. A nice silk handkerchief will also be useful.[7]

This was presumably to be used to wipe away the tears of gratitude. Drury may have taken a leaf from Hannah More's book when thinking about how to dress Clare to play his part. She asserted in *The Shepherd of Salisbury Plain* (1795) that

If I meet with a laborer, hedging, ditching, or mending the highways, with his stockings and shirt tight and whole, however mean and bad his other garments are, I have seldom failed, on visiting his cottage, to find that also clean and well ordered, and his wife notable, and worthy of encouragement. (pp. 4–5)

She would not, however, have approved of the 'frippery of the frill'. This does provide a marvellous emblem for pastoral poetry as a whole. Its fripps and frills were designed to make sure that appearances never proclaimed realities. Indeed, the quaint, quite charming pastoral operetta that was performed at Milton Hall on 5 February is the best example of the politics of pastoral in this period. It is possible to see the way in which an image was actually constructed and then sold. Clare was, of course, an agricultural labourer rather than a 'neighbour' of Lady Milton's. He took his refreshment below stairs with the servants and not with the family. The servants appear to have found this rave from a rural grave highly amusing. They did not see many independent peasants. There was, then, on the surface a pastoral rhetoric of independence and neighbourliness. This was designed to hide the fact that downstairs were subserviently dependent on upstairs, or, at a more general level, that rural England was a society divided against itself. The pastoral rhetoric provided a 'comfortable chain of reflections' in uncomfortable times.

The Anti-Jacobin Review also felt that the discovery of a parochial patriot was of great social significance:

Yet no envious spirit, no carping discontent, is to be traced in Clare's Poems. Resignation to his lot appears to be a prominent feature in his character, combined with that love of his native village, which frequently bears such potent sway in the mind of the unlettered rustic.[8]

Did unlettered rustics really have minds? This review was exactly the kind of response which the public relations machine had been hoping for. The reviewer was actually telling his readers what they wanted to hear rather than offering a particularly accurate assessment of *Poems Descriptive*, for there were poems in it which undermined comforting assumptions about Clare's sense of social place. Drury and Taylor had not been severe enough, yet the readers of pastoral could be just as selective as the writers of it. Wishful social thinking was the order of the day, just as it was the order of the play at Milton Hall. The reviewers and patrons were not so much reading their own hopes and prejudices into Clare's life and poetry, as merely choosing to emphasize one side of his complex, and often rather enigmatic, attitude to rural society. He was, often at one and the same time, fiercely independent and naturally conservative. His conservatism was what appealed to the counter-revolutionary image builders.

This conservatism may be seen in Clare's response to the trial of Queen Caroline, which was the main talking point in the summer and autumn of 1820:

> I am as far as my politics reaches 'King & Country' no Inovations on Religion & government say I . . . . Lord R askd my opinion of the present matters & I bluntly told him that 'if the King of England was a madman I should love him as a brother of the soil' in preference to a foreigner who be as she shows little interest or feeling for England . . . .[9]

'Lord R' was a no-nonsense, cold showers and boxing gloves, muscular christian called Radstock. He was also a counter-revolutionary propagandist, whose *The Cottager's Friend: or, a word in season to him who is fortunate as to possess a Bible or New Testament, and a Book of Common Prayer* (1816) ran into a number of editions. His ponderous style makes even Hannah More appear to be a literary genius:

> For let us ever keep in mind, that it is the property of true religion, not only to make us pious towards God, sober and temperate ourselves, but *useful to the world*. It secures our hands from *violence* and *blood*; our tongues from *falsehood* and *slander*; and our hearts from *fraud* and *cruelty*, it renders us *faithful* to every trust; *firm* to every promise; *sincere* in all our professions; *peaceable* in our stations; *charitable* to our neighbour, and the *most valuable members of society*. (p. 9)

Here endeth the leaden lesson. It was natural that Radstock should try to befriend a real cottager. 1820 was a better year than most for such a public-spirited gesture, since the constitution was in real danger. It was time for all jolly peasants to give the bulls a breather and lumber to the defence of civilization. Radstock came to regard Clare's poetry as a vital battleground, since, if it could be shown that this particular cottager was peaceable in his station, then it could be asserted that all the others either were, or ought to be. Edward Bond captures the spirit of the good Lord's patronage in *The Fool* by comparing it with a prize fight. He suggests that Radstock, like the backers who have arranged the fight, expected to control his man body and soul. There is no difference between the poetic and the pugilistic fancy. Radstock used to carry Clare's letters around with him, so that he could reassure his influential friends that the peasants were not revolting. The Bishop of Peterborough was particularly impressed when he found out what his neighbour Clare really felt about Queen Caroline. Skyscrapers of social theory have been erected upon chance remarks by New York taxi-drivers. Radstock was merely using Clare as a token cottager. Like the taxi-driver who hands out tips for tips, Clare was not averse to telling his patrons exactly what they wanted to hear. He appears, however, merely to have exaggerated his own feelings on this particular occasion. Mrs Emmerson, who was all gush and drama, suggested that Clare could be used to instil virtue below, as well as this much needed confidence above. She pictured the poet making a sound, Hannah More-like contribution to village politics, while drinking a pint of old familiar in the local pub. Clare became the alliance between 'altar, throne and cottage' made flesh.

Radstock was certainly not in the business of helping farmers' boys to desert their stations in life. Clare was just a poor peasant who deserved to be made into a jollier one. All he needed was a comfortable, but very plain, cottage and a few pigs. He would then be able to write effectively for the counter-revolution. The cottager's friend was a commercial asset to Clare, but the price that had to be paid in terms of artistic integrity was a high one. Radstock played the stern father, who demanded total obedience. He was, after all, leading a paternalistic crusade. Mrs Emmerson, who played a somewhat incestuous mother to his bullying father, told Clare why it was essential to remove 'radical slang' from the poems when she copied out one of the good Lord's letters:

It has been my anxious desire of late, to establish our poets character, as that, of an honest and upright man – as a man feeling the strongest sense of gratitude for the encouragement he has received – but how is it possible I can do this if he suffers another edition of his poems to appear with those vile, unjust, and now would be ungrateful passages in them? – no, he must cut them out; or I cannot be satisfied that Clare is really as honest & upright as I could wish him! – tell Clare if he has still a recollection of what I have done, and am still doing for him, he must give me unquestionable *Proofs*, of being that man I would have him to be – he must *expunge*.[10]

An independent but dependently grateful peasant should really not write passages which cursed wealth, such as this one from a poem called 'Helpstone':

Accursed Wealth! o'er-bending human laws,
Of every evil thou remain'st the cause:
Victims of want, those wretches such as me,
Too truly lay their wretchedness to thee:

Serpents have pretty sharp teeth. Although Clare's use of blanket abstractions may strike a modern reader as being rather evasive, Radstock prided himself on being able to sniff out radicalism blindfolded. The process of transforming Clare into 'that man I would have him to be', and thus transforming rural society into the best of all possible worlds, was not a completely negative one. Radstock and others also tried constructively to programme Clare's subject matter for him. The Reverend Plumtre, who was a particularly unpleasant counter-revolutionary sidekick, showered him with tracts in the hope that they might inspire some loyal songs. Mrs Emmerson explained the theory behind this sort of conspicuous patronage when she wrote to Clare in February 1820:

Your extraordinary patronage, will I hope remove from your mind those prejudices against the Great! – which your humble Station has made you *too keenly* feel: you are now my friend – convinced that Greatness-goodness-kind heartedness and benevolence! dwell prominent in the bosoms of the Rich and Great. . . . I beg, you will not consider me, as wishing to dictate to you in the slightest degree – but believe that, I am anxious only, to light up *that beacon* which may lead you to Fame! to fortune, and to happiness![11]

If you just want to paper over the cracks of social injustice, this is what you do. You select very carefully one victim of the system and then reward him with concern and attention. This costs less than money. You then use this microcosm of gratitude to evade wider questions about society as a whole. It is the 'Clapham omnibus', or New York taxi, approach to social criticism.

Fast Eddie Drury, perhaps appropriately, found himself elbowed aside when Clare won fame if not fortune or happiness. Taylor was to continue to act as both editor and manager. The main problem he had was that Clare, unlike Wordsworth, did not believe that the simple always had to be refined and purified. He was thus forced to labour the point that bad grammar and dialect words would seriously limit the range of the audience for Clare's pastoral poetry. Realism did not make good commercial sense. Taylor was not, however, just a publisher and sinner. He had a genuine interest in poetry and was often an excellent judge of Clare's strengths and weaknesses. Those who have waded through the manuscript versions of the poems must feel a great deal of sympathy for him. His 'pruning hook', as Clare realized only too well, was badly needed:

the pruning hook has been over me agen I see in the Vols but vain as I am of my abilities I must own your lopping off have bravely amended them the 'Rural Evening' & 'Cress gatherer' in particular are now as compleat as anything in the Vols . . . you know what sort of a dish will suit the publics appetite better then I . . . .[12]

The public, then as now, did not like down-home, country-style cooking to contain too many of those tastelessly inedible dialect words. It would be dangerous to assume, however, that Taylor was concerned with matters of literary taste, while Radstock was primarily interested in political orthodoxy. The good Lord's equation of slang and radicalism should warn against such an assumption. Taylor certainly gave Clare some moral support when Radstock started to tighten the screws. A commercial publisher and an aristocratic patron were bound to come to blows sooner or later. The prize fight in Bond's *The Fool* is backed by a tradesman and an aristocrat. It is a fight for the control of the literary market. Taylor told Clare to be on his guard against all those who tried 'to screw you up to the squeak of flattery'.[13] It is a memorable description of aristocratic patronage, yet, as Drury pointed out, Taylor suffered from academics' disease. He was 'firm in counsel but weak in purpose & doing'.[14] Despite the memorable descriptions, he tended to give in without too much of a struggle.

Both Mrs Emmerson and Lord Radstock felt it their christian duty to clean up Clare's poetry wherever possible. There were dirty, smutty verses, which lowered the moral tone. Rural society could not be presented as teeming with 'country copulatives'. Clare incurred the wrath of the faithful for daring to suggest that country fairs were so eagerly anticipated because they offered opportunities for sexual freedom and licence. The labourers were more interested in new faces and figures, than ones which reminded them of Wordsworthian community patterns. Clare was to complain that the 'frumpt up misses'[15] who read poetry did not want to be told the truth about rural society. These frumps were, however, Taylor's butter and jam, so he too joined the crusade to make sure that the poems reflected rather than challenged 'the tone of moral feeling of the age'.[16] This meant pruning back 'the language of everyday description'[17] and anything that smacked of vulgarity. It also led to attempts to make Clare look at nature philosophically, in other words, to strive for the universal and the general at the expense of the particular. Peasants were supposed to be the philosophers. Like Hazlitt, Taylor did not believe that a poet should rely primarily on his own confined experience and locality. The publisher inevitably played politician. Taylor made a decision not to publish a poem of social criticism called 'The Parish'. He also edited radicalism as well as slang out of *The Shepherd's Calendar* (1827). Clare's friends and neighbours wanted to preserve an image of rural society.

In the woodshed

Drury had been only too aware that illusions would have been shattered, if Clare's character had been put on parade and inspected too closely. There were some nasty political and religious opinions in this particular cottager's woodshed. Mrs Emmerson was being particularly naive and sentimental when she urged him to argue village politics in the village pub. Clare could not hold his drink very well, even though he liked to suggest in poems like 'The Toper's Rant' that he was the soak of Peterborough. He also had a habit of becoming abusive and radical just before he slid under a table. He had apparently ranted and raved at a reverend gentleman, no less, at a dinner party in London in 1822. When everybody sobered up, a cover-up was mounted to try to prevent the cottager's friends from hearing that he was not quite the man they would have him be.[18] Mrs Emmerson got wind of the incident and was almost convinced that Clare was an ungrateful deist. Perhaps he was even Tom Paine in cottager's clothing. This provides yet another example of the way in which his friends and neighbours twisted various parts of his anatomy to try to make him conform to a particular image. During the early part of his career, Clare was prepared to put up with the twisters, as he was hoping that he might be able to carry off a glittering literary prize or two. Radical sentiments only tended to emerge when drink lifted the constraints of external censorship and Clare's own voluntary self-restraint.

Clare was inevitably rejected by the reading public after their initial curiosity about him had been satisfied. Nobody wants yesterday's elephant man. Caution could therefore be thrown to the winds when he was forsaken 'like a memory lost'. He was not averse to cooking up political opinions to satisfy his friends and neighbours. He told Taylor in 1821:

In politics I never dabbled to understand them thoroughly; with the old dish that was served to my forefathers I am content; but I believe the reading a small pamphlet on the Murder of the French King many years ago, with other inhuman butcheries, cured me very easily from thinking favourably of radicalism.[19]

As this letter contains a number of downright lies, Clare's praise of counter-revolutionary tracts may have been a case of telling the man who is paying for the taxi ride what he wants to hear. His opinion of radicalism may not, however, have been a high one at this time. He recorded in his 'Journal' for 17 March 1825 one of Radstock's many attempts to get him to toady the line:

Receivd a letter & present of Books from Lord Radstock containing Hannah Mores *Spirit of Prayer* – Bishop Wilsons *Maxims* Burnets *Life of God in the Soul of Man* 'A New Manual of Prayer' and Watsons 'Answer to Paine' a quiet unaffected defence of the Bible & an example for all controversialists to go bye were [*sic*] railing has no substitute for argument I have not read Tom Paine but I have always understood him to be a low blackguard.[20]

This is a private statement and so there is little reason to doubt its authenticity. Perhaps Clare had read in a tract that Paine had murdered the French King with his own bare cheek. It is certain, however, that experience made Clare more cynical about propaganda tracts and more sympathetic towards Paine. He described him, in a partially legible manuscript note,[21] as a man of great abilities, even though he disapproved his political partisanship. This was also to be his response to William Cobbett. It seems probable that Clare's own political ideology was influenced by both Paine and Cobbett. He was certainly very close to their analysis of the state of play when he wrote to Taylor at the beginning of 1830:

I think that a universal reduction of tythes, clerical livings, placemens pensions & taxes & all renovated & placed upon a reasonable income suitable to the present decreased value of money & property is the only way to bring salvation to the country . . . heavy burdens with proper assistance become light ones & when there is not so many idly looking on who have no burthens to suffer & immense strength to bear them they ought to bear a part wether they belong to church or state . . . .[22]

Like both Paine and Cobbett, Clare suggested that indirect taxation and tithes took from the poor to give to rich blackguards such as placemen and state pensioners. By the time he wrote to his wife from the Northampton Lunatic Asylum in 1845, Paine had become the only other sane man:

truth is truth and no further & the rights of man – age of reason and common sense are sentences full of meaning and the best comment on its truth is themselves – an honest man makes priestcraft an odious lyar & coward and a filthy disgrace to Christianity . . . .[23]

Paine's three major works are cited by name in this particular outburst against priestcraft. *Rights of Man* is also cited in 'Don Juan', Clare's most politically aggressive asylum poem. The radicalism and sexuality which he had been forced to suppress come welling up to the surface:

Give toil more pay where rank starvation lurches
And pay your debts and put your books to rights
Leave whores and playhouses and fill your churches
Old clovenfoot your dirty victory fights
Like theft he still on natures manor poaches
And holds his feasting on anothers rights
To show plain truth you act in bawdy farces
Men show their tools – and maids expose their arses.[24]

Old corruption is a 'bawdy farce'; it stinks. Politics is just a fraudulent conspiracy: 'Long speeches in a famine will not fill me'. Marriage is a 'driveling hoax'. Society itself is just a shabby casting couch on which tools are brandished and arses exposed. Poets and politicians are whores as well as bores. The poor will never get anything from this bawdy masquerade:

There's much said about love and more of women
I wish they were as modest as they seem
Some borrow husbands till their cheeks are blooming
Not like the red rose blush – but yellow cream
Lord what a while those good days are in coming
Routs Masques and Balls – I wish they were a dream
– I wish for poor men luck – an honest praxis

Cheap food and cloathing – no corn laws or taxes.

Society is founded on foundation cream. Clare looked out from the cuckoo's nest and, with help from Paine as well as Byron, saw the full horror of the theatre of politics.

Clare's concept of 'honest praxis' or fair play was part of his conservative-radical perception of politics. He was, like his father, a stubbornly independent person:

My father's Spirit was strongly knitted with independence, and the thoughts of being forced to bend before the frowns of a Parish to him was the greatest despair; so he stubbornly strove with his infirmities, and pottered about the roads putting stones in the ruts for his 5 shillings a week, fancying he was not so much beholden to their forced generosity, as if he had taken it for nothing.[25]

Although Parker Clare objected violently to charity on principle, he was more likely to accept it from the natural leaders of society than from petty bureaucrats. He believed, in other words, pastoral propaganda which displaced economic blame from the aristocracy. He therefore accepted Lord Milton's help and went to the Sea-Bathing Charity in Scarborough to try to cure his rheumatism. He did not want to become too dependent on his neighbour, so he decided to walk back to Helpston instead of asking for travelling expenses. The journey only made his rheumatism worse. He was thus forced to apply to the frowning parish overseers again. Fast Eddie noted that Clare's father was so crippled by rheumatism that only his eyes moved. Parker Clare had been a champion wrestler in his youth, as well as something of a ballad singer. If only it was possible to zoom slowly in on those eyes, for they could tell us more about rural society than all the fussy folklorists and fusty antiquarians put together. They were, perhaps, proud, suspicious, defiant eyes with just a twinkle of the old vitality and zest left in them. They had seen the unacceptable face of rural society. They had narrowed in pain and defiance at the injuries and insults of the brazen world of agrarian capitalism.

Clare saw his own life in terms of a pilgrimage towards independence. He wrote to Taylor in 1832 to express his anger and frustration at the rumours which were circulating to the effect that Lord Milton was going to give him a smallholding free, gratis and for nothing:

I was in hopes that I was at the end of my pilgrimage & that the shadow of

independance if not the substance was won as all I wanted was to use my
own means to sink or swim as good luck or bad luck might hereafter alow
me . . . .[26]

Clare believed that Lord Milton would be a good landlord, provided
that it was possible to deal face-to-face with him. He wanted to
assert his independence by paying rent to him. The dividing line
between independence and dependence was a fine but crucial one.
Clare was being set up as a small statesman after such independent
cultivators had virtually disappeared from the face of the English
earth. Milton needed to reassure himself that independent peasants
did not fade away. Clare was being used, once again, as a
conspicuous example of a parochial patriot. The cottage
represented the values of the estate and the state itself writ
beautifully small. What Clare objected to was the rumour that the
cottage was actually going to be tied to the estate. Parker and John
Clare did not like being treated as tied cottagers. They stared back
defiantly. Pastoral propaganda referred to independent peasants,
but preferred tied cottagers.

   Clare's obsessions with both honest and independent 'praxis'
dominated 'The Parish', which was his first attempt to write a
sustained, overtly political poem. He claimed that the poem

was begun & finished under the pressure of heavy distress with embittered
feeling under a state of anxiety & oppression almost amounting to slavery –
when the prosperity of one class was founded on the adversity and distress
of the other – The haughty demand by the master to his labourer was work
for the little I chuse to alow you & to go to the parish for rest – or starve – to
decline working under such advantages was next to offending a magistrate
& no oppertunity was lost in marking the insult by some unqualified
oppression . . . .[27]

Although he incorporated some of his early satires into the poem,
the majority of it was written in 1822. He thought it was the best
poem he had written to date. He did eventually manage to get
extracts from it published in a local newspaper, but neither Taylor
nor any of the local publishers would touch it with a pruning hook.
They wanted to keep the woodshed door firmly closed; so do most
modern critics. Although one learned doctor assures us that the
poem attacks wealthy landowners, Clare, true to his
conservative-radicalism, attacks much lower down the social scale.
He sets out his satirical stall and then offers a Cobbettesque

description of the good old farming ways. Oak and pewter symbolize this plain face-to-face society. As with Cobbett, it is difficult to know whether Clare's acceptance of this analysis of rural society was just a rhetorical one. It certainly provides him with the critical vocabulary with which to attack the proud princes of the English hamlets. These princes tend to be mercenaries and interlopers. The gentrification of the local farmers leaves the door open for stewards to abuse their position and the labourers. Clare attacks new men and new religious and political attitudes. The old ways are symbolized by a good old vicar and Justice Terror, who is, apparently a hard man but a fair one. The satire is most effective when it is close to the perceptions of Cobbett, Bamford and Bewick, yet Clare's literary insecurity also led him to take a sideways look at Crabbe. This produces a certain amount of confusion, for, judging by the prose description of the poem, he wanted to write a satire on Crabbe's officious world. He ended up offering passages which endorsed the 'one fate' argument, although this is not used prescriptively against the labourers. Perhaps he was writing with publication consciously in mind. It seems likely, however, that the process was more unconscious. Clare frequently confessed in his early poetry an inability to confront his own experiences as an agricultural labourer in his poetry. This is understandable since poetry was both his intellectual and material escape route from this world. It may be that Crabbe offered a way out of this dilemma by suggesting an idiom through which he could continue to distance himself from it.

Clare extended and developed the conservative-radical side of 'The Parish' in an interesting, uncollected poem called 'The Hue and Cry'. This was knocked off fairly quickly and then published in the Stamford *Champion* on 11 January 1831. Clare's authorship was not directly acknowledged in case it untied the cottager from his remaining patrons. Northamptonshire began to be seriously affected by Swing agricultural disturbances towards the middle of November. Clare is commenting directly and explicitly on these events, although he focuses his attention on counter-revolutionary reactions to the riots rather than on descriptions of their causes and course. A crooked old man represents the legendary Captain Swing. He moves about the countryside with the speed of light:

For some said his clothing was light, lack-a-day,
And some said his clothing was black,

Some saw him as two in a gig that was green;
Some as one on a horse that was black;
Today he sold matches and begged for a crust,
To keep a poor beggar alive,
To-morrow he scares all the dogs in the town,
Driving hard as the devil can drive,
While a day or two's wonder goes buzzing about,
Like a swarm of bees leaving a hive.

The forces of law and order believe that this old man, like Swing, was really a foreigner. It was not quite British to drive so fast and to raise fires wherever you went. Clare is therefore attacking the pastoral interpretations of the riots offered by Fairfax Francklin and Mary Mitford. He also works off grievances against Radstock and the tract-mongers:

Some said it was Cobbett, – some said it was Paine, –
Some went into France to Voltaire, –
And when they got there, – why they got back again,
To discover that nothing was there.
Some rummaged old sermons, some printed new tracts,
And handbills like messengers ran,
Conjectures were many, but few were the facts,
As to who was the crooked old man.

Clare's critique of the other methods of disciplining the rural population is probably the most effective part of the poem. The yeomanry have difficulty actually mounting their trusty steeds. The magistrates suggest various solutions, but are really only interested in buying time:

Fair speakers got up of real goodness to teach,
They had said, – and done nothing before,
And danger, like steam, might force good in the speech,
Which might fall when the danger was o'er.
For the law it still looked upon wrong as its right,
The placemen still hankered for spoil,
And some were for taxes and some were for tithes,
While labour was starving at toil.

It is suggested that a General Fast might starve the country back to its senses. Perhaps it was that dangerous foreign commodity, knowledge, which was leading the jolly bull-baiting peasants astray.

The old man was hunted up hill and down dale like a fox, but the local squires and farmers were unable to catch him. The hunt was actually employed in Norfolk to assist the forces of law and order against the Swing rioters. The old man continues to demand that there should be fair play and 'honest praxis'. Drapers, grocers, publicans, millers, bakers and tailors are all tried in the balance and found lacking. Fair trading was one of the many grievances of the Northamptonshire rioters. The old man is rumoured to be carrying a book with 'Knowledge is Power' boldly inscribed upon it.

'The Hue and Cry' is an uneven piece of work in which both direction and inspiration are lost as soon as they are found. Parts of it could indeed have been written by Dogg, R. L. It is worth wondering, however, whether the canons of the literary church may not have conditioned us to see all radicalism as slang. The content of the poem is certainly worth persevering with since it offers us close-ups of the unacceptable face of rural society. If it is related to 'The Parish' and 'Don Juan', it may be possible to argue against the assumption that Clare was essentially an apolitical poet. Other uncollected poems could be used to strengthen such an argument. Clare attacks the Vachells, Francklins and Twices of the brazen new world in an interesting poem called 'The Summons',[28] which has some similarities with Shelley's anti-clerical ballads. Yet the present-day cottagers' friends may not want the woodshed door to be opened too wide. It would be most ungrateful and unneighbourly of Clare to bite the hands which have lovingly selected and edited his poetry.

Local strengths

Clare was rightly disappointed with his second published volume, *The Village Minstrel* (1821). He felt that he had not been able to describe his own feelings 'strongly or locally enough'.[29] We have seen how he was actively prevented by his friends and neighbours from developing either strong political convictions or an attention to local detail in his poetry. He did, however, write some strong political poetry later on in his career. The shocking realism fallacy still needs to be avoided. Realism must never be seen as just the 'shock, horror, probe' exposures of a particular problem. It is not the divine right hook of overseers like Crabbe. Those who are or have been manual labourers will know that it is only the grave academics who insist that this experience needs to be continually related to crude economic models. What Clare referred to as 'simple pleasures and pastoral feelings' can, and do, exist in what might appear to be the most unlikely circumstances. These circumstances only appear unlikely, if viewed from the splendid isolation of the study or some other 'valley of the shadow of books'. I saw a rose last time I was in Spanish Harlem. If Clare had been born and brought up there, he would have written more poems about roses than slum houses. It would be dangerous to assume automatically that such poems must be unrealistic ones. They certainly escape from the crudely complicated economic models of the study, but that does not make them necessarily escapist. Clare's concentration on 'simple pleasures and pastoral feelings' represents a polemic against officious overviews of rural life. The argument about whether these 'pleasures' and 'feelings' actually existed is an important one, but it must be seen as subsidiary to the polemical assertion that they ought to have existed. The fact that Clare was an agricultural labourer is crucial to both arguments. It ought, first, to make us a little wary of glibly challenging his portrayal of rural society. It ought, second, to suggest differences between Clare's definitions of 'simple pleasures and pastoral feelings' and, say, Wordworth's. Crabbe wrote about the agricultural labourers like a beaky magistrate, whereas Wordsworth often wrote about them like a folklorist. Both approaches must be seen as *de haut en bas* ones and thus distinctly prescriptive. The real question, then, is whether Clare succeeded in portraying what rural society ought to have been like from the point of view of the labourers and the overseen.

Clare was besieged by curiosity vultures after the publication of *Poems Descriptive*. They were often more interested in the sex life of the agricultural labourer than in poetry. He was also bombarded with a great deal of useless literary and social advice. A large number of country clergymen offered their dubious services as guides and redeemers. One correspondent did at least recognize where his strength as a poet might lie:

Yours is not that Panoramic view of Nature, which (imposing while viewed at a distance) only gives an idea of the general effect of the landscape: but you have touched your miniature with the finest pencil; every leaf and flower is there accurately delineatd, & the minutiae of nature's treasures revealed.[30]

In fact Clare's poetry always carried a tension between an overseer's 'Panoramic' view and the overseen's perception of the 'minutiae' of a particular landscape. It tended to be more successful when a concern for detail dominated over the more conventional style of sweepingly selective perceptions from above. Clare's natural history poems represent a very important contribution to the development of a pastoral idiom which could accommodate such detail. I want, however, to pursue the argument in relation to his best long poem, *The Shepherd's Calendar* (1827).[31] This is in many ways a very conventional pastoral poem, which draws on the work of Edmund Spenser and later poets. It contains the familiar pastoral emphasis on refuge:

Old customs O I love the sound
However simple they may be
What ere wi time has sanction found
Is welcome and is dear to me
Pride grows above simplicity
And spurns it from her haughty mind
And soon the poets song will be
The only refuge they can find

Clare is concerned not only to take refuge in the past, but also to provide a refuge for the past. He thus provides long catalogues of wild flowers as he believes that those that have not already disappeared will soon be blighted out of existence. He confesses at one point the tendency for 'every trifle' to catch his eye. This emphasis on cataloguing the 'minutiae' of a landscape means that the poem is descriptive as well as reflective. Such local detail is its strength. Clare does reflect on emotional and temporal distances. The poem is indeed an attempt to evoke the atmosphere of the rural England of his childhood:

Where are they gone the joys and fears
The links the life of other years
I thought they bound around my heart
So close that we coud never part
Till reason like a winters day
Nipt childhoods visions all away

Clare's reflections on the relative merits of past and present, childhood innocence and adult experience lead, as suggested, to attempts at individual rescue. If Clare can achieve some kind of emotional rescue, then it is possible that the kindred spirits who read the poem might be rescued as well. He does not, however, deal very explicitly with a more wide-ranging form of social rescue. He offers a long, Cobbettesque description of the 'thread bare customs of old farmers days', when masters were not distanced from their men. He suggests that this good life may not have disappeared altogether:

The fashions haughty frown hath thrown aside
Half the old forms simplicity supplyd
Yet their are some prides winter deigns to spare
Left like green ivy when the trees are bare

The sense is a little obscure here, since it is difficult to work out exactly what Clare means by 'prides'. Yet the overall message appears to be that there are at least some remnants of the old customs still in existence. These might provide the basis for social rescue and regeneration, once they are recognized for what they are. Even such admittedly qualified optimism is almost immediately compromised and contradicted by requiem:

And ale and songs and healths and merry ways
Keeps up a shadow of old farmers days
But the old beachen bowl that once supplyd
Its feast of frumity is thrown aside
And the old freedom that was living then
When masters made them merry wi their men
Whose coat was like his neighbors russet brown
And whose rude speech was vulgar as his clown
Who in the same horn drank the rest among
And joind the chorus while a labourer sung
All this is past – and soon may pass away
The time torn remnant of the holiday
As proud distinction makes a wider space
Between the genteel and the vulgar race
Then must they fade in pride o'er custom showers
Its blighting mildew on her feeble flowers

Clare also uses the metaphor of the mildewed flower to describe the effects of enclosure. There are still remnants of these old customs, but Clare actually wants them to disappear. He wants to be able to celebrate and praise the past.

The Shepherd's Calendar reconstructs the economic structure of rural society. Although it hints at the unpopularity of parsons and the narrow-mindedness of some of the farmers, the overall perspective is still essentially a blurred long-shot rather than a tight close-up. Clare does, however, seem closer to the perceptions of the overseen in both his descriptions of the variety of rural occupations and in the way in which he seeks to blend work and leisure. He recognizes that 'sullen labour hath its tethering tye', but enters a special plea to the effect that 'toil hath time for play'. Even during the dark days of the agricultural revolution, the toilers in the fields must have had some time for play. Clare's point is also that they should be allowed more. He is thus, as suggested, entering the polemical lists against both Crabbe's and Wordsworth's prescriptive views on the life of the agricultural labourer. *The Shepherd's Calendar* offers a refreshing contrast to 'Michael'. It contains descriptions of work which are not weighed down by an obsession with thrift, frugality and patience. Leisure and pleasure are also viewed less grudgingly and suspiciously. The description of the agricultural community coming back to life again in March after the enforced leisure of the 'dead months' shows most of Clare's local strengths:

The ploughman mawls along the doughy sloughs
And often stop their songs to clean their ploughs
From teazing twitch that in the spongy soil
Clings round the colter terryfying toil
The sower striding oer his dirty way
Sinks anckle deep in pudgy sloughs and clay
And oer his heavy hopper stoutly leans
Strewing wi swinging arms the pattering beans
Which soon as aprils milder weather gleams
Will shoot up green between the furroed seams
The driving boy glad when his steps can trace
The swelling edding as a resting place
Slings from his clotted shoes the dirt around
And feign woud rest him on the solid ground
And sings when he can meet the parting green
Of rushy balks that bend the lands between

Clare is not a dialect poet. He does occasionally use local words and expressions, for instance 'colter' appears to be the local variation on a coulter or the blade of a plough. The passage derives its strength from the onomatopoeic use of such words as 'mawls', 'doughy', 'spongy' and 'pudgy'. Wordsworth wasted much of his, and thus everybody else's, time theorizing about relationships between rural language and society. Clare at least tried, often successfully, to appropriate and cultivate a non-literary language in practice. He is also content in this particular passage to let the poet's, or camera's, eye remain both fixed and close. The overall perspective may reconstruct rural society, but inside this, Clare is nevertheless able to offer some close-ups. Indeed, it is his attention to local detail which transforms and almost reconstructs the conventions. The labourers involved in ploughing and sowing are followed in their turn by the birds:

While close behind em struts the nauntling crow
And daws whose heads seem powderd oer wi snow
To seek the worms – and rooks a noisey guest
That on the wind rockd elms prepares her nest
On the fresh furrow often drops to pull
The twitching roots and gathering sticks and wool
Neath trees whose dead twigs litter to the wind
And gaps where stray sheep left their coats behind
While ground larks on a sweeing clump of rushes
Or on the top twigs of the oddling bushes
Chirp their 'cree creeing' note that sounds of spring
And sky larks meet the sun wi flittering wing

The form as well as the detailed content of this description differentiates it from versions of pastoral prescribed by the overseers of the early nineteenth century. This was, under the counter-revolutionary circumstances, quite an achievement.

Every room has a point of view. I am overseeing a suitably pastoral landscape in the Dordogne valley at the moment. Perhaps it is just as well that I like irony. The guidebook confidently assures me that God might come here for a holiday one day. It does seem idyllic, yet the local château casts a very long shadow over the surrounding area in the late afternoon. I think I know what the jolly peasants really feel about the craftily arty, like myself, who come here in search of refined simplicity, even though my idiomatic French is a little rusty. I spotted a lot of spots on the lowing herd which has just plodded by the window. I have spent my time here trying to murder and then dissect pastoral landscapes, but I am still rather attached to this one. It has been a long, hard summer and we are all entitled to little touches of refuge and rescue. J. Alfred Prufrock found it difficult to propel himself into rooms. I suddenly feel it difficult to propel myself out of this one. Everything looks lovely, provided you can edit out that dark shadow, those dark mutterings and those spotty cows. I would also have to tear up most of what I have written, so I am going to vacate the room for the Almighty as soon as possible. Perhaps it was just the thought of keeping the overseer's overseer waiting which prompted me to think about wasting time shedding tears for the pastoral corpse. I wonder whether they auctioned off the labourers round here in the vestries of the churches. I should really have left my seat by the window and tried to find out. John Clare used to sit by the window in Fleet Street when he came to London to watch the comers and the goers. He had had so much Wordsworthian nonsense about familiarity rammed down his throat, that he was genuinely excited by new faces and places:

one of my greatest wonders then was the continual stream of life passing up and down the principal streets all the day long & even the night one of my most entertaining amusements was to sit by Taylors window in Fleet Street to see the constant successions throng this way & that way.[32]

The flowing, pulsating city streets provided him with a temporary refuge from those inquisitive neighbours' eyes. Yet, as soon as he left this window, he discovered that the London literary village could be as bitchy and parochial as anything he had left behind him in Northamptonshire. Windows in both the country and the city tend to soften the outlines of hard, unacceptable faces.

Part Two
The theatre of politics

everyday life of parliamentary folk would represent the last nail in the coffin of the legal, decent, honest and truthful politician. The brief and tedious of this argument was that it would be suicide to give 'telellectuals' and unelected opinion-mongers so much power. If they were allowed to bone and fillet parliamentary proceedings, then show-business was bound to rear its well-groomed, but empty, little head. Television would inevitably cast politics in its own theatrical image. The viewer would become an insatiable voyeur, craving instant, constant, theatrical titillation. Parliament needed to be protected from the evil television eye.

The most interesting point about this senile chestnut of a debate is that both sides share the same nostalgic, pastoral assumptions. They both hark wistfully back to some ill-defined golden age when politicians were treated with the deference they deserved. Annan and his merry members implied that politicians might regain this paradise, if the great British public could be persuaded to transfer loyalties away from the slick media mob back to the parliamentary priesthood. Both sides remember those good old days before studio chat shows, when politicians had crusading fire in their bellies rather than dry powder on hospitality-ravaged noses. The optimists think that any move out of the studio jungle ought to be encouraged, whereas the pessimists are inclined to the view that containment leads to control. Both positions are authorized versions of pastoral, since they tend to plump for external explanations. The spectre of television is allowed to haunt political argument in the same way that alien cities and commercialism are conjured up to prevent an internal analysis of rural society. Pastoralism slaps a preservation order on rural society so that it remains a far-away country about which we do know next to nothing, but it also seeks to maintain and preserve the distance that lends enchantment to the view of political behaviour. If you are riding the political gravy train, you do not pull the communication cord and announce that politicians have always been show-business performers. You may reluctantly concede that some of them have been corrupted recently by the media.

It would, of course, be misleading to imply that television is just being used as an all-purpose bogeyperson. It has changed the conventions of political theatre by nudging it away from vaudeville to soap opera. Yet this only represents a difference of degree. Conventions may be altered, but this is not the same as creating political theatre at a stroke. Recent American television coverage of judicial proceedings has found itself in the dock, accused of the capital offence of trivialization. The assumption behind the case for the prosecution is that, in those good old days before television, murder trials were solemn occasions without the merest suspicion of theatricality. It would be a waste of time and money to press any edition of *The Newgate Calendar* into the hot hands of such tireless custodians of the political conscience. It might be dangerous as well, since wishful social thinkers are mighty unpleasant on the rare occasions when they are forced to face the facts. I doubt whether I would even have time to suggest that television did not place the theatrical bud around the political worm.

Every generation tends to write political history in terms of a fall from statesman-like grace. Anthony Trollope's political novels, for example, chronicle the undignified attempts of mid Victorian politicians to sell their glorious birthright for a mass of newsprint. The dishonourable gentlemen in *Can You Forgive Her?* (1864–5) are more concerned with tomorrow's headline than today's debate. Trollope preferred pedestrian Plantagenet Palliser because he held fast to values from the good old days before the birth of a mewling and puking popular press. He may not have cut the most dashing figure on his hind legs in the House of Commons, but unnatural theatrical affectation was no substitute for real poise and authority. If you were used to handling a large number of servants, then you did not need to behave like an actor in Parliament. The problem was that vulgar little men like Quintus Slide tried to queer the gentlemanly pitch by asserting that they wanted to rule themselves. Slide, the editor of *The People's Banner*, decides to oppose Phineas Finn and the rest of the 'snobility' at the Loughton Election in *Phineas Finn* (1869). Lady Laura Standish thinks that such action is rottener than the borough itself, since tradesmen, like servants, should be not seen and not heard. This particular tradesman's entrance into politics would upset the natural balance of things by forcing politicians to enter a show-business world of instant profit, reputation and solution. Trollope suggested in *Phineas Redux* (1874) that the old Whig political dynasties had been able to remain aloof from this world because 'something of the feeling of high blood, or rank, and of living in a park with deer about it, remains' (I, p. 334). Only those who had been born with a deer park could prevent politics from becoming the bear garden that Slide and others wanted to create.

Trollope idealized the Palmerstonian period, but he also recalled affectionately late eighteenth- and early nineteenth-century deer parks. One novelist's poisonous buffoon, it would seem, is another's political meat and drink. Trollope, like today's keepers of the political conscience, wanted his genteel readers to believe that political theatre, both inside and outside Parliament, was a recent intruder into the charmed circle. The eighteenth-century Whigs tended to argue the same case when they stressed that the gloriously bureaucratic revolution of 1688 was the state of political grace. It is time to get off Raymond Williams's historical escalator. We have heard twentieth-century placemen trying to convince us that political theatre is the result of television. We have seen a nineteenth-century novelist lay the blame on popular journalistic organs. It is not really necessary to listen to eighteenth-century politicians complaining about the theatrical antics of that devil Wilkes, for it ought to be conceded that political theatre can be seen in all periods when the pastoral beam is removed from the eye of the beholder. All societies are dramatized and dramatizing.

Inside out

Trollope's political novels tow a party as well as a pastoral line. The Conservatives are tarred with the theatrical brush, whereas the Whig–Liberal grandees tend to escape this unpleasant experience. Trollope's perspective is that of a party man, who failed to make the first rung of the political ladder. He contested Beverley for the Liberals in 1868 and his conspicuous failure there overlays many of his political views. The electioneering scenes in *Ralph the Heir* (1871) may be seen as the product of the politics of envy, masquerading as cynical distaste. Divisions between recognized political parties are easy enough to spot in discussions of political theatre. The division between insiders and outsiders is more insidious and thus of greater significance. Trollope, despite forays into the political arena and hours spent in the gallery of the House of Commons, was, by his own unironic admission, a novelist who did not really understand how a Cabinet meeting was conducted. Such admissions of ignorance can provide the political public relations machine with exactly the right ammunition, for it can be suggested that literary and journalistic perceptions of politics lack specialist knowledge about how the system really works. If they emphasize its theatrical qualities, this is only because they are naive, or self-justifyingly cynical.

Walter Bagehot's study of *The English Constitution* (1867)

stressed a distinction between the substance and show of political power. The people, in other words you and me, are only really interested in the latter:

They defer to what we may the call the *theatrical show* of society. A certain state passes before them; a certain pomp of great men; a certain spectacle of beautiful women; a wonderful scene of wealth and enjoyment is displayed, and they are coerced by it . . . . A common man may as well try to rival the actors on the stage in their acting, as the aristocracy in *their* acting. The higher world, as it looks from without, is a stage on which actors walk their parts much better than the spectators can . . . . As a rustic on coming to London finds himself in the presence of a great show and vast exhibition of inconceivable mechanical things, so by the structure of society, he finds himself face to face with a great exhibition of political things which he could not have imagined, which he could not make – to which he feels in himself scarcely anything analogous. (pp. 51–2)

Bagehot's political universe is divided into higher and lower spheres. The higher sphere, which included the monarchy as well as the beau-monde, put on a dignified play to satisfy our desire for spectacles to see beyond the gloomy circle of a vulgar life. Rustics like us might be forgiven for thinking that political life is all pomp and circumstance, but, meanwhile, the Cabinet are efficiently carrying out the business of government. The body politic is in fact two bodies: the ceremonial and the efficient. Like the theory of the king's two bodies in medieval jurisprudence, these bodies should complement rather than contradict each other. We rustics defer to the ceremonial, but are ruled by the efficient.

Such a view of political behaviour is attractive as it appears to offer an equitable division of labour between literary critics and historians. The critic, being an outsider with creative palpitations, is the obvious chap to study the ceremonies and rituals that constitute 'the *theatrical show* of society'. He does not, however, have the qualifications to analyse the substance of government. The historian is the obvious choice to wax prosaical about the dignity of administrative efficiency and the niceties of Cabinet government. There may even be a possibility of conferring at somebody else's expense about connections between the passion play and prosaic realities. There are, fortunately, two problems with this attempt to marry the perspectives of the insider and the outsider. First, ceremonial dignity is in the eye of the beholder. Clare, as noted earlier on, described the passion play as a 'bawdy farce'. Shelley, as

will be seen later, referred to it in 'The Mask of Anarchy' as a
'ghastly masquerade'. Second, it is dangerous to assume that the
efficient parts of the constitution are not themselves permeated
with theatricality. Political theatre may be substance as well as show.
The Black Dwarf, in a long article entitled 'State Theatricals: The
Divorce!', offered a forecast of the inefficient trial of Queen
Caroline in 1820. The tone was similar to Clare's, and, like Shelley,
the author believed that political life in general was a masquerade.
The article is worth quoting at length as an example of the outsider's
perspective, even though some of the particular allusions may be
hard to follow:

A recent melancholy tragedy has fixed the attention of the public *spectators*
at these houses for the last five or six weeks. The gloom now beginning to
lift, the managers have deemed it advisable to terminate the Court
mourning, with a new farcical melodrame called the DIVORCE. . . .
The *machinery* is to be supplied from the *bank* and the *mint*; and the
scenery will embrace some very *distant* and curious views. One of the
performers, it is said, will be engaged from Italy, and the rest, although all
natives, are expected to rival the most experienced performers in 'The Devil
to Pay' . . . Several *processions* will be interspersed, and a great variety of
chorusses by the best performers, both vocul and on wind instruments. A
grand dance of all the parties will finish the piece; and if the spectators are
not tired, a 'mock marriage' will be celebrated on the stage, as a sort of
finale. The *age* of the parties, it is hoped, will be some excuse, if the
performers should not be so dextrous as is expected; but every precaution
that the managers can take to prevent any disappointment, the public may
depend will be most sedulously employed. (no. 46, 10 December 1817)

The article assumes, then, that our masters strategically
stage-manage theatrical shows in order to legitimate and mystify
their control. It refuses to be 'coerced' by such theatrical wheeling
and dealing, which it attempts to send up and packing. Such
refreshing honesty is, I'm pleased to announce, going to make
relationships between insiders and outsiders more than a little
fraught.

A report on the 1980 American presidential election campaign
by David Blundy, of *The Sunday Times,* provides a good example of
a head-on clash between insiders and outsiders. Blundy, while
blazing the campaign trail, found himself being offered unsound
and unsought advice by Richard Allen, one of Ronald Reagan's
aides. Allen was angry that Blundy and other reporters refused to

write about the dignity and efficiency of political life:

the correspondents had not sent full and accurate reports of Reagan's speeches back to their head offices . . . . That means that the British editorial writers only have caricature impressions. (7 September 1980)

He added bitchily that 'you may quote me – if you do so accurately'. This tension between empirical accuracy and 'caricature impressions' is fundamental to interpretations of politics as theatre. Allen, whose political hack record included a spell as Richard Nixon's Deputy Assistant for International and Economic Affairs, seems to be equating objectivity and accuracy with quantity. We should, apparently, never mind about the quality of insight and perception, but, rather, lovingly caress the full width of documentation. The implication of the gospel according to Allen is that political history gets written on the politician's own terms: you may only quote me to illustrate what a man of vision and integrity I am. Interpretations which question the dignity and efficiency of political life are not worth the paper they are scrawled on. Allen, a political speech writer, was obviously peeved that the scribes had decided not to inscribe his efforts for posterity. These speeches were delivered by Reagan, a Hollywood also-rode, from such all-American stages as 'the creaking deck of a Mississippi paddle steamer'. Blundy felt quite correctly that creaking candidates, who attempted to peddle this sort of rhetorical steam, deserved to be sold down the river. He probably did not have a chance to suggest to Allen that, given these theatrical circumstances, 'full and accurate reports' of the speeches themselves would have offered 'caricature impressions' about what was really happening. Empiricism, in other words, is a caricature of events, particularly in the hands of a political public relations machine.

The Labour Party decided, a few years ago, to experiment with the form of its political broadcasts. They offered us a cartoon-strip account of the life and soft times of one Honourable Algernon, an upper-class twit, who was as brainless as he was chinless. He was, however, born with a silver spoon in, I think, his mouth, and so became a prosperous, if not particularly upright, pillar of the financial establishment. The moral of the story was that inherited wealth was a bad thing. The Conservative Party obviously objected to the form and content of this polemical piece. The barons of the Labour Party itself, worried no doubt lest their country cottages should turn to dust when they did, also felt that such 'caricature impressions' were not quite playing the great game according to the rules. So we are still subjected to political broadcasts in which homelier-than-thou uncles grasp at statistical straws. This is usually followed by some carefully orchestrated and castrated *'vox pops'* with anybody who happens to have a loamy, mummersetshire accent. They angle for hearts and votes by using real facts and real people for bait. Yet this approach is just as much of a caricature as cartoons about chinless Algernon, or, at the other extreme, 'pass-the-port' union officials. When Richard Nixon, apparently a real person, wanted to persuade Americans that housecleaners were not whitewashing the files as well as the walls, he appeared on network television. He was flanked by a bust of Abraham Lincoln, real but dead, and a picture of his own all-American family, real but dumb. This fireside chat made Algernon's silver spoon seem like the whole truth.

Few people are even going to borrow second-hand definitions of what constitutes historical accuracy from members of the Nixon administration. It is still important to remember that Allen *versus* Blundy, or the creators of the Honourable Algernon *versus* the political establishment, are being fought every time a political history book is written. John Derry, in his recent biography of *Castlereagh* (1976), attempts to rescue his unlikely hero from 'the false image projected by radical journalists, romantic poets and defunct popular historians' (p. 1). He wants, in other words, to provide a 'full and accurate' survey to combat what he takes to be 'caricature impressions'. If you felt that the reference to 'popular historians' was a pejorative one, you'd be right. According to Dr Derry, history is a job for the professional boys rather than for ungifted amateurs. It is, you see, such a complicated matter. You have to work your way methodically through the sources and be able to file the information away in neat little boxes. You then have to sit in your own neat little box and have little insights. The amateurs do not have the patience to undertake professional, or suburban, research. We are merely spectators, and disgruntled ones at that, of 'the *theatrical show* of society'. The historian, with his privileged access up the back passages of power, is thus always bound to be right. He makes a major contribution to scholarship by trying to convince us that political life is both dignified and efficient. Derry offers the following assessment of Castlereagh:

Restraint allied to insight, perception attuned to political realism, imagination disciplined by intellectual control, conviction matured by experience – these were the secrets of Castlereagh's achievement, and they represented a rich flowering of the eighteenth-century political tradition, as it had been refined and practised by Pitt. The aims for which politicians laboured were limited, but they were not negligible, Castlereagh did not seek to discover a political Utopia: he preferred the modest satisfactions of experience to the wanton delights of the unknown. (p. 231)

This tweedy praise of controlled, disciplined restraint, leading, if you are a good boy, to 'modest satisfactions' tells its own sad story. Schooldays can leave emotional scars for life. I'm sure most people will sympathize. It is much harder, however, to sympathize with the way in which the prim, *petit bourgeois* work ethic of the perspiring scholar and aspiring gentleman is equated with 'realism' and 'experience'. This foolish flannel certainly gives the appearance of being balanced and objective. The yoking together of contrary poles by an unseen narrator is a trick worthy of Jane Austen or George Crabbe. Yet it should not disguise the fact that, like them, Derry merely uses realism as a flag of convenience. He state his own political prejudices, but tries to pretend that they are universally acknowledged truths. Professional history, for all its parade of patient, judicious, petty, sober empiricism, has a habit of offering us 'caricature impressions'.

Castlereagh committed suicide on 12 August 1822. This was certainly not in keeping with the refined and seemingly bottomless Pittite tradition. Montgomery Hyde, in *The Strange Death of Lord Castlereagh* (1959), offers some tentative suggestions as to why he should have taken such an unrestrained step. It is just possible that he was being blackmailed for a sexual offence. This may have been why he chose to liken his predicament to that of the Right Reverend Percy Jocelyn, the Bishop of Clogher. Jocelyn was caught in a state of clerical undress at the White Lion public house in Haymarket on 19 July 1822. His companion-in-arms was John Movelley, a 22 year-old guardsman. There were, apparently, as many as nine witnesses to the activities of the church rampant. As he had a large Irish bishopric and was the third son of an aristocrat, Jocelyn had no trouble in getting bail when charged with unnatural practices at Marlborough Street the next day. He immediately skipped this, changed his name to Thomas Wilson, and, capitalizing on previous job experience as a glorified wine-waiter, became a butler in Scotland. Nobody appears to have been particularly concerned with what this butler had been seen doing. Castlereagh used to haunt the London parks late at night. The Cato Street conspirators had him marked down as an easy target because of these nocturnal activities.[1] One conjecture about his suicide is that his indulgence in 'the wanton delights of the unknown' with prostitutes was a little too well known. He was set up deliberately by a gang of blackmailers, who used a man in drag to lead the leader of the House of Commons to another house of ill repute. He was then, like Jocelyn, accused of unnatural practices.

I am not sure that Castlereagh's identification with Percy's progress was quite as literal as this. I am also worried by the fact that, as it was quite common for politicians to take a leap in the park, Castlereagh's reaction to the threat of exposure must be regarded as an extreme one. I refer to the conjecture, however, partly as an indirect way of attacking Derryism. History is usually more sensational than the historians who write about it. It is also important for characters like Jocelyn to play cameo parts. It is very difficult to appreciate the force of the 'ghastly masquerade' interpretation of political behaviour, unless such characters are allowed to trample over the neat, surburban page. Shelley might have pointed out that Jocelyn was disguised as a bishop, as well as a butler, and that the changes of costume and identity were essentially theatrical. He might even have suggested that Castlereagh was disguised as a politician when he haunted the parks. Public relations men, like Allen and Derry, have vested interests in elbowing aside suggestions that politics is a 'farce' or 'masquerade'. They subject us to fulsome praise for the system that employs them. Derry refuses to accept the validity of Byron's and Shelley's perceptions of Castlereagh, because to do so would be to accept fundamental criticisms of his employers and himself as well. I suggested at the end of the last section that political theatre may be recognized, if the pastoral beam is removed from the eye. I want to conclude this section by emphasizing that the dignity of political life in general, and of 'the *theatrical show* of society' in particular, is very much in the eye of the beholder. Party political biases tend to stand out like Bardolph's nose, but the more general prejudices of the insider are often harder to pick out.

Caricature impressions

The programme for the 1976 Royal Shakespeare Company's

production of *Troilus and Cressida* juxtaposed a number of Thersites's railings with official versions of chivalry and courtly romance. His running commentary on the 'bawdy farce' of the Trojan wars was presented as illiterate, and almost illegible, graffiti, which was daubed on a wall, or actually scrawled over public relations statements made about the war by the other characters. Shakespeare rescued this deformed Greek from the dustbin of history to show how trashy these official accounts really were. Richard Allen would probably have nothing to with such 'caricature impressions'. He might stress that there is no theatre of war, in the same way that there is no theatre of politics. Just wars are, however, just wars to those who die in them to become a public relations cliché or an empirical statistic. Thersites's writing on the wall may not be full and fulsome, but it might be accurate.

Epigrammatic and ideographic approaches to politics need to be taken seriously, since they offer genuine alternatives to middle-of-the-brow political history of the old school. The caricaturist is, thankfully, refreshingly honest about his prejudices and does not usually try to disguise them with bogus nonsense about objectivity. He wears his opinions on the sleeve rather than covering them up with yards of tweed and flannel. Indeed, caricatures and strip cartoons have always been concerned with stripping off such layers of padding. Political hypocrisy may not always be well drawn, but it is usually well hung and quartered. Caricaturists provide important sources of both information and inspiration. It would, for instance, be difficult to interpret Shelley's popular political poetry without reference to the work of William Hone and other graphic satirists. Information about radical iconography can strengthen literary interpretation. I am more concerned here with the way in which caricature offers a general source of inspiration. It provides a strong lever against all forms of cant, and a blend of the perspectives of graphic satirist, popular journalist and radical poet holds out the possibility of being able to evolve alternative grammars and perceptions of politics to those used by the various public relations machines.

Caricature is a source of both information and inspiration as far as the theatre of politics is concerned. Theatrical settings for political events have always been popular. Vicky's cartoon in *The Evening Standard* of 11 December 1958 of Harold Macmillan busking the doleful queues of the unemployed with a song entitled 'You've never had it so good' is one of the best known examples of twentieth-century ideographic satire. Macmillan is dressed as a never-has-been vaudeville comedian. The cartoon depends for its success on a topical reference to John Osborne's play *The Entertainer*, first performed on 10 April 1957. Osborne's Archie Rice and Macmillan are one and the same person. Like Smollett, Vicky wants to suggest that the burlesque comedian and the politician are in the same show and the same business. Politics is a bad music hall act on a wet Monday night.

Vicky's inspiring appropriation of a theatrical setting was part of a well-drawn tradition. It would be possible to explain away the fact that late eighteenth- and early nineteenth-century caricaturists also presented politics as theatre. It could be argued that theatrical settings were merely used to provide easily identifiable and understandable contexts. John Gay's *The Beggar's Opera* (1728) was a particular favourite because it was a favourite with theatre audiences. It may be true that the use of allegory kept some of the prosecuting wolves from the door. It might also be worth stressing the fact that artists often likened their craft to that of the dramatist. William Hogarth once claimed that his pictures were a stage on which various characters acted out a dumb show. These are all plausible reasons for why ideographic satirists drew the theatre of politics. The simplest of all possible explanations is still by far the best. They drew the theatre of politics because it was really there.

John Doyle – pencilname H. B. – portrayed a number of well-known politicians treading the theatrical boards in his *Political Sketches* (1829–43). Sir Charles Wetherell, the Tory member for Boroughbridge, is Macheath in a drawing of 'A Scene from The Beggar's Opera'. Wetherell is doomed to become the 'last of the Boroughbridges' under the provisions of the Whig Reform Bill. Lord John Russell lurks sinisterly in the wings waiting to lead him to the scaffold. Macheath pauses briefly to bid farewell to the leaders of his party, Polly Peachum Peel and Lucy Locket Wellington. If Wetherell had not existed, the caricaturists might have been tempted to invent him. He could never find a pair of trousers that fitted properly and his long fillybusters against the Reform Bills remain among the best comic parliamentary turns. He is another character who deserves to play his cameo part in the history books. Doyle was making a moderately serious point when he cast this likeable showman and entertainer in the role of Macheath. He placed a comedian in a tragic situation to suggest that gloomsday, doomsday speeches against the Bill could be taken with a pinch of snuff. Doyle offers a number of other sketches in which distinctions between the theatre and politics are blurred, if never quite broken down altogether.

Some commentators would argue that Doyle's lithographs do not really belong to the tradition of caricature. The themes may be broadly similar, but the execution of them is very different. Doyle certainly points forward to Victorian illustrative journalism, as well as back to the savage etchings of James Gillray and his school. G. M. Trevelyan, the Whig historian, suggested that Doyle's social curry was so mercifully mild because he

had no party attachments and no personal adulations or feuds. He looked from a side-window at the comedy of high political life and its personages, an amused spectator.[2]

Trevelyan may well be right about the reasons for this difference, but I get a faint whiff of damnation by even fainter praise. Those outsiders, who spectate from the side-windows, can be given a pat on the head, provided that they find the show high comedy rather than low farce. Their viewpoint, however, is bound to be bounded and limited. It can never seriously compete with the views of the professionals on equal terms. Outsiders provide light relief, but that's about as far as it goes. Cartoons and caricatures can be studied to show how the low perceived the high, but rarely as serious political comment in their own right. Yet by noticing and developing *theatrum mundi* themes, Doyle at least got it right.

I want to look very briefly at some other variations on this *theatrum mundi* theme.[3] William Heath's caricatures were sharper and more pointed than Doyle's. He produced a set of drawings in 1829 entitled 'Theatrical Characters', in which George IV was a harassed theatrical manager. He was unable to control the company himself and relied heavily on Wellington, who was his prompter and stage-manager. The perspective is broadly similar to *The Black Dwarf*'s. Lewis Marks explored relationships between political behaviour and *commedia del'arte* in 'The European Pantomime' (1815). Napoleon, or Harlequin, escapes from Elba to destroy the peaceful quiet of Louis XVIII, or Pantaloon. Many caricatures of this period saw politics as a bear garden or a fairground, even though Quintus Slide was not yet a twinkle in his creator's mind. I suspect there is a connection between this theme and the popularity of the political doctor motif. George Cruikshank depicted William Pitt bleeding John Bull dry of guineas in 'Doctor Sangrada

Relieving John Bull of the Yellow Fever' (1795). This was, incidentally, not the best way of improving the constitution. Isaac Cruikshank depicted the Whigs as quack doctors in 'The Westminster Mountebanks or Palace Yard Pranks' (1795). They attempt to peddle quack remedies to all and sundry in the fairground. The political motif is not so explicit in Thomas Rowlandson's 'Doctor Botherum, the Mountebank' (1800), although the fact the presumptuous doctor is decked out in all the rich rags of the fairground does at least suggest comparisons between quacks, political hacks and actors. They are all in the ignoble trade of making sure that the appearance does not proclaim the man. Dr Derry would have us believe that politics has something to do with the art of the possible. The caricaturists suggest that the craft of the plausible would be nearer the mark. This is why the fairground, with its motley crews of quacks and hacks, offered them such an appropriate setting. Charles Williams cast Pitt as a fairground peep-show proprietor in 'Billy's Raree Show – or John Bull Enlightened' (1796). John has his pockets picked by Pitt, while gawping at a political utopia, which was supposed to be just around the proverbial corner. The scene is also set in a fairground in the George Woodward–Thomas Rowlandson 'Preparations for the Jubilee, or Theatricals Extraordinary' (1809). The leading politicians have all set up their booths and they are identified by the title of an appropriate play stuck in a prominent place.

'The Political Drama', which was a series of popular caricatures published between 1833 and 1835, provides a number of interesting treatments of the theatre of politics. 'The Rival Shows' (no. 21), to take just one of them, is set in a fairground. William Cobbett, who is the owner of the radical booth, is trying to get the public to roll up to the show:

Here you will see and hear something worth your money . . . a grand and comprehensive View of corruption in Church and State during which a Pas de deux will take place between the Devil and a Bishop.

I wonder which part Percy Jocelyn auditioned for. The rival booth, which is owned by 'The United Company of Whigs and Tories' also tries to whip up support for a show, which includes

an exhibition of an extraordinary sort of animal, called the Johnny Bull, whose body is capable of bearing any weight, and which possesses the qualities of Fortunatus's purse, that of never failing to produce money when called for.

This is to be followed by a competition to find out whether Wellington or 'Penny Magazine' Brougham is the ugliest freak in the fairground. This theme is broadly similar to William Hone's *The Political Showman – at Home!* (1821). 'The Rival Shows' may appear to be about as subtle as Cobbett himself, but at least it does not itself fall for a fairground patter about the 'rich flowering of the eighteenth-century political tradition'. It also suggests the need to be aware of extensions to Doyle's rather limited conception of *theatrum mundi*. The craft of the plausible is not just practised in up-market political institutions. It permeates every aspect of political behaviour.

The caricaturist's eye catches 'the theatrical show of society', but refuses to dignify it. It also catches the stage-managers in the act of cobbling together a plausible act. Those who despise 'caricature impressions' do so because they are sharp and to the point, pointed.

Looks and purposes

Finally, I want to look very briefly at Shakespeare's presentation of politics. I am not going to argue that he was really an early nineteenth-century dramatist, although such a proposition would almost certainly attract some of the lunatics on the fringes of Shakespearean criticism. I merely want to suggest that an appreciation of certain plays can help to clarify definitions and approaches. It has become fashionable for those of the academic persuasion to import dutifully continental models to help them clarify the clarifications and explain the explanations. I have chosen an old-fashioned English model, since I am heretical enough to believe that theatres are more important places than libraries.

Although *Julius Caesar* was written and first performed in those good old days before the media forced politicians to become actors, it is about the theatre of politics. Elizabethan and Jacobean politics were much less coy than their modern counterparts about admitting, and indeed revelling in, their theatrical shows. Raymond Williams's historical escalator might pass by James I's advice to his son in *Basilikon Doron* (1599). He reminded him that the monarchy, like actors, were expected to give a good performance on the various public stages. Shakespeare captured the conspicuous theatricality of both public and private life in *Julius Caesar*. We are, for instance, introduced to Caesar as he progresses, or processes, towards the games. He indulges in a little stage business to try to convince his audience that Calphurnia is the barren one. He proves that he is not barren of theatrical ability when he gets to the games. The political game, according to Casca, is a variation on hiss the villain, kiss the hero. Caesar has a melodramatic trick for all theatrical seasons. When the conspirators call to escort him to the Capitol, they find that even old troupers get a little touched by stage-fright in the night. They allow Caesar to run through the usual dressing-room emotions of fear, suspicion and contempt, before an appeal to his vanity persuades him to tread the boards again. He slips with effortless ease straight into the part of great man, camply holding court. I suspect that his collection of togas was even more impressive than the array of dressing-gowns worn by Master Coward's Garry Essendine in *Present Laughter* (1942). The conspirators need not have worried quite so much about disguising their intentions, since Caesar only has eyes and ears for his own performance. His famous last words are usually delivered as a breathless, hushed cry of personal anguish. It could be that if you have led a theatrical life, you want, for once, to die an actor's death.

The conspirators, as suggested, had thought it prudent to join Caesar's theatre in order to beat it. Brutus urges them to remember that looks need not necessarily telegraph purposes. The Roman actors should be their model. After the assassination, the conspirators crowd around Caesar's body, which lies at the foot of Pompey's statue in Pompey's theatre. Cassius tries to stir up the shaken by reminding them that this particular scene will be played and played. As Anne Righter suggests in *Shakespeare and the Idea of the Play* (1962), the *theatrum mundi* theme works at a number of levels here. First of all, it provides a plug for Shakespeare's own company and the acting profession in general. Actors are chroniclers of space and time. Second, it hints that the conspirators, like the actors they emulate and hope will emulate them, may only hold the stage for a short time. Third, it sets up a positively bewildering series of permutations. The actors, who play politicians, self-consciously assume theatrical roles. The politicians, who are played by actors, wonder how actors might play politicians in the future. This confusion serves to strengthen the *theatrum mundi* theme, for this kind of reflexivity renders it redundant as metaphor. Politics is not just like theatre: it is theatre. Metaphoric relationships, like platonic ones, always end in confusion.

Brutus is no match for Antony when it comes to giving a performance in the 'common pulpit', for, like Coriolanus, he refuses to indulge the audience with cheap, melodramatic thrills. He urged the conspirators to play parts he had difficulty reaching towards himself. The real problem is that his sense of theatre is too up-market. He expects the audience to be mighty high-minded and pays dearly for such loser's illusions. Antony, who is a great lover of the theatre, has no qualms about making political capital out of wounds and wills in market-places. He would probably have gone into fairgrounds and circuses, if it had been necessary. He knows that it is difficult to fail through underestimating an audience's potential. Some critics are just as gullible as the Roman audience, since they insist that Antony means what he says. Brecht suggests, however, that the funeral oration is a shabbily fine example of the craftily plausible. Arturo Ui employs a hammy Shakespearean actor to provide him with some little touches of class. They rehearse Antony's oration together, so Ui is able to deliver a vamped-up version of it at the end of the play to justify the way in which gangland has banged down the doors to political power. Like Ui, Antony stands and delivers the rhetorical goods downstage, while, upstage, he trims his excesses and stabs his rivals in the back. Indeed, the movement, or flow, of *Julius Caesar* is similar to the way in which *The Black Dwarf* suggested that state theatricals were managed and performed.

It is often assumed that *Richard III* is a propaganda play. It is, however, a play about the use and abuse of propaganda. Richard and Buckingham decide to stage a theatrical show to legitimate their seizure of power. They both revel in the possibility of being able to take the actors on at their own game. Richard plays the part of the godly ruler to perfection. He appears at a balcony, flanked by two priests. He is engrossed in a prayer book and goes through the motions of pretending that kingdoms should not be of this world. He allows Buckingham to persuade him to come out of such monastic retirement in the national interest. The play is designed to show Richard having greatness thrust reluctantly upon him. Richard and Buckingham, by dressing up themselves and the truth in this way, are as much Elizabethan as Yorkist politicians. Shakespeare's audience would have been all too familiar with the way in which private vice could, with the ornamentation of theatrical costumes and props, transform itself into public virtue. Shakespeare's presentation of such state theatricals indicates that he was quite prepared to bite the hand of the orthodox Tudor historians, who fed him his information. Yet the play is not a simple condemnation of this kind of propaganda offensive, for, like Shakespeare, it is impossible for us not to admire Richard as the king of the players. The godly ruler is just one of many parts in an extensive repertoire. Richard plays, among other parts, an ardent lover, a wise councillor, a bluff uncle and an injured innocent. He holds attention and the centre of the stage during his first three acts because of his ability to act everybody else off their hind legs. For Thomas More, the historical Richard's sense of theatre was one of his many weaknesses:

And so they said these matters bee Kynges games, as it were stage playes, and for the more part plaied upon scafoldes. In which pore men be but ye lokers on. And thei yt wise be, wil medle no farther. For they that sometyme step up and playe wt them, when they cannot play their partes, they desorder the play & do themself no good.[4]

More's tone, both here and elsewhere, is distinctly pejorative, but for Shakespeare, the historical Richard's consummate theatrical craftiness could be turned into a strength as well as a weakness. Richard may be demonic, but he acts like an angel. The devil has always been lucky enough to have the best parts and tunes. Thus, Shakespeare's Richard is certainly more exciting than Henry Tudor, who comes across as a smug bookmaker benefiting from a wheel-of-fortune rigged against individuality. Richard, the gambolling gambler, almost won Shakespeare's head as well as his heart.

I suggested, when looking at *Julius Caesar,* that it is dangerous to assume that *theatrum mundi* interpretations of politics are necessarily metaphorical ones. I hope that my equally brief survey of *Richard III* might have indicated that such interpretations are also not necessarily pejorative ones. *The Black Dwarf* and the ideographic satirists certainly open up general questions about political behaviour, but their dogmatic doggerel can close down more specific lines of inquiry. They seem to feel that enough is said, when the theatrical shows of society are shockingly exposed for what they are. This is understandable, given the way in which they had to fight tooth and claw against an official public relations machine just to state the obvious about the current state of the political play. Shakespeare suggests the possibility of a more ambivalent approach. Theatrical shows are tried and tested methods of social and political coercion. It is important to blow the whistle rather shrilly on these antics, but there is also a temptation to blow a trumpet for some of the actors, particularly if they are anywhere near the same league as Richard III or Mark Antony. The look of the show may have theatrical quality, even though the purpose is to propagate seedy propaganda.

7 Catogate

Ruffling the plumage

The second part of Tom Paine's *Rights of Man* was published in February 1792. After a relatively slow start, it began to sell very briskly during the summer months. It was estimated that 200,000 copies had been sold within a year of publication. Many became acquainted with the gospel according to Paine through cannibalized extracts in newspapers and by word of mouth, rather than through the pamphlet itself. *Rights of Man* was, in present-day publishing jargon, an underground best-seller, or one whose remarkable popularity could not have been predicted on publication day. It was also an underground success in the sense that it appealed predominantly to those excluded from the official political nation.

Paine was not saying anything particularly new or original in the second part of *Rights of Man*. He was, even in the famous fifth chapter on 'Ways and Means'. dealing out dog-eared cards from the pack of eighteenth-century political platitudes. His argument must have been shockingly new to many members of his large audience, although it would still be dangerous to assume that the popular political consciousness was a blank page, which was just waiting to be written on by Paine's bold hand. Paine's audience discovered him, as much as he discovered them. His success needs to be seen in terms of what oft was thought, but ne'er so appropriately expressed. His tone, style and idiom were fresh and invigorating, whereas his ideas were a little stale and fusty. This freshness was achieved by constant variation. Paine was the indignant journalist, who was determined to expose the fact that, if there was muck, there must be a rake-off. He could, however, also adopt the light but lethal touch of a vaudeville comic, who satirized and mocked the establishment. He might then cultivate an idiom in which he was plain Paine, the public bar philosopher, who appealed continually to the great God of common sense. He could alternate this with a more pompous style by which he presented himself as cosmopolitan Paine, the first citizen of the brave new world:

I speak an open and disinterested language, dictated by no passion but that of humanity . . . . Independence is my happiness, and I view things as they are, without regard to place or person; my country is the world, and my religion is to do good. (II, p. 106)

He was also scientific Mr Paine and, perhaps his least attractive character, petty Paine, the former Customs and Excise clerk, who wished to cut a factual figure. The secret of Paine's success was that, by alternating the idiom, he was able to please most of the people most of the time. He continually accused Edmund Burke of writing drama instead of history, yet both parts of *Rights of Man* may be viewed as a series, or *tableaux*, of plays, in which Paine played many parts. Politics became a strip cartoon.

The first part of *Rights of Man* (1791) was written in direct response to Burke's *Reflections on the Revolution in France* (1790). If Burke had not existed, Paine would have been forced to invent him, since his oppositional brand of radicalism needed a constant supply of enemies. Many conservative historians claim that this is exactly what Paine did. They do not see even a passing resemblance between their eminently sensible hero and the gothic spectre, which Paine conjured up to haunt the pages of *Rights of Man*. There is, however, a striking resemblance between the sly, feudal shade of Burke, dressed in a creaking suit of armour and clutching mildewed documents in his clammy hand, and these conservative historians. They are merely trying to rescue themselves, as well as Burke, from Paine's invective. Paine's main objection to such historians was that they were so obsessed by the pomp and circumstance of high society, that they did not want to be troubled by mean and vulgar people. He declared, in one of the most memorable of all his catch-phrases, that 'foggy' Burke 'pities the plumage but forgets the dying bird' (I, p. 26). The bird was dying because its strength was being drained away to maintain a useless show. Conservative historians should always remember that the riot of colour at courts and camps depended upon an economic system, which debilitated the rest of the country. Burke's elegantly unintelligent descriptions of the ruffled plumage of French society were strictly for the birds, since he ignored the economic facts of life. Monarchies and aristocracies were merely 'upstart crows', who beautified themselves by stealing another's plumage. They were prostitutes, whose gawdy, bawdy finery barely covered up the ravages of a savagely sinful life. Burke's pompous praise for pomp deserved to be given the bird.

Burke's military parade of the files of evidence also ought to be greeted with hoots of derision, for it was obvious to anybody with an ounce of common sense that these mouldy precedents had only been exhumed to prop up a corrupt body politic. Yet Burke had the nerve to suggest that he was in the profession of 'full and accurate' historical reporting. This was patently ridiculous, since his support for legitimacy was itself illegitimate. He turned a blind eye to any evidence, which might damage the health of his case. The fact that the Normans ruled by military might rather than hereditary right ought, for instance, to make a mockery of arguments in favour of legitimacy. Paine was interested in flaunting the fact that William the Conqueror was a bastard by accident of birth, but the main cut and thrust of his argument was that, when it came to bastardy, all monarchs were self-made men. He was certainly opposed, in theory anyway, to arguments which were based on historical precedent, but was perfectly willing and able to take Burke on at his own game if necessary. This habit of using every available stick to beat dogged legitimists with can only have increased the popularity of *Rights of Man,* since no position was ever categorically excluded. *Rights of Man,* like modern sex manuals, offered a wide variety of positions to pander to all tastes. The main argument was based on natural rights, but radicals of a more historical bent were not offended. Paine's pervasive political pastoralism also meant that few could be actually alienated by his creed. Corrupt government was something that was imposed on the people from outside by dastardly foreigners, like William of Normandy. The fault, dear people, is not in yourselves, but in these ill-starred outsiders, over whom you have no control. If corruption is alien rather than endemic to peaceable civil society, then it really can be removed at a stroke. Paine defined solutions as well as problems with an engaging crudity.

His popularity, then, needs to be related to his ability to flatter his beloved people, only to deceive them. The content of *Rights of Man* may have been on the stale side, but at least it was broad and inclusive. Paine had no time for narrow, exclusive stage armies. He flattered the people by telling them that they could do no wrong. This sort of praise obviously put pride in the collective stride, but such group therapy could only be sustained by avoiding, evading and eluding certain controversial items. Paine was, for instance, able to hold the door to the radical movement open to more or less all comers, since he defined the entrance qualifications in negative terms. Anyone who was not a member of the alien establishment automatically became part of the radical constituency. Masters and men could all be members, one with the other, since it was assumed that they had a common identity of interests against the authority set. *Rights of Man* was an excellent recruitment pamphlet, which really ought to be consulted more often by today's deadly salesmen. The various positions were either defined with breathtaking rhetorical verve and versatility, or else presented in terms of uncontroversial negatives. Paine also managed to engage in some hard selling in 'Ways and Means', where politics was presented as a 'knife and fork' question. He not only held the door to the radical movement wide open, but also made sure that the material benefits of membership were displayed ostentatiously for all to see. This kind of slick salesmanship could win the numbers game, if not the political power game.

Paine's argument was borne along by some superb, hard-hitting, oppositional rhetoric. The monarchy, like the conservative historians who fawned and drooled over them, was presented as the best farce in London:

I compare it to something kept behind a curtain, about which there is a great deal of bustle and fuss, and a wonderful air of seeming solemnity; but when, by an accident, the curtain happens to be open, and the company see what it is, they burst into laughter. (II, p. 36)

Stout parties like George III will just collapse, when exposed to this kind of universal ridicule. Like the ideographic satirists, Paine often felt enough was said in just noticing the theatre of politics. If the people can only grasp this simple truth about political behaviour, then they will laugh and hiss the show off the stage. Parliament will lose both credibility and power when it is perceived to be merely a long-running farce. Similarly, the aristocracy will be laughed out of court, as soon as it is realized that their obsession with titles is similar to children calling each other nicknames. If the people were amused rather than bemused by the theatre of politics, then its days were numbered. It was, after all, merely a 'puppet-show' (I, p. 38), which ought, before the end of the play, to bore rather than awe the people. Then all they have to do is unkindly to ask old corruption to leave the stage, taking its prison locks, stock exchanges and rifle barrels with it. Paine even suggested, in one scenario, that the people could watch passively the funeral of the old disorder:

The fraud, hypocrisy, and imposition of governments, are beginning to be too well understood to promise them any long career. The farce of monarchy and aristocracy, in all countries, is following that of chivalry, and Mr Burke is dressing for the funeral. Let it pass quietly to the tomb of all other follies, and the mourners be comforted. (II, p. 161)

Paine always confused perceptions of the problem with solutions to it. He pitted himself against the plumage of society, but could do little in practical terms for the dying bird. He could catch a phrase and an audience with the best of them but was, ironically, caught in at least two minds when it came to political ways and means.

Paine's ambivalent attitude to social change was the result of his perceptions of property. He was in fine rhetorical fettle when he asserted that the monarchy and the aristocracy had acquired their property by raping, looting and pillaging the country. He cried havoc at the way in which they maintained and increased their property through more legalized forms of plunder, such as indirect taxation. He gave them the rhetorical bum's rush, but his heart was never quite where his mouth was. The problem was that, after these hounds had been sent packing, there was a danger that all property rights would disappear. The expropriators could find themselves expropriated. Paine's constituency was as broad as it was bottomless. It included farmers, manufacturers, merchants, tradesmen and clerks, as well as labourers. The 'men of small or moderate estates' (II, p. 105) wanted protection, rather than redistribution, of property. Paine was their champion when he argued that the church and state ought to get off the backs of the people. Government intervention, through charters, monopolies and taxation, only led to stagnation. Civil society, which literally produced the goods, ought to be protected from those who were merely interested in consumption. The aristocracy were just glorified rent-collectors, who knocked down people as well as doors. Despite the rhetorical flourishes, Paine was only really suggesting that a more free-wheeling economic system ought to replace the crooked deals and clogged wheels of the existing restrictive practices. He wanted to cut the stays that restricted such a loose and flowing economic movement. This freedom would actually facilitate the accumulation and security of property. Paine was potentially more subversive when he suggested that natural rights ought to be protected in the same way that portable property was. Yet these natural rights were absorbed into the nexus of the contractual relationships of civil society and did not necessarily offer a lever against them.

The abrasive rhetoric promises goods, which are ultimately not delivered. Paine's ability to be revolutionary in word, but not in deed, allowed him, yet again, to please most of the people most of the time. This credibility gap undermines the effectiveness, if not the popularity of 'Ways and Means'. Paine proposed a progressive wealth tax, which would squeeze the rich until the pips squeaked. Yet only a very radically reformed Paliament could realistically elicit such howls of financial anguish. Paine did not offer his supporters the practical ways and means of bringing about such a state of affairs.

It is tempting to relate such credibility gaps to present-day radicalism. The modern radical's heart may usually be on the left, but his chic wallet is often on the right. Such a comparison would, however, be unfair to Paine, for, unlike those whose little thoughts find their way into little radical journals, he at least had the literary ability to write for a mass movement. He believed rightly that stage armies were for stages, or obscure sages. His pen almost created the modern radical tradition by stroking the people and lashing their opponents. His rhetorical virtuosity certainly sustained the tradition. He hacked away at the establishment and its flannelling historians with admirable ferocity. When Paine caught somebody with a phrase, he or she stayed caught. Burke had described the proceedings of the French National Assembly in his *Reflections* as being farcical:

They act like the comedians of a fair before a riotous audience; they act amidst the tumultuous cries of a mixed mob of ferocious men, and women lost to shame, who, according to their insolent fancies, direct, control, applaud, explode them; and sometimes mix and take their seats amongst them; domineering over them with a strange mixture of servile petulance and proud presumptuous authority . . . . Who is that admires, and from the heart is attached to national representative assemblies, but must turn with horror and disgust from such a profane burlesque, and abominable perversion of that sacred institute? (p. 102)

Such taunts stung Paine into his attempt to expose the 'seeming solemnity' of a farce called old corruption. He exposed the theatrical nature of establishment politics, but was a star performer in the theatre of politics himself. He strutted and fretted through the pages of *Rights of Man* in a number of costumes. He was plain Paine and cosmopolitan Citizen Paine. Like John Wilkes and William Cobbett, he believed that popular politics needed the constant interjection and projection of personalities. The aristocracy had their 'puppet-shows', so Paine gave the people an irreverent one of their own. It was called 'Court Acting: or, where Burke can put his plumage' and it is still being performed, somewhat imperfectly, today. It is an end-of-the-pier show, which never quite succeeds in ending the peerage.

The way to Cato Street

The second part of Paine's *Rights of Man* took the byways, if not the the highways, of Great Britain by storm in 1792. It compelled many to look for a radical fold to enter. Paine left his disciples with the problem of providing such organizational ways and means. There were, very crudely and very simply, three alternatives on offer in the late eighteenth and early nineteenth centuries. The first may be described as working within the system. Its politics were reformist and gradualist, and it emphasized that common sense was no substitute for moral and educational rearmament. It maintained that the people needed to prove themselves worthy of the vote. Like E. P. Thompson, I tend to associate this position with Francis Place and the right wing of the London Corresponding Society in the 1790s. It can also be seen in the committees which organized the radical election campaigns in Middlesex and Westminster at the beginning of the new century. It was Painite in the sense that it accepted that there was an identity of interest between all those excluded from the charmed political circle. Yet Paine's cocky, truculent tone gets lost in this particular attempt to forge links between plebeian and patrician radicalism. His direct approach was replaced either by witty, patrician, rhetorical foreplay, or by the leaden prose of committee men committed to murdering the English language.

The second alternative was to try to pressurize the political establishment into conceding demands. Although committed committee men certainly played an important part in organizing, maintaining and sustaining this particular response, its principal manifestations were petition, platform and journalistic politics. The tone of the protests could be more-constitutional-than-thou, but this merely represented the velvet glove of radical politics. The iron fist was the sheer force of numbers, who signed petitions, attended platform meetings and read the alternative political press. This approach did take the constitutionalists on at their own game, but it usually managed to retain something of Paine's aggressively populist tone as well. It prided itself on being in touch with, and able to touch, the common people. This tradition of protest may be associated with the great platform demonstrations, such as at Copenhagen Fields (1795), Spa Fields (1816) and Peterloo (1819). It found an organizational voice in most of the corresponding societies and some of the Hampden clubs. Its strengths and weaknesses are demonstrated in the journalistic career of William Cobbett and the political career of Henry 'Orator' Hunt. Hazlitt, perceptive as ever, referred to Cobbett as the fourth estate made flesh. Hunt was very much the fifth estate, or the platform, personified.

The third approach was to try to smash the establishment by force of arms rather than by persuasion, argument or threats. Sabres should be used instead of rattled indignantly. The gaffers ought to be blown up. English radicalism tended to import theoretical models for bloody revolution from France. Babeuf's conspiracy became a particular favourite. Yet such models only began to make practical sense when the Government closed down the political options associated with the fourth and fifth estates. The counter-revolution of the 1790s made it increasingly difficult to sprawl over this middle ground. The left wing of the London Corresponding Society became interested in the viability of a *coup d'état* and, perhaps unwisely, plunged into the thicket of Irish politics to look for additional support. Colonel Despard was executed in 1803 for allegedly attempting to co-ordinate an armed uprising. Officers were not quite the gentlemen they used to be.

The Cato Street conspirators, like the revolutionaries at the turn of the century, took the plunge when it appeared to be the only way out of the radical dilemma. They certainly enjoyed discussing plans for a *coup d'état*. A spy informed his pastors and masters in 1817 that Arthur Thistlewood was noisier than most during such discussions:

– and it was suggested by Thistlewood, that the best way of effecting this infernal and very Diabolical proposition was at a Cabinet, or publick Dinner *where the Privy Council & Prince Regent* attended. But this was not

to be attempted if they had *numbers sufficient* to undertake a more noble
and general *enterprize,* but as the *last resort*.[2]

Such reports need to be treated very sceptically since, as Shelley,
Hazlitt and others pointed out, spies had a distinct personal interest
in the existence of such extreme forms of radicalism. Their
occupations would be gone if there was a meek and mild acceptance
of the *status quo*. Yet this particular report, with its emphasis on
assassination as a *'last resort'*, does ring truer than most. Other
reports in 1817 confirm that advanced radicals were both nudging
themselves, and being nudged, towards bloody revolution.

   Such theorizing and posturing only became a distinct practical
possiblity when the Government closed down, yet again,
middle-ground options. Thistlewood and his disciples were
involved in the great platform demonstrations against the
Government, which inevitably followed the end of the Napoleonic
wars. Thistlewood, as indeed he proved at Spa Fields in December
1816, was usually plotting some violent side-show to accompany
these mass protests. There is still a sense, however, in which his style
of protest may be related to middle-ground radicalism. He just felt
that muscles could be used, as well as flexed, to put pressure on the
Government to concede political demands. Such a connection
between the Cato Street conspirators and mainstream radicalism is
crucial, since it then becomes harder to write off the conspiracy as
the antic disposition of a few psychopaths. If Thistlewood was
leading the last of the radical flock, rather than a motley crew of
apolitical lunatics, then the theatrical form of the conspiracy may be
related to the radical tradition in general.

   The voices calling for a *coup d'état* certainly became shriller after
the massacre at Peterloo in August 1819. Yet Thistlewood kept a
foot in both radical camps throughout the latter part in 1819. He did
toy with plans to shake and stir the Government once and for all, but
he also continued to organize demonstrations against their
repressive policies. The spies' reports allow us to go behind the
scenes at these protest meetings. We learn, for instance, about the
preparations for one of the many meetings at Smithfield:

They afterwards surveyed the ground in Smithfield, for the most
convenient spot for the erection of the stage – the center [sic] would not do –
as the military could surround them, but appointed the situation directly
opposite Cloth fair there being so many alleys there to retreat to . . . .[3]

The stage-managers were obviously concerned to protect entrances and exits. Such descriptions suggest comparisons between radical political theatre and the Elizabethan touring companies. They both utilized inn yards or similar locations for performances from wagons or mountebank stages. They both also regarded flags and banners as the most essential stage props. A report by John Stafford of Bow Street indicates the crucial symbolic importance of flags in the theatre of politics:

Just at the conclusion of the business a mob of a most desperate description joined the meeting (supposed to have come from Smithfield) bearing a black flag on which was inscribed '*Let us die like men and not be sold as slaves*' underneath a *death's head and cross bones* – This was considered a very improper as well as suspicious reinforcement and by general consent the meeting was brought to a hasty termination. The *Whigs* & co retreated to the coffee house & the flag was torn down by the Westminster boys but the staff & a small fragment was carried off by the gang who had brought it.[4]

Thistlewood and his followers had sallied forth from Smithfield to attempt to disrupt a meeting being held at Covent Garden by Sir Francis Burdett and the Westminster Committee. It was a clash between plebeian and patrician radicalism. When the Smithfield boys entered, stage left, it was their standards which immediately identified them as a rival army. Thus the 'Westminster boys' felt that, if they could capture and destroy these flags, they would demoralize the whole army. It may be that a variation on these tried and tested military tactics ran through the minds of the yeomanry at Peterloo. The flags, whose inscriptions represented the iron fist of radicalism, certainly appear to have been red rags to these yeomanry bulls. The seizure of these inflammatory symbols was given as the reason for the charge of the right-wing brigade on the wagon, or stage, in St Peter's Fields. Stafford indicates that the 'Westminster boys' behaved exactly like the 'zigger-zagger' boys do at a modern football match. Football supporters inflict a form of ritual humiliation on their rivals by dragging scarves and banners through the mud. Often it does not matter if anybody is attached to them. Thistlewood, in common with many other radicals, was particularly conscious of the need to stage-manage platform meetings. The spies' reports allow us to eavesdrop on several conversations about the manufacture, storage and movement of flags and banners.[5] It is no exaggeration to say that radicals were obsessed with arranging symbolic clashes.

By December 1819, if not before, advanced radicals like Thistlewood were beginning to despair about the effectiveness of platform and petition politics. The Whigs and patrician reformers could sit safely and smugly in their coffee houses, but Thistlewood needed the freedom of the streets. He was, after all, involved in street theatre. Yet this was one of the many freedoms which was severely curtailed by the repressive legislation, usually referred to as the Six Acts, which came into force with force in December 1819. It effectively eroded the middle ground. It was time for the cloaks and daggers to come out of the radical costume department. Conspiratorial behaviour may seem exceptionally theatrical, yet it has to be remembered that it developed out of a radical tradition which was obsessed with the theatre of politics. This connection can be displaced by putting too much emphasis on Thistlewood's private vendetta against Home Secretary Sidmouth. There was certainly a clash of personalities. Thistlewood appears to have held Sidmouth personally responsible for the fact that he was forced to sweat his heart out in 1817 on a High Treason rap, which was later dropped. The Home Office records indicate that Sidmouth had Thistlewood under more or less constant surveillance for the best part of three years. The fact that Thistlewood knew that big brother's minions were watching him was not guaranteed to improve personal relations.[6] This was probably why he challenged the Home Secretary to duel with swords or pistols in January 1818. Home Secretaries usually have other weapons at their disposal, and so Thistlewood found himself languishing in Horsham gaol for a year. This personal clash ought, however, to reinforce rather than displace the level of radical political consciousness of the Cato Street conspiracy.

Thistlewood was a land reformer, but it would be wrong to see him as just a single issue campaigner, for he coveted the mantle of the 'old jack' or Jacobin. This meant that he was also a loyal republican and a confirmed deist. It is difficult to piece together his biography, as he liked to vary it each time he found somebody gullible enough to believe his tall stories. Matters are not helped by the fact that, after the conspiracy had been discovered, the government press was eager to present him as all warts. He was born and brought up in Lincolnshire, where he became a lieutenant in the local militia. Although he was prudent enough to marry for money, the lawyers made sure that he only inherited debts when his first wife died in childbirth. He left the splashy fens of Lincolnshire for the flashy dens of London. Some accounts suggest that he made his first trip to France to escape his gambling debts, although political curiosity may also have played a part. He certainly developed a passion for French political models. It is probable that this soldier without much fortune fought for the French while he was over there. His luck changed, however, when he inherited property in Lincolnshire. He set himself up as a gentleman farmer, but went bankrupt in a short time. Early nineteenth-century radicals obviously liked being bossed about by farmers. Both Cobbett and Hunt very self-consciously dressed and acted the part of the independent farmer of substantial means. Thistlewood returned to London and became, somewhat ironically, an active land reformer.

His followers, far from being apolitical, also belonged to the London underground of republicanism and deism, which was nourished by Tom Paine, *The Black Dwarf* and the publications of Richard Carlile and William Hone. The Reverend David Ruell, Chaplain of the House of Correction at Clerkenwell, examined most of the conspirators on their religious beliefs immediately after they were arrested. His report, which, needless to say, was passed straight to the Home Office, reveals that many of them were familiar with the writings of the sceptical eighteenth-century *philosophes*, as well as with Tom Paine's *The Age of Reason* (1794).[7] James Ings, a prime mover in the conspiracy, had kept a republican coffee house for a brief period. This degree of political consciousness was underplayed at the time. The radicals were naturally reluctant to claim Thistlewood and his followers as kith and kin, as to have done so would have been political suicide. Liberals were willing to take the conspirators' part against the Government, but were uncomfortable with the proposition that violence could be part of any political creed. Leigh Hunt's *The Examiner* was content to present them on 5 March 1819 as 'paupers who have been driven to desperation in unconstitutional times'. It would be more accurate, however, to see the conspiracy as one attempt to solve some of the radical riddles, which Paine had posed back in the 1790s. Paine spoke with tongues of Jacobin fire, but was more moderate and Girondist when it came to political ways and means. Thistlewood was attempting to bridge this kind of credibility gap. A *coup d'état* was one of the most obvious theoretical ways in which Jacobin rhetoric and policy could be reconciled. The solution became more of a practical possibility each and every time the Government closed down the middle ground of popular political protest. It would be wrong, then, to displace the Cato Street conspiracy from the radical tradition. I shall indeed be suggesting that it might be possible to see it as emblematic of the whole radical, oppositional theatre of politics in the early nineteenth-century.

Lofty scenes

Internal developments within the radical tradition suggest that some attempt at bloody revolution was almost inevitable in 1820. The Government's repressive policy aggravated an already potentially dangerous situation. Yet the timing of the attempt that was in fact made, owed as much to the specific external agency of the Government, as it did to these more general developments. This interesting fact should emerge during the course of this brief summary, or programme note, of the main events associated with the conspiracy.[8]

Twenty-five men gathered in a loft in Cato Street, which was just off the Marylebone Road, in the early evening of 23 February 1820. They had a large quantity of arms and ammunition, most of which had seen better days. One of the conspirators later set the scene, in terms of which Mary Mitford would have approved:

The look of the place with the arms lying about put him in mind of a Banditti at the Playhouse. There were pistols, cutlasses, cartridges.[9]

The plot, which had been thickening for the past two months, was to assassinate as many members of the Cabinet as possible at a dinner being held that night, and then to proclaim it from the housetops and billboards that a Provisional Government had taken over. The conspirators laid some rather haphazard plans to capture strategically important buildings in London that same night, and they hoped that news of their success would trigger off a nationwide series of uprisings against the forces of law and order. They were probably in direct contact with advanced radical groups in West Yorkshire and Scotland.

The Government, through its network of spies, knew this plan even better than the conspirators did. They even announced that there would be a Cabinet dinner at Lord Harrowby's on the night of 23 February, so that they could provoke the conspirators out into the open. Thus, as Thistlewood and his merry men were preparing to sally forth, the Bow Street runners plodded in for the kill. The runners were meant to be backed up by thirty Coldstream guards. These guardsmen, somewhat predictably, entered the street from the wrong end and so failed to rendezvous on time. The Bow Street boys, ever eager to chase promotion as well as villains, heroically decided to go it alone. George Ruthven climbed up to the loft with two of his men, while the remainder of the force took up positions below. Ruthven told the conspirators that the game was up and advised them to come along quietly. A scuffle took place and Thistlewood ran through one of the runners. The other two beat a hasty retreat. By this time the guardsmen had started to arrive on the scene. The front of the building was surrounded, but many of the conspirators managed to slip out the back way. Only nine were in fact arrested that night. They were bundled into hackney cabs and taken to Bow Street. The theatres were just turning out as they reached their destination. There was a new farce on at Covent Garden called 'Too Late for Dinner'.

The arrest of the conspirators stirred the great British public's ghoulish instincts. The lofty scene in Cato Street quickly became a tourist attraction, and large crowds assembled whenever the prisoners were shunted about London to be examined or committed for trial. Gaolers supplemented paltry pittances by charging the public more than a few pence to gawp at this political peep-show. The press was deeply shocked and horrified that such potentially violent events could ever take place in England. They were not that interested in probing the bumbling incompetence with which the arrests had been made. They probably felt that accounts of such Dogberry-like activities might damage the breakfast, digestion and circulation. They settled instead for fearless policemen and flawless guardsmen. Robert Birnie, who had been the Bow Street magistrate in charge of operations, placed stories along these lines in the blankly objective journalistic notebook. *The Morning Chronicle* dutifully reported on 25 February that he had 'exposed himself everywhere . . . whilst the balls were whizzing round his head'. Bow Street stringers found themselves being plied with drinks so that they would be in a position to sniff and snout out some really good stories. The hacks themselves had something of a field day trying to cap each other's sensational stories. An ace reporter, in a hole for a really punchy description, decided that nine arrests was not good enough. The readers of *The Times* were therefore informed on 24 February that 'nearly ten' had been captured. The sound of dog barking louder than dog was positively deafening. Foot-and-mouth in the door journalism reached epidemic proportions. It was a great chapter in its chequered book, as the story remained top copy for just over two months. They really did build things to last in those days.

The organs of the Government, such as *The Courier* and *The New Times*, presented the arrest of the conspirators as a damned close-run thing. The Government and civilization itself were lucky to have survived such a wicked plot. Anybody who ventured to criticize anything was immediately suspected of being at Cato Street on that fateful night. *The Courier* was in no mood to pull punches and duck important issues on 25 February:

Well may we call this sanguinary conspiracy a part of the system of radicalism, whose object was to uproot all our venerable establishments; unloose all the bonds that hold society together; and involve the whole country in one scene of confusion, plunder, butchery and bloodshed.

The more liberal papers, such as *The Times* and *The Morning Chronicle*, found this hard line hard to take. They wagged their inky fingers at these sycophantic journals and tore off a few column inches against journalistic prostitution. *The Times* noted, with refined distaste, on 3 March the way in which the conspiracy was 'feasted and revelled in' by the Government's journalistic tools. It was not just ministerial papers that gorged themselves on juicy details. Popular Sundays, such as *The Observer*, went to town and country on the conspiracy. They carried illustrations of the main locations and characters, as well as showing their readers exactly what kind of weapons Thistlewood and the others had had at their disposal. The liberal press was worried by the Government's hypocrisy. The ministers went through the motions of being appropriately stunned. The Reverend Knapp officiated at a service of thanksgiving in the Chapel Royal, St James's on 27 February. Sidmouth was among those who thanked God for mercifully delivering him in the nick of time from butcher James Ings's chopper. Yet was this a case of praying and praying, and still playing the villain? For, as *The Times* put it on 2 March:

instead of 'social order' being shaken in this empire by the formulation of *Thistlewood's* plot, there is not a man in office who can refrain from rubbing his hands, and heartily congratulating his next neighbour on the lucky *lift* which the Cato-street business has given to ministers on the eve of this general election.

Perhaps this 'lucky *lift*' was really why they were lifting up their voices thankfully to that great politician in the sky.

Although *The Times* was much too polite to say so, it was in fact hinting that the Cato Street conspiracy may have been little more than a cunning election stunt. The death of George III meant that the Government had to purchase good opinions and angle for votes again. Their domestic policy meant that their image was a little tarnished. Thus, as *The Times* suggested, the discovery of the Cato Street conspiracy was remarkably convenient. Parliament was kept sitting a little longer because of the domestic crisis and then dissolved. The national interest is always a trump card at election time. The Prince Regent's dissolution speech made the conspiracy a major election issue. If he could conveniently forget about *sub judice*, then everybody else could do so as well. The message from the throne was an unequivocal piece of electioneering:

Deeply as his majesty lamented that designs and practices such as those which you have been recently called upon to repress, should have existed in this free and happy country, he cannot sufficiently commend the prudence and firmness with which you directed your attention to the means of counteracting them.

If any doubt had remained as to the nature of those principles by which the peace and happiness of the nation were so seriously menaced, or of the excesses to which they were likely to lead, the flagrant and sanguinary conspiracy which has lately been detected must open the eyes of the most incredulous, and must indicate to the whole world the justice and expediency of those measures to which you judged it necessary to resort, in defence of the laws and constitution of the kingdom.[10].

The final reference is to the Six Acts. *The Times* huffed and puffed away at such crude party political broadcasting. A leader on 29 February decided to mince the uncrowned King's words:

It is not unusual to say that certain measures of Government have prevented certain evils from occuring, which would invevitably have taken place; but to prove the efficacy of the measures by the actual occurence of the evils which the measures were intended to prevent, appears to us, at least, to be a very perverted system of logic.

This 'perverted system of logic' nevertheless helped to carry the day at the subsequent elections.

The radical press was not quite so willing to accept that the discovery of the conspiracy might have been a lucky accident, on which the Government strategically capitalized. It was inclined to the view that Sidmouth's magic circle, like Prospero's, was not a place where accident and coincidence were encouraged. *Wooler's British Gazette* put this case on 27 February:

It is indeed *boasted*, that all the movements of these *Conspirators* were *known* to the ministers, to such exactness, that they could place their hands upon them at any period; and the facility with which they discovered those who escaped from the first attack, is additional proof that they had nothing to fear, from conspirators whose every movement was known to the parties against whom they were conspiring.

This interpretation led to the conclusion that the whole affair had been cued and prompted by the Government to suit their own devious designs:

The theatrical effect of seizing upon them in consultation, with the machinery of the performance about them, was perhaps good policy; but the mode in which it was executed, has cost a life, which was valuable, and might have been spared.

An election victory at the cost of one life was, however, very cheap at the price.

It gradually began to emerge that the Government was staging yet another state theatrical. Some strange facts emerged when the radical press and others started digging to find the headlines behind the headlines. The warrant for the arrest of the conspirators had contained the name of Edwards. Yet he was not picked up on the 23rd, or rounded up subsequently. Nobody appeared concerned about the one that got away. A spy was spied. Did he help stage-manage the whole show? The official spokesman said nothing. It was a 'no comment' situation. The Home Office files contain the story that would have made any journalist a lunchtime legend in 1820.[11] Edwards was indeed a spy. He managed to evade arrest on the night of the 23rd by making sure that he was on sentry duty outside Lord Harrowby's house. He helped the Bow Street boys to locate the conspirators who had slipped through the net, including Thistlewood himself. He was then hidden in various supposedly safe houses in London. He was for a time holed up in the grubby street of ink itself, right under all those sniffers and snouters. He was consulted on points of information by those engaged in building up the case against Thistlewood. He may have been packed off, appropriately enough, to Cambridge when the conspirators were actually put on trial. He was then exiled, all expenses paid, to Guernsey, and from there probably made his way to the Cape of Good Hope. The course of justice like systems of logic, could easily be perverted.

Thistlewood's trial for high treason and murder began on 17 April. Reporting restrictions were not lifted, although *The Observer* decided to publish and be fined £500. Thistlewood was found guilty on 19 April. It was then only a matter of time before the four other leading conspirators joined him in the condemned cell. James Ings, John Brunt, William Davidson and Richard Tidd were all given separate trials. Sentence of death was passed against the infamous five conspirators on 28 April. The condemned men were then taken along the underground passage, which connected the Old Bailey with Newgate. They spent their last days being harrassed by the Church of England. They were executed before a large crowd on 1 May. Five other members of the Cato Street gang were transported to New South Wales the following day. The charges pending against other suspects were eventually dropped. The Government had, by this time, had a good electoral run for their money.

The Solicitor-General, summing up for the Crown against Thistlewood, attempted to ridicule the idea that the conspirators had been manipulated. They were not just patsies, but evil men. The defence had got its briefs in a twist by believing such silly stories. The dinner party, which was announced in *The New Times* on 22 February, was not a bluff designed to call forth murdering hands. The defence, however,

supposed, that no dinner was intended; that the whole was a fiction; that some person behind the scenes, who possessed great influence over the prisoner, and could move him like a puppet, had for his own purposes inserted this article in the paper; but when the affair comes to be investigated, the cloud is at once dispelled.[12]

Yet, when the sordid affair is investigated properly, Sidmouth's role in it as a political puppeteer becomes fairly apparent. The Cato Street conspiracy was an election stunt, in which Sidmouth, through Edwards when necessary, pulled most of the strings. Robert Shaw's dramatization of these events, *Cato Street* (1972), is a disappointing one. The clumsy, but trendy, substitution of Susan for Arthur Thistlewood does at least leave the stage open for Sidmouth to dominate it. Edwards suggests that the Home Secretary could exploit the conspiracy in such a way that radical chaps would have to roll themselves up for at least twenty years. Sidmouth snaps back that he does not need to be told his job: 'I am an authority on show and precept' (2.51). He may appear to be rather an unlikely manager of stage theatricals as he had the manner and bearing of a punctilious country doctor. Yet, if the Cato Street conspiracy proves anything, it is that such appearances can be deceptive. Vile politicians are never going to dress as such. The show must go on.

Lawful espials

Polonius defines the essential trick of the spy's trade in *Hamlet* as the ability to use 'indirections' to 'find directions out'. He regarded it as perfectly legitimate for a father to employ a servant to shadow a wayward son. Such standards are, of course, set by Claudius, who enlists the dubious services of Rosencrantz and Guildenstern to monitor Hamlet's moody movements. The eye of Claudius is everywhere. Hamlet, like the early nineteenth-century radicals, sees these supposedly 'lawful espials' as so many dirty rats behind the arras. They are employed by villains like Claudius, whose public relations smile is as flashy as it is forced and false. Home Secretary Sidmouth, like Claudius, believed that the maintenance of paternalism necessitated, and thus legitimized, the use of such 'espials'. A London jury disagreed with him in 1817, when they acquitted Dr Watson of a charge of high treason for his part at the Spa Fields demonstrations. This jury really had no alternative since the chief prosecution witness, one Castle, had been brilliantly sieged and demolished by the defence. Castle had made figures and models at one time in his varied and unillustrious career, but was employed by the Government to mould the leading radicals into prosecution fodder. His credentials were good. He had had experience at forging bank notes, which was usually referred to as 'uttering forged notes'. He was also connected with an infamous Soho brothel. This experience of faked currency and orgasms may have stood him in good stead as a spy, for he had to utter forged political notes in the hope that the leading radicals would try to cap his outrageous statements. Although Henry Hunt was being wise after the event when he came to deal with Castle's activities in his

Memoirs . . . (1820), it may have been true that this fake's radical progress seemed outrageously over the top at the time. His brand of melodrama was, however, indistinguishable from Thistlewood's. Castle thus found a theatre for operations against the radicals in which he was accepted at face value. He was able to wave the tricolour with one hand, while he planted incriminating evidence with the other. The Government was desperate for a conviction against the radicals, so it tried to give Castle every chance in court. It bought him new clothes to try to make sure that he cut a suitably impressive figure in the witness box. The rich men with their Castle were, however, unable to put poor men behind prison gates on this particular occasion.[13]

This public humiliation did not stop the recruitment and employment of 'espials'. Oliver, alias Richards, alias Pendrill, was used as an *agent provocateur* before the Pentridge rising of 1817. He later claimed in a long narrative written for the Home Office that, although he had not created the spirit of disaffection, he had been able to help to organize and co-ordinate it.[14] The Government continued to stand by its spies, even when their cover had been blown inside out. Hazlitt was amusingly not amused by such a stand. He ripped Castlereagh's arguments to shreds in two articles 'On the Spy-System'.

The Cato Street conspirators were caught squarely, if not fairly, in a tangled web spun by the Home Office and its 'espials'. George Edwards, like Castle, had been a figure-maker and modeller. He was sometimes described as a seller of images. As suggested, he was employed to spy on the conspirators so that the Government could peddle an image of a country on the brink of civil war, and thus justify its policy of reaction rather than action. Edwards was not just a snapper-up of informational trifles. The Home Office and Bow Street had had their agents twisted into Thistlewood's gang for some time. He was used as a *provocateur*. The evidence suggests that Thistlewood was perfectly capable of working out an assassination plan himself. We shall never know, however, just how capable he would have been of executing such a plan alone and unaided, for Edwards stepped in with money and boundless enthusiasm. He was always there to lend a helping hand when the going got tough. The conspirators appear to have accepted this modeller of men into their midst because of his connections with the Spenceans. Edwards's brother was a prominent member of one particular group. The conspirators did not know, however, that this brother was also on the Bow Street payroll. There may well have been more agents than radicals present at some meetings. There may, for aught we know, be more television reporters roughing it on the Embankment on full expenses than real down-and-outs.

It was usual for spies to learn their job by trial and error. It is just possible, however, that Edwards received a rudimentary training in tradecraft from Major-General Taylor.[15] His technique was nevertheless not particularly subtle. He tended to leave his messages at safe houses and presumably received instructions through them as well. He would not have lasted very long during the cold war. Edwards did not need any training when it came to acting the required parts. He was a small, insignificant man, who only appeared to come alive when acting these parts. Thistlewood described at his trial how Edwards loved to change his identity in this way:

This Edwards, poor and pennyless, lived near Pickett-street, in the Strand, sometime ago, without a bed to lie upon, or a chair to sit in. Straw was his resting place; his only covering a blanket. Owing to his bad character and his swindling conduct, he was driven from thence by his landlord. It is not my intention to trace him through his immorality; suffice it to say, that he was in every sense of the word a villain of the deepest atrocity; his landlord refused to give him a character; some short time after this he called upon his landlord again, but, mark the change in his appearance, dressed like a lord, in all the folly of the reigning fashion. He now described himself as the right heir to a German baron, who had been some time dead; that Lords Castlereagh and Sidmouth had acknowledged his claims to the title and property; had interfered in his behalf with the German government, and supplied him with money to support his rank in society.[16]

It is impossible to verify the accuracy of this splendid account, but also rather unnecessary. Edwards's landlord would have found it difficult to give him 'a character', as he preferred the plural to the singular. His repertoire may have included this preposterous German baron. We know that it also included the part of down-at-heel rebel with a burning cause. It is perhaps ironic that our portrait of Edwards playing this particular part comes from the reports of other spies and agents, who hovered on the fringes of the Thistlewood gang. We find him brandishing his sword-stick to make a point and swearing that he will bring down the Government single-handed if necessary. All spies wear well-trimmed, reversible turncoats. They fight in a looking-glass war in which the appearance must never proclaim the man. Thistlewood used to refer to Edwards as his aide-de-camp. This privileged position meant that Edwards was at the very centre of the conspiracy. The evidence suggests that he was as theatrically camp as the proverbial row of tents. It is doubtful, however, that Thistlewood himself needed much aid, or stage coaching, in this department.

Castle, Oliver and Edwards are obviously members of the *dramatis personae* of the theatre of politics. Yet their activities only represent an easily identifiable variation on the commonest theme of political behaviour. The establishment and the radicals were also members of the cast. Polonius is, after all, as much a master of political disguise as Reynaldo is. Claudius is infinitely more accomplished than Rosencrantz and Guildenstern. Hamlet is usually at least one theatrical trick and costume change ahead of the 'espials'. Shelley was right to suggest in 'The Mask of Anarchy' that spies needed to be seen as part of a much wider pattern of political behaviour:

And many more Destructions played
In this ghastly masquerade,
All disguised, even to the eyes
Like Bishops, lawyers, peers, or spies.

The spy masters also fight in this looking-glass war, as do the spied upon.

There only seems to be a slight difference of degree between the activities of George Edwards and those of George Ruthven. It seems likely that Ruthven spent most of the afternoon of the 23 February keeping his beady eye on the comers and goers around Cato Street. He holed up in the Horse and Groom public house immediately before the arrest. He must have taken steps to blend in with the scenery of the area, for it was exactly the kind of working-class slum in which policemen stuck out like big feet. It may well be that his first words on reaching the loft, which were 'We are officers, seize their arms!', were necessary to identify himself. It is certainly true that he found no difficulty blending in with the conspirators, when the lights went down and the struggle ensued. Thistlewood apparently shouted 'Kill the buggers, throw them down stairs!' Ruthven's footwork was, however, remarkaby fast for a policeman:

I heard a rush at the stairs, and I joined in the rush saying 'Ah kill them', and got down. I heard it, for I could not see it . . . . I did not observe any thing till I got into John-street, and there I met with the soldiers, and returned with them. There were a great many shots fired before I got down.

Ruthven was helped by the encircling gloom, but it is still interesting that he took the precaution to assume the identity of a conspirator. It may take a thief to catch a thief, but it also takes an actor to catch another one. This was by no means the first time that Ruthven had employed a little disguise. He admitted that he had been employed to trail and tail Thistlewood in the weeks immediately before the arrest. Yet it is even more significant that in 1817, under an alias, he attended Spencean meetings to try to come up with incriminating evidence against Thistlewood. He may, then, have actually needed to insist that he was playing the officer on the night of 23 February. The conspirators could have been forgiven for thinking that this staunch land reformer, who seemed vaguely familiar, was coming to throw in his lot with them.[17]

It may be that Thistlewood took a leaf out of Ruthven's book and made his escape from Cato Street by impersonating a police officer. *The Courier,* in an exclusive on 4 March, claimed that he jumped out of the back of the loft and made his escape through one of the houses:

he called to them that he was an officer in pursuit of the villains who had just quitted the loft, and if the door were not instantly opened, he would break it down, as on such an occasion, he had authority to do so. His audacity vanquished their scruples, and believing him to be the person he represented himself to be, they no longer refused to permit him to enter.

Some doubt is cast on the authenticity of this account by the fact that Mrs Wallis, the owner of the house, appears to have later identified Ruthven as the man who stormed through her house.[18] So the only thing that we can be really sure about is that there were a lot of people in and around Cato Street on the night of 23 February, who were not what they represented themselves to be. An identity parade would have been very confusing, since it would have been difficult to know which of several identities was actually being paraded at any given time.

Cloaks and daggers

The Cato Street conspirators enjoyed dressing up just as much as spies and policemen seem to have done. Thistlewood's performance as the English Napoleon was probably just as good as Edwards's impersonation of a German baron. Thistlewood liked to exaggerate his military appearance. He had a good scar on his right jaw and liked wearing military sashes. He enhanced his political and personal virility by carrying a French cut-and-thrust sword, which was at least a foot longer than usual. His passion for French political models was complemented by a preference for French dressing. He owned a set of prints of Napoleon's major battles, as well as portraits of the great man. It is probable that he asked his tailor to copy one of Napoleon's uniforms, when he decided in 1817 to get a general's uniform run up.[19] He wanted to lead the English revolution in style. The casualties of both war and peace who joined him followed his choice of suit. They too went in for the military and the paramilitary. They resembled down-market versions of the swaggering swordsmen, who teamed up with the Earl of Essex against Elizabeth I. Butcher Ings liked to hang military hardware on both sides:

He was preparing himself in the manner he intended to enter the room where their lordships were, he puts a black belt round his waist, in order to contain a brace of pistols; he puts another black belt on to hang a cutlass to his shoulder; after this, there was a bag hung to each shoulder, a large bag to each shoulder, in the form of a soldier's haversack. When these bags were on, he placed a brace of pistols, one on each side; he hung a cutlass; he viewed himself and said, 'Damn my eyes! I am not complete now – I have forgot my steel!' With that he pulled out a large knife, and began to brandish it about . . . as if he were in the act of cutting the heads of those he intended to cut off, he would bring away a head in each hand . . . .[20]

It seems incredible that he could move at all underneath this mighty arsenal, yet the utility of the outfit was rather unimportant. Ings, like all those of the political persuasion, was primarily interested in a narcissistic form of self-dramatization: he wanted to view himself. He also liked acting out charades before an appreciative audience. Paine believed that the political establishment was a group of overgrown children, who indulged in nursery games. His own followers are not immune from the same accusation. There is only a difference of degree between Ings's antics and those of, say, Cobbett and Hunt on the radical platforms.

The conspirators were mostly masters of disguise. Richard Tidd earned a dishonest living during the Napoleonic wars as a bounty-hunter. He signed on with as many regiments as possible under different names. It was not just the spies like Edwards, or the bishops like Jocelyn, who had a limited use for a particular name. Identity was fluid and could be changed as easily as clothes. Thistlewood managed to evade the thief-takers for a couple of months in 1817 by assuming a variety of disguises. He was finally picked up trying to board a ship to America. He was wearing a padded coat and a broad-brimmed hat. His furtively antic disposition continued to frustrate the 'espials' in the weeks before the discovery of the conspiracy. The Government found itself having to pay out bad money from the slush-hush fund, just to be told that Thistlewood could slip an unwelcome follower by slipping into a different costume. Yet disguise could in fact be a form of self-conscious advertisement. We learn that at one meeting in December 1819

[the] greatest part of them had swords under their coats amonst others Bryant & Hartley . . . . Wilson had on a long Spanish Blue Cloak with two capes, to disguise a long sword & white belt . . . .[21]

The modern equivalents of the 'long Spanish Blue Cloak with two capes' might well be the black berets, dark glasses and combat-jackets, which seem to be absolutely *de rigueur* for adults who still enjoy playing at soldiers.

The conspirators enjoyed viewing themselves and doing a few twirls for their friends, but they also hankered after louder applause and wider acclaim. The sight of Thistlewood haring and tearing through the streets of London was so familiar that it almost became a tourist attraction. He still needed to play street theatre. His followers were just the same. They turned up at meetings with looks that could not help but betray their purposes. A studied carelessness about the effectiveness of disguise was an essential part of the conspiratorial frame of mind. Such carelessness may eventually cost lives, but, in the short run through the streets, it both casts and confirms roles. It casts ordinary lives as dramatic political parts. Most of the accounts of the battle of Cato Street commented on two aspects of it. First of all, that these ragged-trousered radicals and ancient pistols, when stripped of their paramilitary paraphernalia, looked embarrassingly ordinary. *The Times* stated on 25 February that they

had nothing extraordinary in their appearance. They were for the most part men of short stature, mean exterior, and unmarked physiognomy.

Second, although some papers vamped up their descriptions of the action, there was a fairly general consensus that, with the obvious exception of the cutting and thrusting Thistlewood, the conspirators found great difficulty in actually using their much cherished equipment. They would have had difficulty blowing up a paper bag, let alone fighting their way out of one. Their tragedy was that they ever moved, and were moved, from 'fumble through' and dress rehearsal to the real thing.

State theatricals

The newspapers made a certain amount of play of the fact that the conspirators had evolved a society within a society. They had their own flags, oaths of allegiance, passwords and slang.[22] Yet Eastcheap complements the political practices of the court, even though it also seeks to contradict them. The conspirators' obsession with ceremony and costume was paralleled by the rites and rituals of orthodox political life. The freemasonry of this world ought to seem just as absurd as anything practised by Thistlewood and his cronies. It would be very dangerous to fall into the trap of assuming that George IV's use of a military champion on ceremonial occasions was normal, whereas the conspirators' love of military styles was not. Butcher Ings might have seemed faintly ridiculous when dressed to kill. So did hanging judges, who dressed themselves up to look like unshorn sheep in plush dressing-gowns.

Show trials are usually defined as ones in which the defendants are given a fair trial and then hanged. The trial of the conspirators was no exception to this general rule. It was also a show trial in the sense that the full ceremonial weight of the establishment was coercively brought to bear upon society as a whole. Those of the pastoral persuasion may like to kid themselves about the solemnity of nineteenth-century judicial proceeding, but there is no reason why they should kid us as well. Some of the seats at the Old Bailey were reserved for interested parties, such as students, the press and those connected with the trial in question. Such seating arrangements were handled by the court administrators. Members of the public gained admission by buying tickets from a private organization, which owned some of the boxes and seats inside the court. Such tickets were being sold for a guinea or more for Thistlewood's trial. A number of young men, who dressed as Regency bucks, toured the streets trying to persuade the public that this was really cheap at the price. The touts appear to have miscalculated. The massive pre-trial publicity may have overkilled the event itself for some people, while others were just not prepared to be robbed in the daylight by the flashmen. There was, nevertheless, enough of a 'big match' atmosphere to disturb the conscience-mongers. *The Times* declared on 19 April their forlorn hope

that the city of London is the only part of England, and the Old Bailey the only part of the city, where the solemn spectacle of a fellow-creature standing on trial of his life or death is turned into a public exhibition, open to all who choose to pay for it.

Yet state theatricals were concerned with the 'public exhibition' of right and wrong. It was also rather prissy of *The Times* to draw attention to the box office. The theatre of politics always needed an audience.

The stage-managers had to take extreme care to see that only the acceptable face of the establishment was exhibited to the public at this show trial. If Edwards was put into the witness box, there would be little chance of his being able to clear his deep throat. He was put through a number of dummy cross-examinations, just in case he had to become part of the case.[23] The Government was particularly concerned to cover itself against allegations that it had, through Edwards, indirectly funded the Cato Street boys. Edwards presented a real problem. It might, for instance, be difficult to get a conviction without his evidence, yet he could be torn to shreds like Castle was. Robert Adams, one of the conspirators, came to the rescue. He was persuaded to hang his friends rather than himself. He turned King's evidence. John Stafford, the Chief Clerk at Bow Street, had the arduous task of coaching Adams, until he was word perfect in the authorized version of the conspiracy.[24] A super-grass was never going to be a particularly credible witness, but at least Adams only put on the reversible turncoat after the conspiracy. The prosecution worked very hard on its case during March and the early weeks of April. It studied the treason trials of 1794 and 1817 in the hope of learning from past mistakes. It was determined to make its case as legally hard as it was morally fast and loose.

The prosecution could itself be accused of a number of things, but never of being idle. The defence, by contrast, was hopelessly and helplessly out of their league. The prisoners had not been given much of a chance to collect their thoughts. Thistlewood's request

for pens, ink and paper was turned down on 12 March. He was given
a bible instead. Two guards kept a constant watch on him in his cell
in the 'Bloody Tower' and he was not allowed access to the kind of
friends who might have helped him.[25] An action group, which was
supported by Leigh Hunt, opened a fighting fund for the prisoners,
but this does not appear to have done very well. Thistlewood
eventually engaged John Adolphus to defend him. Adolphus
pointed out in court that he was only given one day, which was a
Sunday, to study the case. *The Law Magazine*, however, paid tribute
to the way he acquitted himself, if not the defendants:

an accomplished and impressive speaker, whose eloquence takes the lead in
persuasive rhetoric. He spoke with such perfect ease as always to impress
his hearers with the idea how easy it would be to do the like. He affected his
auditors as it is said Garrick did his spectators – 'This is not acting,' said
they, 'it is a mere exhibition of ease.'[26]

Eloquent actors, like Adolphus and Garrick, still need a chance to
learn their lines. Despite this glowing tribute, Adolphus's career
had not been a particularly successful one. He was probably too
charming for his own good. He was, rather curiously, a reasonably
close personal friend of Sidmouth's. He had received a government
salary earlier on in his career for political services rendered. His
daughter proudly recorded that he frequently visited Sidmouth at
his house in Richmond Park.[27] There is no evidence to suggest that
plots were thickened there prior to the trial of the conspirators, just
as there is none to suggest that they were not. Adolphus's lack of
preparation seriously damaged his handling of Thistlewood's case.
He improved with practice. His cross-examinations of Adams at the
subsequent trials were both cross and examining, but then it was too
late. Thistlewood's conviction was the one that mattered.

It would have been difficult for Adolphus, or anybody, to have
reversed the trend after Thistlewood's conviction. The same jurors
had a habit of turning up at the different trials. Eight members of the
jury which convicted Thistlewood were empanelled for Brunt's
trial. The jury caused the stage-managers a certain amount of
concern, for it was imperative that they should not just be of more
than average stupidity, but also more than averagely loyal. The lists
were scrutinized with due care and attention. Potential jurors were
labelled as 'very loyal', 'loyal' and 'disloyal'. Peter Fish was
considered to be such a threat to judicial impartiality that he was
labelled 'very bad a radical'.[28] The prosecution and the defence

were both perfectly within their rights to object to jurors. The jury which convicted Thistlewood may not quite have been vetted, but it was subjected to more than average scrutiny.

Those who paid a guinea to see these state theatricals probably got their money's worth. Charles Abbott, the Lord Chief Justice, was on splendid form. He really enjoyed squeezing urbane amusement out of such names as Brunt, Tidd and Ings. I'm surprised that he did not rest the case after referring to the Hole-in-the-Wall passage, which was one of the many significantly named locations. If the Bow Street runners were shown a gallery, they were usually more than happy to play to it. They showed off their scars and told stories which made Cato Street seem like Agincourt. Even the guardsmen, who were resplendent in dress uniform, cut suitably impressive figures. The grand finale to the prosecution's case was a ritualistic production and exhibition of ancient pistols, cut-and-thrust swords and hand-grenades. It was even hinted that these hand-grenades might go off in court. Curwood, Adolphus's junior, tried to be scathing about this ploy, when he addressed the very loyal jury:

You have, to garnish the case lying before you, an affected display of rusty sabres, broken pistols, and a great many other things.[29]

He must, as a lawyer, have known that the game was up, as garnish and affectation were all. The prisoners, with the exception of Ings, were garnished with leg-irons when they stood to receive sentence. The legal beagles decided to garnish themselves with special scarlet robes on 25 April, during Brunt's trial, to celebrate the King's birthday. Byron was right to notice the uncanny resemblance between legal bullies and Shakespeare's Parolles.

The prisoners were not allowed to steal the show, but they did turn in some good supporting performances. Butcher Ings, who was dressed in black for his trial, broke down while addressing the jury. All the prisoners tried to make Adams's long bouts of Government-sponsored perjury as difficult as possible for him. Although the public galleries apparently shuddered as he told his terrible tale, the prisoners attempted to hiss at him. Davidson developed a nervous laugh, which he used to interrupt the flow of Adams's evidence. Adams's task, which was never going to be an easy one, was not helped by the fact that his appalling squint did not endear him to the jury.

Thistlewood was an 'old jack', who had seen productions in the theatre of law before. He affected to treat the proceedings with the contempt they undoubtedly deserved. If the judge could camp it up theatrically, then so could he:

This awful appeal, delivered by the judge in the most impressive manner, was wholly lost on Thistlewood, who, with apparent careless indifference, pulled out his snuff-box, some of the contents of which he took, casting his eyes round the court, as if he were entering a theatre. His indifference was the more conspicuous when contrasted with the solemn manner in which the Lord Chief-Justice addressed the prisoners.[30]

Thistlewood, rather ironically, came alive during his trial. He had turned in a few defiant performances after his arrest. He refused to take his hat off when being examined by the Council called the Privy on 3 March. Yet he became distinctly faded and jaded as the weeks dragged by. Old pros seldom die, theatrically anyway, before a large audience. Thistlewood began his speech to the jury, which was written out on several sheets of paper, in a quavering voice. He was, however, very soon giving a performance for his life:

With respect to the immorality of our project, I will just observe, that the assassination of tyrants has always been deemed a meritorious action; Brutus and Cassius were lauded to the very skies for slaying Caesar; indeed, where any man, or any set of men, place themselves above the laws of their country, there is no other means of bringing them to justice than through the arm of a private individual. If the laws are not strong enough to prevent them from murdering the community, it becomes the duty of every member of that community to rid his country of its oppressors.

Abbott, who was obviously worried that Thistlewood might be stealing the show, interrupted at this point to remind him that it was not possible to justify assassination in a theatre of law. Thistlewood continued unadmonished:

High Treason was committed against the people at Manchester, but justice was closed against the mutilated, the maimed, and the friends of those who were upon that occasion indiscriminately massacred. The prince, by the advice of his minsters, thanked the murderers, still reeking in the gore of their hapless victims. If one spark of honour, if one spark of independence, still glimmered in the breast of Englishmen, they would have rose to a man; insurrection then became a public duty, and the blood of the victims should have been the watch-word to vengeance on their murders.

Abbott intervened again, but Thistlewood pointed out that he only had 'a few lines more' of this carefully prepared speech to stand and deliver. These, incidentally, included a reference to the *theatrum mundi*:

I shall soon be consigned to the grave, my body will be immured beneath the soil whereon I first drew breath. My only sorrow is, that the soil should be a theatre for slaves, for cowards, for despots.[31]

Anybody who can give such a good performance before dying deserves to be saluted. Parliament was formally opened on the same day that Thistlewood was formally sentenced to death.

The execution of the five conspirators was the final act in Sidmouth's 'ghastly masquerade'. The day before it, which happened to be a Sunday, was spent in erecting a suitably impressive stage. Uninformed speculators suggested that this might actually be placed on top of Newgate itself, although it was eventually erected in the usual place beside the Debtor's Door. The workmen took longer than expected and had to finish by torchlight. The presence of these stage-hands on the set must have provided something of a curtain-raiser for those who had arrived early to avoid disappointment. The touts and flashmen did a brisk trade throughout Sunday. It was money for old rope, when compared with trying to flog tickets for the trial. Window seats were fetching two to three guineas a time. Sidmouth decided that, as distance was badly needed to lend some enchantment to the view, actors and audience ought to be kept as far apart as was theatrically possible. Thus, as Mayday dawned, the forces of law and order tried to make sure that the crowd kept their distance. While John and Jenny Bull jockeyed for position, an assortment of the great and the good were being escorted around the condemned cells. Sidmouth was too theatrically superstitious to watch the last act of the masquerade himself. He therefore had to rely on a description by the Lord Mayor:

the execution has taken place in perfect quietness – when Tidd came on the platform there was a little shouting and when Ings came on he gave three cheers which were partially and faintly returned, but the Prisoners did not address the populace and if they had the distance from the place of execution would have prevented any bad effects. There was by far the most dissatisfaction expressed at the decapitation, but it was but momentary – on the whole there has seldom been a more tranquil Execution witnessed – the Troops were so dispersed that in whichever way the populace approached the Old Bailey they must be seen in force sufficient to deter any attempts at rescue – the mob are beginning slowly to disperse and unless any thing fresh were to occur I think it will be unnecessary to trouble your Lordship with any further account of this unpleasant business.[32]

The conspicuous deployment of troops was very much part of Home Office house style. They had provided the iron fist to the velvety legal rhetoric during the trials. They were used at the execution to underline the point, just in case anybody had missed it, that the Government had powers of life and death.

It might be worth troubling all but the most squeamish reader with a few incidental details about the way in which the theatre of violence was acted out. The church militant, represented by the Reverend Cotton, led the prisoners out of Newgate. Then they mounted the scaffold one at a time. As each one reached the top of the steps, he was seized by a masked executioner. A rope was tried on for size. When all five were neatly in a row, the drop fell. Sidmouth's puppets dangled on the end of their strings. Their legs were occasionally pulled, literally of course, to make sure that they were not going to cheat the hangman. They were hoisted back on to the main part of the stage after about half an hour. The mysteries of the executioner's art were then demonstrated to the crowd. The executioner wore a black mask over the upper part of his face and used a handkerchief to conceal his mouth. He also wore a broad-brimmed hat. His job was to decapitate the corpses with a dagger. Like Adolphus, he apparently needed a bit of time to get his eye in. An apprentice in this dying trade then exhibited each head to the crowd and pronounced their recent owners to have been traitors. The execution team then placed both the trunk and the head in a coffin. The coffins had been at the front of the stage throughout the proceedings. These coffins, which remained open, were then carried slowly offstage. The speed had nothing to do with feelings of dignity or respect for the prisoners. The set was almost knee-deep in sawdust, which was used to try to absorb the blood, so it was necessary to proceed with a certain amount of caution. The show was over. The crowd dispersed to have a nice day. They were welcome to it. Curtain.

Conclusions

Sidmouth must have been rather disappointed by some of the reviews he received. He had, after all, devoted time, effort and money to his masquerade. He had given the public a sensational arrest, a show trial and a bloody good execution. What more did they want? Some muttered darkly that the Government had cloaked its activities with great skill. Others noticed that the masked executioner had used a dagger to decapitate the corpses. Were members of the Government the real cloak and dagger boys? Alderman Matthew Wood persisted in quibbling about the cast list. Why was Edwards not included among the performers? Wood demanded that Edwards, presumably dressed in his reversible turncoat, should be forced to attend at the bar of the House of Commons to answer some searching questions. The honourable Members, who had probably been attending bars in more public houses, came to the aid of Sidmouth's masquerade and brayed with laughter at such a silly suggestion.

Thistlewood was dead, but Sidmouth found it difficult to bury him. Some extreme radicals went so far as to crown him King Arthur. Even Byron, who was simply appalled by the very thought of the people themselves coarsening the nobility of revolution by taking matters into their hard, horny hands, felt that Thistlewood's death, if not his life, had a certain nobility. Sidmouth must have been irritated by the tiresome, almost scholastic, pedantry of the reviewers. They wondered, on the one hand, whether the conspiracy was against the Government, and, on the other, whether it was a conspiracy by the Government against the people. State theatricals were meant to please and police all the people all of the time. Where had Sidmouth gone wrong?

My own review of the events follows the lead of a hard-hitting leader in *The Examiner* on 30 April, which suggested that at least the sordid 'machinery' of politics had been exposed for what it really was. The particular event provided a key to unlock general secrets about political behaviour. This interpretation is confirmed by the evidence that has come to light since 1820. The reasonably 'full and accurate' range of evidence in the Home Office files confirms interpretations of political behaviour, which the public relations boys would prefer to dismiss as 'caricature impressions'. The 'machinery' of state theatricals, both on and off the stage, is there for all to see. A reactionary reaction to such an interpretation might be to suggest that exceptional events do not prove general rules. Yet the Cato Street conspiracy may be more representative than the placemen are prepared to admit. The propaganda offensive which followed the arrest of the conspirators was part and parcel of a long tradition of counter-revolutionary activity. The radicals of the 1790s would have had little difficulty working out what was going on in 1820. Similarly, show trials at both the national and local level were very well-tried methods of containing and coercing radicalism. The execution of the conspirators was hardly the first production of Government-sponsored theatre of violence in this period. It is also important to remember that Thistlewood and his followers were members of the radical flock. Their obsessions with dressing the parts and arranging symbolic clashes were the rule for those who attacked establishment rule. *The Examiner* was right to suggest that the Cato Street conspiracy was emblematic of early nineteenth-century political behaviour. If all political activity is a fraudulent conspiracy, then it has a much wider significance. Establishment and oppositional theatricals are exposed in ideographic detail. That is not a paradox. The spies, the spy-masters and the spied upon allow us to glimpse the true 'machinery' of politics. Those who take exception to my abuse of what they still regard as an exceptional event are doubtless already warming up some of Dr Derry's clichés on the substitutes' bench. Perhaps Derryisms are substitutes for the real thing.

Butcher Ings told the jury at the end of his trial that he was being 'sold as a bullock into Smithfield-market'.[33] The whistle ought to be blown on vile politicians of every persuasion, who sell us to the slaughterhouses to keep themselves in power. This is often difficult to do, since auctioneers are such plausible people. They have a way with words. Their footwork is as fast as it is furious. Whistle-blowers are inevitably coerced by theatrical brilliance. We may not be political auctioneers, but perhaps we all want to be. Sidmouth, whom I have presented as the iron man behind these state masques, did get some bad notices. Yet it has to be noticed that he proved himself capable of putting on a jolly good show. Perhaps his critics were just jealous. The theatricals were, on the whole, exceedingly well timed and effective. So, of course, were Italian trains and German gas ovens. That's the problem.

8   Carnival turns 1820

Rule and misrule

Thistlewood and Sidmouth may have wished to appear to be political poles apart, but they shared the same obsessions with military, ceremonial and symbolic aspects of politics. The oppositional theatre of politics reflected the codes and conduct it tried to reject. All the evidence suggests that the establishment very self-consciously waged a ritualistic offensive at both local and national levels during this period. Social attitudes which might have been implicit in these rituals before the 1790s became much more explicit. The counter-revolution was first and foremost a psychological war. Joseph Arch's father was humiliated by the Church of England, yet this humiliation was ritualistic. The church service mirrored the social attitudes of the dominant class as well as the limited expectations of the subservient class. The war on the home front was being fought for control, discipline and containment. No psychological quarter was given. The counter-revolution did have a more tangible side to it. It is still possible to visit some of the grim barracks, which were hastily thrown up in the potential danger zones. It is also possible to kick the obscene little tracts, which tried to pretend that early nineteenth-century England was the very best of all possible worlds. Yet the full weight of the counter-revolutionary punch only becomes painfully apparent when its various political, religious and judicial ceremonies are actually recreated and restaged. These were the real belting blows below the belt.

Radicals parodied and burlesqued these ceremonies in the hope that inversion and perversion might lead to total subversion. William Hone's *The Political Litany* . . . (1817) was an attempt to turn church services upside down:

From an unnatural debt; from unmerited pensions and sinecure places; from an extravagant civil list; from utter starvation,

> Good Prince, deliver us!

From the blind imbecility of ministers; from the pride and vain glory of warlike establishments in time of peace,

> Good Prince, deliver us! (pp. 3–4)

Richard Carlile also made the militancy of both church and state his target in *The Bullet Te Deum* (1817):

To thee all Placemen cry aloud:
The Treasury and all the clerks therein,
To thee Pensioners and sinecurists continually do cry,
Bullet, Bullet, Bullet: from thee our power floweth. (p. 4)

A society which is steeped in liturgical ritual inevitably produces an opposition which exploits these rituals. William Hone and other satirists flooded the country with parodies of litanies, liturgies and the whole bag of counter-revolutionary theatrical tricks during the trial of Queen Caroline in 1820. Caroline's private life was publicly tried because it was felt that it would be dangerous to include her by name in church services. Such ceremonies would lose their coercive psychological force, if they started to provoke knowing winks and coarse nudges among the audience. The traditional prayers for the Royal Family would be open to mockery, if Caroline were allowed to continue her relationship with an Italian waiter. The Government probably realized that it would always have to deal with the dislikes of Hone and Carlile. It appears to have been concerned, however, about the possibility of Caroline's inclusion in church services providing the satirists with a captive audience. It might appear to be a thankless task to try to defend the managers of this particular state theatrical against the charges of political incompetence and miscalculation, which were levelled against them by *The Black Dwarf* and others. It could be submitted, nevertheless, that as they were committed to a ritualistic offensive, they did not really have any alternative. They had to try to purge the liturgy of anything that might be offensively used against them. The Queen's name was incidentally removed before her trial. As will be seen later on, the Government found itself hoist with its own ceremonial petard during the Queen Caroline affair.

It is possible to get a sense of the way in which the rituals of the right were set against them from pamphlets by Hone, Carlile and others. Yet, just as an exclusive concentration of Hannah More and Legh Richmond leaves vast tracts of the counter-revolution unexplored, so these radical pamphlets do not provide the best guides to the oppositional theatre of politics. Drama always needs to be studied in performance, or as performance. There was a serious cholera epidemic in Manchester in the autumn of 1832. The mutilated body of a child was discovered in one of the overcrowded cholera hospitals. Major-General Bouverie explained to the Home Office what happened when the authorities tried to bury this child with indecent haste:

The mob seized upon the coffin at the place of interment and paraded it with the body through the streets, and a piquet of cavalry was employed to rescue them, which was accomplish[d] without difficulty.[1]

It seems likely that this particular popular protest took the appropriate form of a savage parody of funeral processions and possibly even burial services as well. If so, then the protestors were drawing on the traditions of carnival. Le Roy Ladurie has shown in his important study of *Carnival: A People's Uprising at Romans 1579–1580* (1980) that mock funeral processions were an integral part of the carnival activities. They flouted not only the authority of the church, but also of death itself.

The sermon was also a target for both inversion and subversion. Radicals tried to beat suppressive, repressive legislation by pretending to hold religious rather than political meetings. This form of mock worship caused the Home Office a certain amount of concern in December 1819. John Stoddart, the editor of *The New Times*, whom Hone nicknamed Dr Slop, forwarded a letter to them about one such meeting, which had taken place in Lambeth. The mock preacher placed

himself in an attitude which I cannot better describe than the view given in the picture shops of these Boxing men when having what they technically call, *a set to*. He commenced pouring forth a torrent of the most abusive language . . . on the *Bishops & Clergy* of the present day designating them all as *murderers & knaves* charging them with every crime that men are capable of being guilty, and attaching to them every epithet which the most scurrilious language could suggest.[2]

The radicals found it necessary to hold these mock services to avoid the watchful eyes and spies of the Government, but they contrived to make a virtue out of this necessity. The political meeting itself took the form of a parody of a religious service. The preacher was a mocking as well as a mock one. He appears to have had a good line in sending up muscular christianity.

Carnival festivities were originally pagan fertility rites, but they were absorbed into the framework of the Roman Catholic church without too much difficulty. Carnival was allowed to be in season immediately before Lent, so its celebrations tended to culminate in *mardi gras* parades and pageants. Emotions, which had been bottled up during the winter and were to be again during the purges and scourges of Lent, were allowed to fizz away for a brief but frenetic period. Plebeians were allowed to mock patricians and they, in turn, either mocked themselves or the power of church and state. There were two reasons why the fizzy, dizzy carnival spirit did not necessarily undermine authority. First of all, it was licensed or sanctioned by the authorities themselves. They removed the stopper to stop the bottle being smashed altogether. The release of emotions and grievances made them easier to police in the long term. Second, although the world might appear to be turned upside down during the carnival season, the facts that Kings and Queens were chosen and crowned actually reaffirmed the *status quo*. Carnival was, however, Janus-faced. Falstaff is both the merry old mimic of Eastcheap and the old corruptible who tries to undermine the authority, or rule, of the Lord Chief Justice. The carnival spirit, in early nineteenth-century England as well as in sixteenth-century France, could therefore be a vehicle for social protest and the method of disciplining this very protest.

Banbury Cross

Late eighteenth- and early nineteenth-century parliamentary elections were usually strong theatrical stuff. Parson Woodeforde described the triumphal entry of Sir John Wodehouse into Norwich during the 1784 campaign:

About 10 o'clock the Market Place and Streets in Norwich were lined with People and almost all with Wodehouse's Cockades in their Hats. After breakfast I went to Mrs. Brewsters and got 6 Cockades all for Wodehouse – 3 of them of blue and Pink with Wodehouse wrote in Silver on the blue, the other 3 plain blue and Pink for my Servants at home. About 11 o'clock Sr. John Wodehouse preceded with a great many Flaggs and a band of Musick, made his public Entry on horseback, attended with between two and three Thousand Men on Horseback, They came thro' St. Giles's, then thro' the

Market Place, then marched on to the Shire House on the Castle Hill and there Sr. John Wodehouse with Sr. Edward Astley were unanimously chosen Members for the County. After that they had dressed themselves handsomely and were chaired first round the Castle-Hill and then three times round the Market Place amidst an innumerable Number of Spectators and the loudest acclamations of Wodehouse for ever.[3]

Parliamentary elections were sometimes concerned with burning local or even national issues. The bone of contention on this particular occasion was that most unholy of unholy alliances, the Fox–North Coalition. Yet patterns of electoral performance should never be neglected in favour of more orthodox interpretations of content.[4] Woodeforde draws our attention to the importance of such stage props as horses, flags, cockades and musical instruments. Although the sense of the description is a little obscure, he also suggests that politicians made their calling and election sure by paying particular attention to costume. Wodehouse and Astley appear to have managed a quick costume change after the election result had been declared. It was quite common throughout this period for handbills to advertise an election in the same manner as a play. After Sheffield had been enfranchised in 1832, the inhabitants were given a list of the forthcoming attractions at 'The New Borough Theatre'. These included a burletta entitled 'Professions!! or, Believe us who may'.[5] It would be possible to come up with plausible explanations for such equations between politics and theatre, yet rather unnecessary since politics was theatre. The theatre of electoral politics was particularly widespread in this period. The social historians argue convincingly that popular recreations and festivities were brutally sacrificed to the great gods of work discipline and social control. A parliamentary election thus became one of the few occasions on which carnival could legitimately show its painted face.

The inhabitants of Banbury became exceedingly cross on 10 March 1820. Most of them did not have the vote as they lived in what was known as a corporation borough. The Mayor and Corporation elected a Member of Parliament. The political party did, however, lay on a jolly good party for the people on election day. They provided beer, cockades and all the other trappings of the political circus. They did not have to buy votes, but they may have felt that it was still worth buying collusion and acquiescence. If you took the precaution of buying the people a few drinks, they were anybody's. Mr Sarcastic and Sir Oran Haut-Ton, in Peacock's *Melincourt* (1818), give the citizens of Novote plenty of beer, otherwise known as 'frothy rhetoric', so that they will be in good humour during the election for the ancient borough of Onevote. It was decided that it was no longer necessary to have such a costly circus in Banbury Town in 1820. Work discipline and business efficiency appear to have claimed another victim. The people felt cheated of their undemocratic rights and so decided to stage their own circus.

Robert Brayne, the Mayor, the Honourable Legge, the sitting Member and the Corporation assembled at the Mayor's private house between ten and eleven on the morning of 10 March. The plot usually took the form of a seemingly solemn procession to the Town Hall. The election then would be carried out on the steps. The voters stood at the top of these steps, descended to cast their vote and then ascended to cast their eye over the adoring multitude. Injustice was seen to be done, provided that you were not too drunk to notice or indeed care. It was then well past time for the honourable gentlemen to roll out a few more barrels. The chimes of midnight probably sounded somewhere in the muddled distance, as the people, caked with ale, rolled themselves back home.

The election took on a very different complexion in 1820. As the local worthies made their way to the Mayor's house, they began to sense that the natives were restless. Instead of the usual gruntled oafs, they saw louts loitering about with suspicious intentions. Why were these natives wearing cockades made out of wood shavings in their hats and forelocks? Perhaps they intended to make a mockery of the whole dignified and efficient procedure. The emphatic answer came in the form of a hail of stones, which smashed Mr Mayor's windows. The worthies stiffened their lips with a stiff drink and decided that the show must still go on. It was crucial to show the natives that you made no bones about their sticks and stones. It may be that some sort of trouble had been anticipated, for when the procession eventually set out for the Town Hall it was accompanied by thirty special constables. It was still given a rough, unceremonious ride. The chains of office and command appeared to have snapped. Matters were very definitely out of soft hands by the time Brayne and the others had fought their way to the steps. Their entrance was blocked by a carriage, which was twisted into the railings. The special constables managed to remove it, but the natives then used it as a battering ram against the gentlemen and their officers. Brayne decided to hold the election behind closed doors. The mechanicals were rude enough to force the Corporation to move from room to room by keeping up a heavy bombardment of sticks and stones. The shutters were put up in the Council Chamber and the Honourable Legge was duly elected for the said constituency. The voters were then forced to spend some time with their backs against the wall, since the multitude swinishly broke down the shutters after a determined assault. Brayne later described how the Corporation had been forced to secrete themselves in various nooks and crannies around the Town Hall. Somebody then had a bad idea. If the mob were given something to drink, perhaps they would return to their usual state of passive intoxication. The tubs of beer merely provided them with more ammunition. After spending three hours holed up in the Town Hall, Brayne decided to sound a retreat. The Corporation slipped out down back passages and tradesmen's exits. This was, after all, marginally more dignified than being beaten into corners. Legge was recognized and chased by an angry herd of people. He just managed to get to the local bank before injury was added to insult. Although the bank was then put under a state of siege, Legge eventually managed to get back to the Red Lion Inn. He saddled up his trusty steed and rode hell for leather out of Banbury. Instead of being chaired around the town, he was chased out of it. Most of the other worthies managed to escape unharmed. They regrouped, appropriately enough, at the Dog and Gun public house at eight o'clock in the evening. Mr Mayor decided that it was time to read the Riot Act and send for Major Stratton and the yeomanry boys. All was much quieter on the Banbury frontline by about eleven o'clock that evening.

This riot was an act, or play, which followed the conventions of carnival. Brayne later described how, on the morning of 10 March, he had

observed a chaise drawn by several men and accompanied by a large concourse of People making a great noise – huzzahing and shouting 'No Legge' 'No Legge' . . . and wearing in their hats cockades made of shavings.

This chaise then came to rest outside Brayne's house. He

saw a man dressed in a Smock Frock and wearing a cockade of shavings whose name as the examinant hath been informed is William Castle but called Mettle get into the chaise . . . .[6]

It may be that the natives were merely staging a mock election on this particular occasion to protest about the fact that the beer was off. They elected their own candidate, who happened to be the local idiot, and paraded him through the streets to parody the form of the parliamentary election. Yet a funny thing happened immediately after the idiot had started to play the conquering electoral hero. He bowed to the Mayor and the Mayor bowed back. It was then that the first volley of stones thundered against the windows. It is possible that there was a tradition of licensed political carnival associated with parliamentary elections in Banbury. The natives had been allowed to elect their carnival MP, provided that the implied spirit of misrule and mischief was light and festive. Such licensed misrule may indeed have been one of the ways by which collusion and co-operation were guaranteed. Mr Mayor may have bowed back because he thought he was just confronting such a licensed tradition of political misrule. It was only after the first salvo had been fired across his bow that he realized that the festive safety-valve had blown. He may have bowed back in the hope that his gesture would in fact license a potentially subversive situation.

The carnival MP was then dragged off towards the Town Hall. As in genuine elections, the chaise was pulled by a team of enthusiastic supporters. Brayne estimated that by this time the crowd had grown from 200 to nearly 1000 people. He and his colleagues spent about half an hour debating whether they should actually provoke a direct confrontation between rule and misrule. They had to put up with a lot of bad-natured heckling, as they attempted to reassert their control over the mean streets of Banbury. The swine were not, however, just content to grunt abuse. They were determined to get their trotters on the very symbols of insolence and office. The mace-bearer, who presumably led Brayne's ceremonial counter-offensive, managed to remain attached to his bauble, but the constables and special constables were not so lucky. Their staffs were taken from them by the natives, who then passed them back in triumph into the crowd. Although cobble stones were the main weapons in the battle of Banbury, the broken reeds and staffs of office were thrown back at the worthies as they cowered in the Town Hall. There is no humiliation quite as satisfying as ritual humiliation. The natives of Banbury had won a ceremonial battle. Carnival was King for a few hours on 10 March 1820, yet the establishment, here and throughout the country, won the ceremonial war.

The way to Oldham

William Cobbett was duly elected in 1832 to serve as a Member of Parliament for Oldham, which was a gritty, northern constituency on the road to Wigan Pier. His parliamentary career was not a successful one. He did speak quite effectively in favour of factory legislation in 1833 and fought against the Poor Law Amendment Act in 1834. His championship of these causes suggests that his particular brand of conservative-radicalism had an appeal for both north and south. The personification of rural England could represent the hopes and aspirations of his constituents in the new industrial wasteland. Cobbett was often branded as a fire-raising demagogue. His enemies presented him, particularly during the Swing riots, as a real barn-burner of a public speaker, to appropriate one of Tom Wolfe's phrases. Although some of Cobbett's rustic harangues appear to have been well received, he was still rather a wooden public speaker. Unlike Henry Hunt, he never really discovered the way to hold a large, live audience. Journalism was undoubtedly the best medium for his message. He had been a keen student of parliamentary debates for most of his adult life, but the fact that he was 69 when he finally had the chance to put theory into practice only served to underline his limitations.

Cobbett had unsuccessfully entered the parliamentary lists at Coventry in 1818, while he was still in exile in America. This was just an attempt to keep his name in the public eye. He selected Coventry because radical candidates often managed to have a good run for their money in the constituency. He returned to England towards the end of 1819 with the intention of finding himself platforms from which to recapture the heady days of his heyday. He was, however, never able to turn the clock back to the immediate post-war period, when his *Political Register* set the style and tone for the radical movement as a whole. He hoped that his comeback would be aided and abetted by Tom Paine's bones which he brought back from America with him to exhibit at radical meetings. The Government press had a lot of fun at Cobbett's expense when they learned that the bones of a deist were being treated with what appeared to be religious reverence. It was tantamount to devil worship. For Cobbett 'dem bones' had great symbolic importance. The establishment had its rites and rituals, so he tried to provide radicalism with all the trappings of a secularized religion. He literally resurrected Paine in order to foster the religion of radicalism.

The franchise at Coventry was held by the freemen of the city. You became a freeman by serving a seven-year apprenticeship in or around the city. It was estimated that there were around 3000 voters in 1820. As some of these no longer lived in Coventry, Cobbett was able to do quite a bit of canvassing and campaigning in London. He declared himself a candidate in January 1820 and in the early part of February held meetings in London for such freemen as cared to attend. He also started bombarding Coventry itself with election addresses. His message was that indirect taxation was bringing the country to its ankles. He tried to cover his election expenses by setting up a fighting fund which was monitored by *Cobbett's Evening Post*. It stood at just over £242 on 12 February. Among the subscribers listed were '18 red hot ragged radicals', who had given 5s. between them. The fund was not a success, as thousands rather than hundreds were usually needed to win an election. The travel expenses of non-resident voters was just one of many heavy items of expenditure. Cobbett managed to make the best of a bad throw. He assured his supporters that money would come pouring in, when the radicals read about the way in which he had been treated like a king and drawn in triumph through the streets of Coventry on 14 February.

His triumph did not go unchallenged. *Cobbett's Evening Post* reported on 18 February the events of the previous day in the lists at Coventry:

Jack Cherry, and other turned out cobblers, thought they would make a desperate push to expose themselves, and accordingly they got together a cart, a drum, a fife and some flags, with about twenty or thirty dirty boys, and a prize-fighting butcher at their head. This formidable host, with a standard and flags bearing portraits of the Devil, proceeded with due solemnity to the sound of the kettle-drum, to assault the electors, who were by this time assembled and listening to a speech from Mr Cobbett.

Jack Cherry and his gang had been parading round the streets since crack of dawn trying to whip up anti-Cobbett feeling. Their activities seem to be remarkably similar to those of the late medieval guilds in Coventry, who toured the streets from dawn to dusk with nativity plays such as *The Pageant of the Shearmen and the Tailors*. These plays were performed in wagons on the street corners and the arrival of the troupe was announced by the beating of a drum. Flags played an important part in the Coventry election, despite the attempts to legislate against their use. The Devil was calling for the return of Tom Paine's bones on the flag that was being used on this particular occasion by Cherry's troupe. A flag bearing the inscription 'No Cobbett No Thistlewood' made an appearance later on in the campaign. Cobbett's supporters apparently had no trouble getting rid of these unwelcome intruders on 17 February. *Cobbett's Evening Post* concluded its description of the meeting by drawing attention to the process of ritual political humiliation:

The whole apple cart was upset, and the drummers and fifers driven off; Hudibras [i.e. Cherry], in his escape was caught and brought back to receive a most sound pummelling, and his standard carried and presented to the speaker. Cobbett shook his head, and the poor relic was cracked to pieces.

Cobbett used to place these spoils of war in a prominent place on the carriage, which he used for his triumphal processions through Coventry. He left the city shortly after this meeting, but returned to begin his campaign in earnest on 28 February. He entered Coventry on the footboard of his carriage, waving his hat to all and sundry.

The election itself did not begin until 8 March. Although it is probable that the other candidates, Edward Ellice and Peter Moore, stage-managed demonstrations against Cobbett with the help of their agents, they did not in fact arrive in Coventry with their carpetbags until 6 March. Cobbett described their entry in terms of a military parade. Ellice was a stock-jobber and Moore a retired colonial civil servant, so Cobbett was meeting his traditional enemies face-to-face. They established their campaign headquarters at the Craven Arms. Cobbett topped the poll at the end of the first day and toured the city to celebrate his victory. It was, however, a short-lived one, for he was back in third place at the end of the second day. He complained throughout the rest of the campaign that his potential supporters were intimidated by bully boys hired by Moore and Ellice. Voters had to run the gauntlet on their way to the polling booths. Their coats were ripped and there was verbal as well as physical abuse. Cobbett himself had two tactics for dealing with the heavy mob. He described in his *Political Register* of 25 March 1820 how he used

to stand and look upon the yelling beasts with a most good-humoured smile; turning my head now and then, and leaning it, as it were to take different views of the same person, or same group. I now and then substituted something of *curiosity* instead of the general total *unconcern*, that was seated upon my face.

His second approach was a little more direct. He traded punches with 'the yelling beasts'. He remained in third place at the end of the third day as well. His opponents obviously felt that now was the time for him to leave Coventry with his tail between his legs. As they had bought off the supposedly independent candidate, Captain Close, by offering to pay his election expenses, they would win as soon as Cobbett gave up the unequal struggle. They knew to their cost that elections were expensive and did not want to prolong this one longer than was absolutely necessary. They probably also wanted to get back to London as soon as possible. Cobbett pointed out that under electoral law he could keep the polling booths open for a maximum of fourteen days. He tenaciously kept the booths open for a fourth day on Saturday 11 March. *The Sun* described on 12 March some of the attempts that were made to try to get him to take his bones out of Coventry:

The first indication of riot was on Friday, when a parcel of the Spur-street ruffians got drums and fifes, and began to rally about half-past three, just before the closing of the poll for the day, carrying a wooden skeleton on a pole, and several minor exhibitions of bones on three large sticks – a cow's head all bloody, with the skin on another pole &c. which they paraded round the booth with, and through the streets, several times. On Saturday they got a stone-mason's handbarrow, and laid a man upon it, covered with a great coat, face blacked to appear dead, with mock parsons before and mourners with black cloaks after, carried by four men, and a lamb hung upon a pole by the neck with the skin on, with states of the poll, and other inflammatory placards, on different poles, and being supplied with plenty of gin, they were roused up to a state of savage frenzy *more like demons than men*.

They then launched a fierce attack on Cobbett at his lodgings. He withdrew from the contest on 14 March. Although it is likely that the Spur Street boys were using animal bones, rumours did circulate about graveyards being robbed of the dead at night. These bones and the skeleton were obviously parodying Cobbett's exhibition of Paine's bones. They also conveyed an unsubtle hint that Cobbett himself would be a skeleton, if he remained in Coventry much longer. The cow's head was probably meant to resemble the head of a traitor after a masked executioner had been to work on it. The head was on one pole, while the skin, or body, was on another. There may, then, be a connection between this emblem and that of the lamb that was hung on the pole with its skin on. This may have been intended to suggest that Cobbett would be hanged, before he was decapitated. These emblems can probably in turn be related to craft and apprenticeship rituals in Coventry. The mock funeral procession is the most interesting aspect of the Spur Street version of political street theatre, for such processions were one of the ways in which the authority of the church, and often the state, was turned upside down. This flouting of ceremonial authority could be taken to subversive extremes, as indeed it was at Romans in 1580 and Banbury in 1820. Yet it was originally intended actually to strengthen such authority. As suggested, a licensed tradition of misrule at least insured against the possibility of grievances and grudges festering away for too long. Carnival gave vent to such feelings and thus tamed and controlled them. It could be, then, both an agency of social control and a vehicle for social protest. Cobbett's opponents at Coventry appear to have quite deliberately orchestrated a carnival spirit to support their political stand for greater social discipline and control.[7]

I'll be your queen

Caroline of Brunswick married George, Prince of Wales, on 8 April 1794. This marriage of convenience proved to be decidedly inconvenient. The couple positively sailed apart, even before the birth of their daughter, Princess Charlotte. George fled to the often ample bosoms of various maternal, society ladies. Caroline was not averse to saying hello to high-ranking sailors. This eccentric conduct was the subject of a supposedly delicate investigation in 1806. She was not so much promiscuous, as independent and forthright. Such conduct was regarded as unbecoming for a woman, who also happened to be a member of the Royal Family. Caroline's problem was that she did not seem to understand that English society was based on double standards. She had had more than enough of gossiping columnists and pillars of the establishment by 1814 and decided to go on her travels. She was actively encouraged to do so by certain leading Tories, who were worried by the way in which she allowed herself to become a focal point for the Opposition. Caroline based herself in Italy. She cruised around the Mediterranean and made grand tours of the mainland. She was very much Byron in minor key, with all the enthusiasms and eccentricities but none of the genius. Her constant companion on these exotic, picturesque journeys was one Bartolomo Pergami, who had originally been engaged as her butler or head of household. It soon became apparent that they were mixing business with a bit of pleasure on the side. Caroline and her handsome servant used to dress up in Greek and Turkish costumes. Like Byron, Pergami had a passion for colourful military uniforms. Mistress and servant slept together on deck while sailing for the Holy Land. It was obviously a close working relationship.

Caroline might have been allowed to keep no Italian waiter waiting, if her husband had remained Prince Regent. When his eventual succession to the throne itself seemed inevitable, however, her romps began to appear all the more scandalous. Sir John Leach was therefore appointed in 1818 to lead a team of dirty diggers to inquire into the private life of this most indelicate of princesses. The diggers were referred to as the Milan Commission. The dirt on the Princess was placed in a 'Green Bag'. If Caroline had been prepared to be reasonable and British about the state of her *affaires*, then this Green Bag might have been allowed to gather mould. Yet, after the death of George III on 20 January 1820, she began to feel the urge to come home. She had obviously had enough of playing the sultry Mediterranean madame and wanted top-billing as Queen of England. The negotiators worked out a plan to buy her off. She was offered the princessly sum of £50,000 a year; no questions would be asked about her private life, which was, after all, her own, she would just have to renounce her title and agree not to darken any royal doors in England. It was such a reasonable deal that only a silly foreigner would dream of turning it down. Caroline told the crooked dealers what they could do with their dotted line and sent them packing.

She eventually arrived in London on 6 June 1820, having been treated like a conquering electoral hero since setting foot in England. Alderman Wood offered her his protective wing, so she stayed briefly at his house in South Audley Street. Wood was shrewd enough to realize that Caroline offered him a much stronger lever against the Government than the late, lamented King Arthur Thistlewood did. Cobbett and other radicals were quick to hitch their battered wagons to the Queen's star. *The Black Dwarf* summed up very succinctly the reasons behind Caroline's immense, intense popularity: 'Shouts in favour of the Queen insult the

Monarch in his own palace.'[8] The Queen offered the radicals an opportunity to revenge the humiliations of Peterloo and Cato Street. The Government had to proceed with a certain amount of caution in the face of such slaps in the face. There had been some talk about the possibility of open debates in both Houses of Parliament on the Queen's conduct. It was even hinted that spicy beans from the Green Bag might be spilt. This was primarily a negotiating tactic to try to frighten Caroline into taking the money and running. Such open government would obviously leave the Government open to criticism. So a secret committee started to sift through the evidence on 27 June. They reported back on 4 July. It was decided that only the peers should peer into the murky depths of Caroline's private life. A Bill of Pains and Penalties was cobbled together and given a first reading in the Lords on 5 July. The second reading, which demanded the presence of the Queen and the host of witnesses against her, was eventually fixed for 17 August.

Their Lordships, spiritual and temporal, were being asked for their finite wisdoms on three related matters. First of all, they had to listen to the examination of these witnesses and decide whether Caroline had actually committed adultery with Pergami. Second, they had the task of reminding Caroline that such pleasures carried pains and penalties, which in this particular case meant divorce. Third, by voting in favour of divorce, they were effectively stripping her of all titles. The highest court in the land was given the job of legally and morally chastising the highest courtesan in the land. Caroline was the victim of a number of double standards. Although her husband complained that she was butch and masculine, the dirty diggers came up with a bagful of evidence to the contrary. Her conduct, which would have been regarded as racily rakish for a Regency buck, was put on trial because even hints of female sexuality would really have ruined those roués. She might have got away with it, if she had gracefully and discreetly granted favours to odd members of the English aristocracy. Her preference for foreign servants, however, undermined civilized values. One's wife and servants would be simply impossible to control, if the Queen of England's social intercourse was so vulgarly familiar. The stately homes of England would be turned upside down, if downstairs was always upstairs in my lady's chamber. An acquittal of Queen Caroline would represent a butler's charter. It was perfectly reasonable for Byron to pass wet days at Newstead chasing and embracing the servant girls – that was what servants and wet days were for. If there was no sport to be had outside, then it was only natural that young masters should keep themselves in trim with touches of horseplay. Caroline's conduct was both unreasonable and unnatural. It was whoreplay. She really ought to have thought a little bit more about England when she lay back, if lay back she did, under those dangerously decadent Mediterranean skies.

While the stage-managers ducked and weaved about preparing their case, Caroline's supporters transformed her into a carnival, or people's queen. She was used quite deliberately to flaunt and flout the ceremonial dignity and authority of the state. The cross citizens of Banbury elected the local idiot as their Member of Parliament. Londoners could easily have crowned some Eastcheap hostess as their carnival queen. Mistress Quickly briefly assumes the role of Queen to Falstaff's King when the Boar's Head mocks the court in *Henry IV, Part I*. Yet Caroline herself was both willing and able to play the part. Carnival is based on an inverting parody, which may become subverting in the hands of the opposition. Its levels and meanings become even more complex when the real Queen and the carnival queen are one and the same person. Poor Caroline took the volume of support for her as an indication of her personal popularity as Queen of England, while it was given to her in her role as people's queen. When the carnival was over, she too was forsaken 'like a memory lost'. Idiots and Members of Parliament have much in common, just as East End molls and real Queens do. It would still be fair to say that Banbury staged a broad burlesque of the theatre of electoral politics. The Londoner usually likes to prove that he has more sophisticated theatrical tastes than the country cousins from the sticks. Carnival metropolitan-style took the form of allowing, and indeed actively encouraging, Caroline to be more regal than the rest of the Royal Family put together. She had a state carriage built for her as quickly as possible. *The Observer* felt it unfair to spare any details on 20 August 1820. This carriage was apparently

finished in a style of great splendour. It is, properly speaking, a landau, and may be used either closed or open, with equal convenience. The colour of the body is maroon, or deep claret, a colour which was chosen by the Queen as being similar to that of the private carriages of his late Majesty. The pannels of the doors, and those before & behind, are richly emblazoned with the armorial bearings of her Majesty, executed in a style of singular excellence . . . the tout ensemble has certainly a very beautiful appearance.

It was meant to have, since it was a crucial stage prop in this sophisticated parody of court ceremony. Caroline and her supporters wanted the royal ensemble to be complete and so postilions were stuck into yards of livery, which, like the carriage itself, had been run up at lightning speed.

The Queen was now in a fit and proper state to meet the double standard bearers in the House of Lords. She had taken up residence at Brandenburg House in Hammersmith for the weeks before the trial. It was here that she held court and received the numerous petitions and addresses of support. She made St James's Square her campaign headquarters during the trial itself. She took a house next door to Castlereagh, who was not amused as he had to put the shutters up to prevent her supporters from doing too much damage. She left St James's on 17 August in style. *The Observer* estimated, perhaps a little rashly, that there were 10,000 people in the Square alone to cheer their carnival queen. She certainly played the part well. *The Observer*, in the same front page spread, described how she

> bowed and smiled with great condescension to all who pressed towards her carriage with a view to have a nearer look at her countenance, and seemed to maintain her confidence throughout the extraordinary scene.

The progress or procession found itself slowed down to a very dignified pace indeed by the huge crowds outside the House of Lords. The radicals were in festive mood, again according to *The Observer:*

> Waddington, and one or two other persons whose names have become familiar of late in crowds in the metropolis, had procured a pole on which they fastened a large green bag, that had suspended from it a caricature drawing, which was intended to illustrate some of the measures adopted against her Majesty. The exhibition of this bag caused a great deal of laughter: it was carried both in the crowd and among the soldiers without any interruption being offered to the bearer.

Waddington was the master of radical ceremonies. He used to tour the streets blowing a horn to announce meetings. He also kept and manufactured flags for Thistlewood and others.[9] The procession itself had all the reverence and solemnity of state pageantry, yet this 'caricature drawing' was a reminder that parody was the order of the play. Sophisticated and broad parody existed side by side on this occasion.

It would be very dangerous to assume that such demonstrations of support for Caroline were entirely spontaneous. Even before she had arrived in England, preparations were well under way to make carnival a vehicle of social protest. An espial reported that

some are preparing flags, engaging musicians &c And that even Horn boys are in a state of requisition . . . .[10]

Another report described how Major Cartwright and the leading radicals had

sent to the North instructions to get flags and standards made & they have dictated various mottoes, but particularly the following –

'THE QUEENS RIGHTS, THE PEOPLES LIBERTYS'

It is also intended to wear buttons with the *cap of liberty* on them . . . .[11]

The radicals were well prepared for 17 August.

Government stage-managers had also been busy. They tried to make the House of Lords a theatrical set fit for the trial of a queen. New galleries were erected to accommodate the broad bottoms of the backwoodsmen, who were under strict instructions to attend the proceedings. Only the Roman Catholic peers, undesirables like Lord Byron and those with genuine domestic excuses were listed as being able to give the trial a miss. The stage was dominated by the throne. *The Observer* played Enobarbus on 17 September, when it described how this throne

was erected at the commencement of the reign of the present King. It far surpasses, in point of splendour, that of his late Majesty. The pillars which support the canopy are fluted & richly gilt. The crown & cornices of the canopy are likewise brilliant with burnished gold. The hangings are of crimson velvet, looped up with golden ropes, & trimmed with costly gold lace. In the back are the royal arms, embroidered on crimson velvet, and above them the letters GIIII.

The King himself maintained the lowest of profiles during the trial itself, which was no mean achievement for somebody of his bulk. The majesty of majesty was, however, conspicuously on display. Even the flunkies who manned the entrances and exits were dripping with royal insignia. Scarlet was the colour of both kings and whores.

The case against Caroline, which was conducted at the bar of the House opposite the throne, was a particularly tricky one actually to prove. The state became very interested in the state of her bed. If the linen was dirty, then, well it was as good as catching her in the act. Her reputation would be stained, if the sheets were. A succession of chambermaids, tavern door-keepers, cooks and lackeys were asked for their considered opinions on such delicate matters. These witnesses, the scum of Europe, were, according to Cobbett, brought into the House of Lords by an underground passage to prevent them from being lynched. If Caroline's bed, and not Pergami's, had been tumbled in, to appropriate one of the many euphemisms from the trial itself, then all loyal men and true must nudgingly infer that she was indeed a scarlet harlot. If she was actually seen through a keyhole fumbling with Pergami, then her little game was up and no mistake. The defence, which was spearheaded by Henry Brougham and Thomas Denman, was not convinced by arguments based on such clouds of knowing innuendo. It wondered whether those who had paid the witnesses' expenses were calling forth these salacious tunes. It was surprised by the way in which those who accused Caroline of tumbling and fumbling groped in the dark themselves under cross-examination. These witnesses appeared only to remember what they wanted to, or what they had been told to.

The trial itself showed all the signs of becoming the longest running farce in the West End. It was adjourned on 9 September after twenty-one full days to give the defence more time to prepare its case. That was the official reason, although all the actors probably needed a breather by this stage. Brougham certainly returned to the fray with great vigour on 3 October when he delivered a long set-piece oration on the Queen's conduct. Denman explained why the Green Bag gave off such a powerful stench. The Milan Commission had 'ransacked filthy clothes-bags . . . raked into every sewer, pried into every water-closet'[12] to get their evidence. Such fighting talk was not enough, however, to save Caroline. When the vote was taken on 6 November, the prosecution had a majority of twenty-eight on the Second Reading of the Bill of Pains and Penalties. It also secured a majority of sixty-seven for the controversial divorce clause. The discrepancy between the figures is explained by the fact that the Lords spiritual were unwilling to put asunder what the good Lord had joined together. Caroline's supporters claimed that such relatively slender margins represented a moral victory for her moral conduct. This interpretation proved to be correct. The Bill only scraped through the Third Reading by a mere nine votes. The Government, particularly Prime Minister

Liverpool who had played an active part in the proceedings in the Lords, was obviously disappointed that it could not thump the Queen with thumping majorities. The Bill was officially put in mothballs on 10 November. Cobbett described in his *History of the Regency and Reign of King George the Fourth* (1830) how bells were rung, cannons fired and candles lit throughout the night to celebrate the victory of the carnival queen. Caroline decided to celebrate by going in state to St Paul's Cathedral on 29 November. The church militant had tried to exclude her name from its liturgies and rituals, but it could not now exclude her from its buildings. George IV continued to skulk and sulk at Windsor and only began to re-emerge into society at the beginning of 1821. Caroline's triumph, like her carnival crown, was ultimately a hollow one. When her husband's coronation finally took place on 19 July 1821, she was turned away by a prize fighter who had been hired for the day as a bouncer. Most accounts assume the boxer to have been genuine, although he may just have been a particularly muscular christian. Caroline's vocal supporters had melted away by this time. She had, after all, served her theatrical turn. She died on 7 August 1821 and, at her request, was buried in Brunswick. The double standards she flouted are, of course, still alive and kicking.

Queen Caroline was the talk of both town and country for six months in 1820. Although interest and support obviously ebbed and flowed during such a long time, it is remarkable that the carnival spirit was maintained and sustained throughout this period. Caroline was carnival queen for months rather than days. As suggested, the carnival took at least two distinct forms. First, Alderman Wood and others staged a sophisticated parody of court ceremonials. They deferred to Caroline's dignity rather than her husband's. Second, radicals such as Waddington and Hone supported her in a more irreverend way. They tried to subvert all forms of state pageantry through a more direct kind of mockery and inversion. The country cousins were also determined to get in on the act. George Wells reported that the West Country was flooded with hawkers selling pamphlets which supported the Queen.[13] Once again, such pamphlets are no substitute for examples of carnival in performance. Caroline's supporters in Cheltenham broke into the churches and rang the bells to celebrate her victory. They also pasted up placards and caricatures.[14] Caroline had been put on trial to try to preserve the rites and rituals of the Church of England from universal derision, but the carnival spirit which was unleashed by this

9 Shelley's theatre of politics

Rogues' gallery

Although Shelley liked to embrace a brace of sisters, he could be more than a touch puritanical. He cast disapproving glances in the direction of those who did not share his particular perversion. He was, for instance, genuinely shocked by Byron's coarse assaults on the Venetian population. He felt that this sexual merchant of Venice hazarded too much in the pursuit of adventure. He also found Queen Caroline's conduct distastefully unbecoming. He described her, mixing his puritanism with an equally unendearing snobbery, as a 'vulgar cook-maid'.[1] Such a remark would not have been out of place at Field Place, the family abode. He suggested that England should not allow itself to be used as a theatre for such a common little Punch and Judy show as the squabble between Caroline and her husband. He piously informed Peacock that Caroline was 'rather indecorous', 'vulgar' and 'low'.[2] She was still, unfortunately, the best weapon available against the establishment. Shelley was therefore forced to swallow some of his puritanical scruples. He implored a God he did not believe in to save a Queen he despised in 'A New National Anthem'. He also knocked off a drama, *Oedipus Tyrannus or Swellfoot the Tyrant,* in which Caroline was cast as the heroine. Shelley began work on this satire on 24 August 1820. It may have taken him only six days to write. The vigilantes were even quicker in their responses when the drama was eventually published in December 1820. They burnt the whole edition, apart from the seven copies which had been sold before they had had time to stoke up their fires.[3]

It is therefore impossible to tell whether Shelley had succeeded in adapting his philosophical views on politics to a more popular idiom. The title itself suggests a tension between classical erudition and popular satire, which runs throughout the play. The vigilantes may, however, have been right to take no chances, for Shelley's appropriation and exploitation of ideographic satire amply made up for some rather ponderous classical allegory. Shelley had contributed £5 in 1818 towards a fund to help William Hone fight the good fight against the judicial system. Some critics have speculated about whether he was specifically drawing on Hone's drawings when he came to write *Swellfoot*.[4] This interpretation has some plausibility, as Shelley is certainly very close indeed to both the style and idiom of Hone's satire when he deals with the infamous Green Bag. There are, however, two problems with it. First of all, Shelley was in Italy during the trial of Queen Caroline and there is no record of any caricatures being sent over there to him. Second, *Swellfoot* was actually completed before many of these caricatures were. He also appears to be drawing on an older tradition of caricature in the imagery of the play. Edmund Burke's unfortunate reference, in the House of Commons as well as in his *Reflections*, to the activities of 'a swinish multitude' (p. 117) provided both opposition and establishment caricaturists with a rich seam of imagery. James Gillray caricatured those who supported the people as little better than a swinish multitude themselves. Charles James Fox and the other leading Whig politicians are represented as swine in 'Pigs Meat, or – the Swine Flogg'd out of the Farm Yard' (1798). The theme recurs in later caricatures such as 'More Pigs Than Teats or the New Litter of Hungry Grunters Sucking John Bull's Old Sow to Death' (1806) and 'The Pigs Possessed – or the Broad Bottom'd Litter Running Headlong into the Sea of Perdition' (1807). Shelley may have been influenced in general terms by Hone, but *Swellfoot* appears to borrow much more specifically from Gillray. Shelley did not, of course, share Gillray's rather ambivalent anti-Jacobinism. My speculation runs along the lines of Shelley's appropriation and inversion of Gillray's anti-Jacobin imagery. The image of a swinish multitude never ousted John Bull from his position in the centre of the caricaturist's stage. Shelley produces his own variations on John Bull as well as the swinish multitude in *Swellfoot*. Although the play does contain a number of topical references, it is also firmly located in the caricatures of the late eighteenth and early nineteenth centuries.

Mammon explains that the contents of the Green Bag will transform everybody into 'a ghastly caricature/Of what was human' (I.I.372–3).[5] The message of the play as a whole is that those who handle this kind of poison every day of their political lives are themselves ghastly caricatures. Shelley's favourite method of making this criticism of vile politicians was to suggest that, although they wore human masks, they were ghastly and inhuman underneath. *Swellfoot* is not, however, a critique of masked men in the same tradition as 'The Mask of Anarchy', since inhumanity is presented as being clearly visible. Shelley starts off by offering us caricature impressions rather than by pointing to the human face of inhumanity. The play opens with Swellfoot, or George IV, entering the Temple of Famine. He surveys his 'kingly paunch' (I.I.3) and admires its expensive, expansive qualities. George's figure, or rather lack of it, had been the butt of the satirists for a number of years. Gillray had mocked his tasteless tastes in 'A Voluptuary Under the Horrors of Digestion' (1792). Swellfoot ironically chats away to Famine in terms of easy familiarity:

Thou to whom Kings and laurelled Emperors,
Radical-butchers, Paper-money-millers,
Bishops and Deacons, and the entire army
Of those fat martyrs to the persecution
Of stifling turtle-soup, and brandy-devils,
Offer their secret vows! (I.I.11–16)

The 'radical-butchers' are the yeomanry troops at Peterloo, although Shelley is obviously playing with definitions of a radical butcher here. James Ings was a radical butcher as far as the Government press was concerned. Swellfoot is disturbed by a multitude of very thin swine, who are shadows of their former selves:

If 'twere your kingly will
Us wretched Swine to kill,
    What should we yield to thee? (I.I. 33–5)

Swellfoot jestingly replies 'Why, skin and bones, and some few hairs for mortar' (36). This confirms earlier suggestions that the plight of the swine is similar to that of the Jews in Egypt. Swellfoot, like Pharaoh, has captured and enslaved his workforce. George's extravagant tastes in Oriental architecture meant that comparisons with Oriental despots came easily enough to the satirists. Shelley was drawing more specifically on the radical tradition in this comparison of England with Egypt. Major Cartwright and others hammered away at the fact that the people of England were fair-haired and fair minded Anglo-Saxons, who were forced to put up with the yoke of a Norman tyranny. The Egyptian yoke did not achieve the same popularity as the Norman yoke in radical circles, although it was a particular favourite among the Spenceans. The swine start off by being ever so humble but they are still concerned to remind Swellfoot that a bit of paternal concern would not go amiss:

Now if your Majesty would have our bristles
  To bind your mortar with, or fill our colons
With rich blood, or make brawn out of our gristles,
  In policy – ask else your royal Solons –
You ought to give us hog-wash and clean straw,
And sties well thatched; besides it is the law! (I.I.61–6)

Swellfoot immediately gets a pungent whiff of 'sedition, and rank blasphemy' (67) and instructs the gelders to sharpen their knives. These gelders are all Jews: 'Solomon the court porkman,/Moses the sow-gelder, and Zephaniah/The hog-butcher' (69–71). According to Shelley's version of the Egyptian yoke, Moses was a problem not a solution. He had presented the great commander as being in league with a vengeful God in *Queen Mab* (1813). Here Moses is clearly identified as belonging to the tribe of Parson Malthus, whom Shelley had castigated earlier on in the summer of 1820 in his 'A Philosophical View of Reform'. The attack on Malthus as the 'arch-priest of Famine' (77) has some similarities with Cobbett's harangues against the reverend gentleman. Shelley found himself becoming increasingly attracted towards Cobbett's brand of populist politics, almost against his better judgement, or at least against the Whiggish judgements of Field Place. The fact that Malthusians are presented as Jews may also owe something to Cobbett.

The swine exit pursued by a gelding knife and Mammon and Purganax enter to discuss the state of the state. Purganax is obviously Castlereagh, although there is some doubt about Mammon. He may be either Parson Malthus or Lord Liverpool; he could be both. Purganax is the kind of politician who does not sleep at night. He is a natural pessimist. Mammon, by contrast, exudes the kind of confidence which comes naturally to those drunk with both political power and alcohol. If the economy is in a bad way, then the simple solution is to print your way out of trouble, or 'coin paper' (104). Shelley supported Cobbett in his attacks on the real tigers who used and abused paper money. One of Gillray's most famous caricatures depicted 'Midas Transmuting all into Gold Paper'

(1797). Midas was William Pitt, just as Shelley's Mammon was probably Lord Liverpool. Shelley, Gillray and Cobbett were all in favour of the golden age of gold. Radicals and conservatives could form a united front against attempts to paper over economic cracks. It is Mammon who weaves together the two hardy perennials of the caricaturist, the swinish multitude and John Bull:

And these dull Swine of Thebes boast their descent
From the free Minotaur. You know they still
Call themselves Bulls, though thus degenerate,
And everything relating to a Bull
Is popular and respectable in Thebes. (139–43)

Swinish pastoralism took the form of nostalgia for the good old days when they were freeborn and ranging bulls. Purganax then explains how the Milan Commission will prevent the swine from forming an alliance with Iona Taurina, or Queen Caroline, and thus from being able to reassert their rights. Shelley's depiction of the Leech, or Sir John Leach, and his henchmen, the Gadfly and the Rat, is remarkably similar to their presentation by William Hone and other satirists. Such similarities may have been the result of the fact that both Shelley and the ideographic satirists were operating from within the same alternative grammar of politics. *Swellfoot* and *The Queen's Matrimonial Ladder* (1820) overlap with each other because they both present politics as a ghastly farce. Shelley's presentation of Sir John Leach also needs to be related to one of the more grotesque images in his grotesque 'Sonnet: England in 1819':

An old, mad, blind, despised, and dying king, –
Princes, the dregs of their dull race, who flow
Through public scorn, – mud from a muddy spring, –
Rulers who neither see, nor feel, nor know,
But leech-like to their fainting country cling,
Till they drop, blind in blood, without a blow, –

The Leech in *Swellfoot* is also a sucker who refuses to give the country an even break.

Various plots are thickened to try to prevent the swine from running amok. There is talk of packing a jury against the Queen with loyal pigs and true. Something has to be done pretty quickly since, as Laoctonos, or Wellington, points out, there is a danger of the swine forming an alliance with the military:

What is still worse, some Sows upon the ground
Have given the ape-guards apples, nuts, and gin,
And they all whisk their tails aloft, and cry,
'Long live Iona! down with Swellfoot!' (320–3)

Shelley is returning once again to the themes which preoccupied him in 'A Philosophical View of Reform'. Mammon comes to the rescue with his 'Divide and rule' (344) brand of politics. He masterminds the scheme whereby Purganax persuades the 'Gentlemen and Boars' (II.I.1.) in Parliament to accept a trial by ordeal. Iona must be made to agree to have the contents of the Green Bag sprinkled over her. If she is as innocent as the lean boar faction, or Whigs, pretend, then she will be transformed into an angel. It is a pity the vigilantes burnt *Swellfoot*, since Purganax's speech might have provided Castlereagh with some helpful hints on how to manage a disgruntled audience. The Queen agrees to this medieval form of justice and the stage is set for its execution in the Temple of Famine. Swellfoot and his sidekicks assemble for the feast of Famine. Shelley may have had some specific examples of the Prince Regent's conspicuous consumption in mind, such as the fête at Carlton House on 21 July 1814 to celebrate victory over Napoleon. This kind of juxtaposing of famine with feasting was a familiar theme in the caricatures of the period. The feasters are often presented as gorging themselves on the starving people. Shelley develops this theme at the end of Part Six of 'Peter Bell the Third' and hints at it in *Swellfoot* when Laoctonos claims that claret reminds him of blood. While the Queen is preparing for her ordeal, Liberty appears to deliver the gospel according to Shelley about the true relationship between famine, or necessity, and freedom:

FREEDOM calls *Famine* – her eternal foe,
To brief alliance, hollow truce. – Rise now! (II.II.101–2)

The stage directions indicate how old corruption corrupts itself:

PURGANAX, after unsealing the GREEN BAG, is gravely about to pour the liquor upon her head, when suddenly the whole expression of her figure and countenance changes; she snatches it from his hand with a loud laugh of triumph, and empties it over SWELLFOOT and the whole Court, who are instantly changed into a number of filthy and ugly animals, and rush out of the Temple. The image of FAMINE then arises with a tremendous sound, the PIGS begin scrambling for the loaves, and are tripped up by the skulls; all those who EAT the loaves are turned into BULLS, and arrange themselves quietly behind the altar. The image of FAMINE sinks through the chasm in the earth, and a MINOTAUR rises.

Shelley was not usually able to bury his misgivings about the influence of famine on the revolutionary course quite as easily as this. The Minotaur is none other than John Bull. The Queen, wearing 'boots and spurs, and a hunting-cap, buckishly cocked on one side', leaps on his back and sets off in pursuit of the ugly animals. She is the kind of Joan Hunter-Dunne, whom every subaltern falls in love with. Shelley's earlier misgivings about Caroline's character seem to lie behind his presentation of her as a rather butch Goddess, who will use her spurs on poor old John Bull. Shelley buffs, like the literary widow herself, tend to be too protective towards the great man. They would be happier if Shelley had not written *Swellfoot*. It is true that he had misgivings about the status and importance of popular political satire. This may have been why he relied so heavily on the existing tradition of ideographic satire. He was perfectly prepared, however, for the play to be published. Its visual qualities might have guaranteed it a certain popularity, if the vigilantes had not moved in and burnt the rogues' gallery.

Masked men

It is sometimes assumed that Shelley took both the title and theme of 'The Mask of Anarchy' from a report on the Peterloo Massacre, which appeared in *The Examiner* on 22 August 1819. Peacock posted this off to him in Italy and it arrived on 5 September. He probably began work on what Richard Holmes has rightly described as 'the greatest poem of political protest ever written in English'[6] round about 9 September. The report asked

with what feelings can these men in the Brazen Masks of power dare to speak lamentingly of the wounds or even the death received by a constable or a soldier or any other person concerned against an assemblage of Englishmen initiated by every species of wrong and insult, public and private?

The novelty of the idea of the 'Brazen Masks of power' can hardly be said to have struck Shelley with the full force of a cavalry sabre. His interest in Platonism meant that he had been exploring relationships between shadow and substance, veil and reality, mask and man, a long time before the radicals were butchered at Peterloo. He had, for instance, drawn attention to the acceptable face of unacceptable power in *Queen Mab*, an early poem of uncontrolled political fury. When a King hears

The tale of horror, to some ready-made face
Of hypocritical assent he turns,
Smothering the glow of shame, that, in spite of him,
Flushes his bloated cheek. (III, 41–4)

The compendious notes to the poem also contain a clear reference to politics as masquerade, or theatre. The soldier, for both Shelley and William Godwin,

is like the puppet of a showman, who, at the very time he is made to strut and swell and display the most farcical airs, we perfectly know cannot assume the most insignificant gesture, advance either to the right or the left, but as he is moved by his exhibitor. (p. 802)

Shelley also refers to the theatre of politics at the beginning of *A Proposal for Putting Reform to the Vote* (1817):

An hospital for lunatics is the only theatre where we can conceive so mournful a comedy to be exhibited as this mighty nation now exhibits: a single person bullying and swindling a thousand of his comrades out of all they possessed in the world, and then trampling and spitting upon them, though he were the most contemptible and degraded of mankind, and they had strength in their arms and courage in their hearts.[7]

The fact that he used Tom Paine's imagery of the 'plumage' and 'the dying bird' in the subtitle to *An Address to the People on the Death of the Princess Charlotte* (1817) indicates his awareness that the pageantry of society disguised, masked or veiled a multitude of sins. *The Cenci*, which was written during the early part of the summer of 1819, returns to the subject of the theatrical masks, or 'ready-made faces', which are worn by the actors on the political stage. The vacillating Orsino reaches for masks to cover up his own inadequacies. He can, however, never disguise himself from himself. Beatrice refers to a life blighted by 'the breath/Of accusation' (IV.IV.142–3) as merely a mask. She also feels that, given the corrupt nature of Italian society, 'white innocence' is pressurized into wearing 'the mask of guilt' (V.III.24–5). The first three acts of 'Prometheus Unbound', which were also written before the Peterloo massacre, contain Shelley's most sophisticated treatment of the 'Brazen Masks of power'. Act III ends with the Spirit of the Hour reflecting on the overthrow of Jupiter's tyranny:

The painted veil, by those who were, called life,
Which mimicked, as with colours idly spread,
All men believed or hoped, is torn aside;
The loathsome mask has fallen, the man remains
Sceptreless, free, uncircumscribed, but man
Equal, unclassed, tribeless, and nationless,
Exempt from awe, worship, degree, the king
Over himself; just, gentle, wise: but man
Passionless? – no, yet free from guilt or pain,
Which were, for his will made or suffered them,
Nor yet exempt, though ruling them like slaves,
From chance, and death, and mutability,
The clogs of that which else might oversoar
The loftiest star of unascended heaven,
Pinnacled dim in the intense inane. (III, IV, 190–204)

Tyranny is a 'loathsome mask', but it is a self-imposed one. The slave is master of the slave. Jupiter's power is given to him by those who do not see that they are in fact kings over themselves. If we give the Jupiters, the Castlereaghs and others their masks of power, then we can take them away. According to the theatre of the mind interpretation of 'Prometheus', these tyrants are figments of a warped imagination. They are a part of us which can and must be destroyed.

Shelley did not need a report in *The Examiner* to alert him to the existence of a complex theatre of politics. He might actually have been more interested in descriptions of the meeting as carnival, or gala, than in a rather clichéd reference to the 'Brazen Masks of power'. The radicals were butchered to stop them having a holiday, or political carnival. He had juxtaposed festivity and butchery in 'Lines Written During the Castlereagh Administration'. The political gravedigger is asked to listen to the 'festival din':

Hearest thou the festival din
Of Death, and Destruction, and Sin,
And Wealth crying *Havoc*! within?
'Tis the bacchanal triumph that makes Truth dumb,
Thine Epithalamium. (Stanza IV)

The theme is developed in more detail in 'The Mask of Anarchy'.

The masquerade is 'ghastly' and the dance is the dance of death.

The poem opens with Shelley apparently commenting on his own political inactivity and inertia:

As I lay asleep in Italy
There came a voice from over the Sea,
And with great power it forth led me
To walk in the visions of Poesy. (I)

1818 had been a year of domestic crises and upheavals. Shelley had, nevertheless, written 'Julian and Maddalo', the account of his relationship with Byron, as well as working on his translations of Plato. He had also begun 'Prometheus Unbound'. It may be that he felt that, although his intellectual commitment to political issues was strong, he had allowed the more active and practical side of his political nature to lie dormant for too long. He had, after all, attempted to play an active part in Irish politics in 1812, when he delivered a political speech in a Dublin theatre. He was involved in a number of attempts to create a political heaven on earth after his return from Ireland, most notably at Tan-yr-allt. He continued to write political pamphlets on the immediate issues of the day after the failure of his various communitarian schemes. The news of the Peterloo massacre reawakened his desire for a greater degree of political involvement. Yet Shelley had also reached the conclusion by 1819, if not before, that the poet could only fulfil his role as 'unacknowledged legislator', [8] as he put it in 'A Philosophical View of Reform', by retaining a certain detachment from the political arena. His task was to visualize and prophesy changes beyond the immediate change. The poet's dream was more important than the politician's programme. The first stanza of 'The Mask of Anarchy' raises, through its rather awkward tone, this contradiction between the dormant activist and the prophesying poet.

The poet's vision takes the form of a nightmarish dance of death, or less specifically, a *danse macabre*:

I met Murder on the way –
He had a mask like Castlereagh –
Very smooth he looked, yet grim;
Seven blood-hounds followed him:

All were fat; and well they might
Be in admirable plight,
For one by one, and two by two,

He tossed them human hearts to chew
Which from his wide cloak he drew. (II–III)

Murder and Castlereagh both wear masks to disguise their real intentions. There is more than a hint that these masks are one and the same. The 'Seven blood-hounds' represent the European nations who belonged to the Holy Alliance. If the disguises are stripped off, the Holy Alliance becomes an unholy, or hellish, one. The bloodhounds are in reality dogs of war, or hounds of hell, who spread havoc rather than peace. They are remarkably similar to the Furies in 'Prometheus Unbound':

We are the ministers of pain, and fear,
And disappointment, and mistrust, and hate,
And clinging crime; and as lean dogs pursue
Through wood and lake some struck and sobbing fawn,
We track all things that weep, and bleed, and live,
When the great King betrays them to our will. (I, 452–7)

Castlereagh, like the villain in a melodrama, opens 'his wide cloak' to feed these hounds of hell. The imagery of the dance of death suggests that Castlereagh may reveal that he is just a skeleton when he draws the 'human hearts' out of this cloak. Fraud is the next figure to dance by in Shelley's nightmarish vision. He bears more than a passing resemblance to Vice-Chancellor Eldon. Shelley's description of his particular *bête noir* is similar to Hone's representations of Bags in *The Political Showman – at Home!* (1821). Indeed, there are a number of interesting comparisons between Shelley's imagery at the beginning of 'The Mask of Anarchy' and Hone's cabinet of political curiosities. There is, for example, a bloodhound which destroys liberty:

When it scents a human victim it follows his track with cruel perseverance, flies upon him with dreadful ferocity, and, unless dragged off, tears and rends the form until every noble feature of humanity is destroyed. It has an exquisite smell for blood.[9]

Shelley and Hone appear to be drawing their imagery from common radical sources. Hypocrisy follows hard on the heels of Fraud:

Clothed with the Bible, as with light,
And the shadows of the night,
Like Sidmouth, next, Hypocrisy
On a crocodile rode by. (VI)

Bible black is the true colour of the thought police. It would be possible to relate Shelley's *danse macabre* to other early nineteenth-century variations on the theme, such as Thomas Rowlandson's illustrations to *The English Dance of Death* (1816). It may still be important to try to visualize the poem in terms of medieval iconography, for Shelley's political nightmares, both here and elsewhere, often shaded over into medieval gothic. When viewed in this context, Castlereagh, Eldon and Sidmouth wear the masks of modern politicians, whereas in reality they still belong to a medieval world of superstition and tyranny.

Murder, Fraud and Hypocrisy are not the only figures in the dance, but just the ones who stand out most clearly in the nightmare:

And many more Destructions played
In this ghastly masquerade,
All disguised, even to the eyes,
Like Bishops, lawyers, peers, or spies. (VII)

Shelley's long-standing anti-clericalism ensured that the 'Bishops', or rather the forces of anarchy passing themselves off as saintly old men, played a part in the 'ghastly masquerade'. The 'lawyers' and 'peers' are included because the Old Bailey and the House of Lords were such obvious stages for the theatre of politics. Early nineteenth-century masqueraders were, incidentally, quite fond of passing themselves off as lawyers. Mary Shelley felt that a lawyer was the best performer at the carnival in Pisa in 1822. Although Shelley had been toying with 'Charles the First' since 1818, he did not begin working on it seriously until the beginning of 1822. There may, then, be a connection between Mary's thoughts on the carnival and Shelley's presentation of the masque at the Inns of Court. The Third Citizen comments sourly

When lawyers masque 'tis time for honest men
To strip the vizor from their purposes.
A seasonable time for masquers this! (I.I. 76–8)

Shelley provides some of the reasons why the lawyers are included in the 'ghastly masquerade' in the first scene of this unfinished play. As there is still a tendency for him to be presented as an ineffectual, but angelic, intellectual, it is important to notice that the lawful espials are probably included for a specific reason. Shelley's *An Address to the People on the Death of the Princess Charlotte* (1817) is a savage indictment of Oliver's orchestration of the Pentridge rising. His bitterness may have been partially conditioned by the fact that Lord Sidmouth's agents had their beady eyes on him for some time after his return from Ireland, particularly when he was at Lynmouth. Spies do not waste their time watching lyric poets.

Anarchy is the last but by no means the least Destruction to appear. He is the lord of the dance of death:

Last came Anarchy: he rode
On a white horse, splashed with blood;
He was pale even to the lips,
Like Death in the Apocalypse.

And he wore a kingly crown;
And in his grasp a sceptre shone;
On his brow this mark I saw –
'I AM GOD, AND KING, AND LAW!'

With a pace stately and fast,
Over English land he passed,
Trampling to a mire of blood
The adoring multitude. (VIII–X)

Revelations describes Death's horse as being pale. The white horse is in fact ridden by the Conqueror, while the red horse is mounted by the Destroyer of Peace. Shelley's reworking of the Apocalypse poses two interesting questions. First of all, why is Anarchy only 'Like Death in the Apocalypse'? Why, in other words, isn't the poem entitled 'The Mask of Death'? One possible answer is that Shelley wanted to present the political system itself as being essentially anarchic. The 'Destructions' themselves appear to be controlled, like puppets on a string. They are performing a dance of death, but it is one that appears to be out of their control. Who is pulling the strings? Who can possibly control Anarchy? Shelley appears to be pointing towards some sort of anarchic void at the very centre of political life when he poses these questions. Murder wears a mask, but Murder itself may well be just another mask. If everyone and everything is thoroughly unmasked, then there might be nothing at the end of the process. Shelley seems to be dropping hints in this direction in 'Prometheus Unbound' as well. In Act One the Fifth Spirit comments on the encroachment of the counter-revolution. He is no longer able to see Love, as 'hollow Ruin' (768) now yawns behind it. 'Ruin', like the 'Destructions' in 'The Mask of Anarchy', may be a hollow, yawning void. The Spirit of the Earth describes to Asia his impressions of the world before the overthrow of tyranny towards the end of Act Three.

. . . among the haunts of humankind,
Hard-featured men, or with proud, angry looks,
Or cold, staid gait, or false and hollow smiles,
Or the dull sneer of self-loved ignorance,
Or other such foul masks, with which ill thoughts
Hide that fair being whom we spirits call man; (III.IV 40–5)

The old order is hollow to the very core. The figure of Anarchy itself is a mask which covers up the hollow void, or black hole, at the centre of political life.

The second question posed by Shelley's reworking of the original account of the Apocalypse points in the direction of a more straightforward reading of the poem. If Anarchy is 'Like Death', why does he ride a white horse splashed with red, rather than the traditional pale steed? The Hanoverians imported white horses from the fatherland for ceremonial occasions. Shelley obviously wanted to equate the figure of Anarchy with that of the Prince Regent, who, as Thistlewood pointed out at his trial, had actually added insult to injury by thanking the yeomanry for butchering the radicals at Peterloo. Such an equation is rich in satirical irony. The Regent was so gross that he had to be winched into the saddle like a medieval knight. Anarchy, true to the imagery of the dance of death, was a skeleton.[10] The crusaders for law and order might appear to have as little to do with anarchy as an incredible bulk has to do with a skeleton. Yet the establishment perpetrates political and social anarchy. Appearances are meant to be deceptive. The Prince Regent provides a corpulent mask for Anarchy. Monarchy is Anarchy. Gillray mounted William Pitt on the horse of Death in his 'Presages of the Millenium' (1795), a caricature which alluded to the popularity of chiliastic sects in that year. The horse, which resembles those used on ceremonial occasions, carries the embroidered saddle cloth of the Hanoverians. Although Gillray's anti-Jacobinism is certainly compromised by this portrayal of Pitt as Death in the Apocalypse, it is perhaps more significant that he is riding over a swinish multitude of Foxite Whigs. Some of them are being kicked back into Hell by the horse's hooves. After the death of Anarchy, Shelley describes how 'The Horse of Death' trampled over his own followers:

And Anarchy, the ghastly birth,
Lay dead earth upon the earth;
The Horse of Death tameless as wind
Fled, and with his hoofs did grind
To dust the murderers thronged behind. (XXXIII)

Both Gillray and Shelley opt for a white horse rather than a pale one. They both depict it destroying groups of people. Such similarities form the basis of my speculation that Shelley appropriated and inverted Gillray's imagery.

Anarchy rides throughout the country rather like a Tudor monarch. His progress is described as a 'Pageant' (XIII), yet it is a particularly destructive one. The dignity of state pageantry was very definitely in the eye of the beholder. The people have been coerced into believing that the Monarchy really does represent law and order. This is why 'The adoring multitude' allows itself to be pulped to death by state ceremonials, which are merely an extravagant mask for a society 'red in tooth and claw'. Monarchy begins to reveal his true identity when he arrives in London, for the people are now 'panic-stricken'. Their hearts with 'terror sicken' (XIV). The Home Office wrote to a clerical magistrate called Hay on 12 August 1819 to explain what constituted unlawful assembly:

a meeting of many men, attended with such circumstances as strike terror into the minds of the King's Peaceable subjects falls under such a denomination.[11]

Hay and his fellow magistrates, armed with this information, initiated the Peterloo massacre a few days later. Shelley's point throughout the opening stanzas of 'The Mask of Anarchy' is that, although the law and order brigade pretend to be moving in to prevent terror and panic, they are in fact the very people who 'strike terror' in the hearts and minds of the population. I suspect that Shelley would have been well aware of this definition of unlawful assembly. Anarchy's train is swelled by soldiers, lawyers and priests as he marches through the streets of London. King Arthur Thistlewood and his cronies were charged with high treason in 1817 for allegedly attempting to storm the Bank of England and the Tower of London. Yet this is exactly what Anarchy and the motley crew of lawyers and priests in holy orders attempt to do:

So he sent his slaves before
To seize upon the Bank and Tower,

And was proceeding with intent
To meet his pensioned Parliament. (XXI)

Anarchy stormed the bastions of the establishment a long time
before December 1816. The parody of legal language, 'proceeding
with intent', only serves to confirm his guilt.

If the Prince is Anarchy, then it is not surprising that everybody
else is in masquerade dress as well. Despair is decked out as Hope.
She lies down in the middle of the road and waits patiently to be
trampled to death by Castlereagh, Eldon and the Prince Regent.
Shelley's presentation of the 'adoring multitude' and this kind of
patient acquiescence raises issues that are explored in more detail in
'Prometheus Unbound'. The people must take some of the
responsibility for the dance of death because they have granted it a
licence to perform. They have not realized that they can rule
themselves. Hope is prevented from achieving a spurious fame
through martyrdom by the appearance of 'a Shape':

It grew – a Shape arrayed in mail
Brighter than the viper's scale,
And upborne on wings whose grain
Was as the light of sunny rain.

On its helm, seen far away,
A planet, like the Morning's lay;
And those plumes its light rained through
Like a shower of crimson dew. (XXVIII–XXIX)

It is this 'Shape' which destroys Anarchy. Shelley does preach his
own particular brand of passive resistance towards the end of the
poem, yet this does not always ring true given the way in which he
almost revels in the bloody overthrow of Anarchy. The death of
Anarchy is followed by a long battle hymn of the Republic delivered
by Earth. She urges the people to

Rise like Lions after slumber
In unvanquishable number,
Shake your chains to earth like dew
Which in sleep had fallen on you –
Ye are many – they are few. (XXXVIII)

This stanza is brought back like a refrain at the very end of the
poem. It may appear to support the argument that the passive
resistance of the many will eventually overcome the tyranny of the

few. The message is deliberately ambiguous, however, since in the context of the poem dew is virtually synonymous with blood. The chains may be like dew in the sense that they will be covered with the blood of a civil war. The fact that these chains have fallen on the people while they have been asleep confirms the nightmarish qualities of the 'ghastly masquerade'. Shelley, asleep in Italy, experiences this nightmare, yet he is able to employ the poet's vision to escape from it. Earth claims that once the people recognize that they are free 'tyrants would flee/Like a dream's dim imagery' (LII). 'The Mask of Anarchy' suggests a number of reversals and inversions. The Monarchy is really Anarchy and what we believe is reality is in fact a nightmare. The poet's dream thus becomes the sanctuary for reality. Earth's main problem is in trying to convey this reality in positive terms. She starts off by defining freedom solely in terms of its opposites and the stanzas in which her approach is more positive are some of the weakest in the poem:

For the labourer thou art bread,
And a comely table spread
From his daily labour come
In a neat and happy home.

Thou art clothes, and fire, and food
For the trampled multitude –
No – in countries that are free
Such starvation cannot be
As in England now we see. (LIV–LV)

Similarly, the positive call for a 'vast assembly' of the people seems to lack the power of the early sections of the poem. This is why Richard Holmes is right to describe it as a poem of political protest. Shelley was protesting against the fact that politics was a 'ghastly masquerade'. He is not listened to by political historians because they have, rather like Wordsworth in 'Peter Bell the Third', been bought by the Devil and are footmen in his service. Their bad prayers are still adored by the multitude.

10 Lord Byron's speaking part

Speaking parts

I wonder whether aspiring politicians still take William Hamilton's *Parliamentary Logic* (1808) to bed with them. I suspect that they may feel a 'single-speech' orator, like a one-book professor, is not a particularly credible person. Hamilton's only claim to fame may appear to be a brilliant maiden speech, which bowled the Commons over in 1775. His advice on how to perfect the craft of the plausible should still not be underrated. He knew a bit about defending the indefensible:

> When you cannot convince, a heap of comparisons will dazzle . . . Have a method; but conceal it . . . . If your cause is too bad, call in aid the party: if the party is bad, call in aid the cause. If neither is good, wound the opponent.

Those accustomising themselves to public speaking might find the section in which Hamilton explains how to *'hesitate and appear to boggle'*[1] in the middle of a carefully prepared speech of particular interest, for they could then make a virtue out of necessity.

Byron preferred his orators, like his women, to have had a little more experience. He was particularly impressed by the parliamentary career of his friend, Richard Brinsley Sheridan. Sheridan entered the Commons in 1780, after a spell as a dramatist, which was as brief as it was dazzling. He soon established himself as both a cut-and-thrust debater and set-piece orator for the Whigs. His finest hour, or, to be more precise, five and a half hours, was probably the speech he gave during the proceedings against Warren Hastings on 7 February 1787. He gave a repeat performance of it the following year before the House of Lords. This time it took him four sittings to get through the speech. The setting, as well as the delivery, of these speeches indicate that parliamentary theatre is hardly an invention of popular newspapers and television cameras.

There were overnight queues in 1788 and there was, apparently, chaos when the doors were finally opened. Those with tickets might have paid up to £50 for them on the black market.[2] Coleridge, in his sonnet on Sheridan, described him as the 'Apostate by the brainless rout ador'd'. Sheridan did win a closely contested popular election at Westminster in 1806, but could never really be described as a platform orator. The 'rout' he appealed to were the 'brainless' people who went to Drury Lane and the other London theatres, instead of wrestling with Coleridge's poetry.

Boy Byron was fond of reminding people that, when he grew up, he was going to blaze a trail of rhetorical glory through the House of Lords. Harrow is at least half way up the political hill. Byron studied classical oratory there and took part in rhetorical competitions. Robert Peel, a future Prime Minister, was one of his contemporaries. Byron later made a study of the speeches of great modern orators and listened to some parliamentary debates from the gallery. He took his seat, with his usual embarrassed bravado, on 13 March 1809 and attended a few debates. His parliamentary career only really began, however, after Childe Byron had returned from his travels. He wanted to initiate a new golden age of oratory. According to his particular version of political pastoralism, dead politicians were great performers rather than staid statesmen. 'The Curse of Minerva' was primarily concerned with suggesting that Lord Elgin ought to lose his marbles, but his shabby conduct is also presented as part of a wider pattern of decay and corruption. Parliament is not immune from this general trend:

Then in the senate of your sinking state
Show me the man whose counsels may have weight.
Vain is each voice where tones could once command;
E'en factions cease to charm a factious land: (273–6)[3]

'Hints from Horace', which was also written before Byron took up his parliamentary duties, contains further references to the rotten state of political oratory.

Byron resumed his seat on 15 January 1812 and lost his parliamentary virginity on 27 February, when he made an impassioned plea on behalf of the Luddites. He was on his hind legs again on 21 April to deliver a speech on the treatment of Irish Roman Catholics. It would be dangerous to take Byron's apparent cynicism about his parliamentary affairs too literally. He always affected to despise what he really wanted. Grapes turn sour, so he liked to turn sourly on them before they did so. He dug himself a hole, but really wanted to be pushed out of it. His attendance record during 1812 was good and he appears to have been just as keen to play the orator as the rising famous author. There were a number of people, notably Lady Oxford, who believed that a new political star might be born. Byron continued to attend debates in the Lords in 1813 and used to listen to ones in the Commons as well. He delivered a short speech on 1 June in favour of the activities of the veteran reformer, Major John Cartwright. When Lady Oxford left England shortly afterwards, however, his interest and enthusiasm began to wane. Peccadilloes in Piccadilly became more important than performances in Parliament. The Senator became a *salon* centaur. Byron, like his hero Don Juan, was a surprisingly passive person. He preferred careers and girls to find him rather than to seek them out. Enthusiasm was also rather bad form for an aristocrat. Cynical disdain and lethargy, however, masked a strong desire to succeed in Parliament.[4]

The evidence for such an interpretation comes partially from the later poetry, in which the failure to win a glittering political prize smoulders away beneath the apparently light-hearted surface. One of the house guests at Norman Abbey, in Canto XIII of *Don Juan*, is a bright, young orator. Byron pokes fun at his laboured eloquence. Byronic parody is, however, usually self-parody. Norman Abbey is probably Byron's beloved Newstead, but the actual gathering of the beau-monde which is being satirized here is probably one of the country house parties Byron attended during the summer recess of 1812. It may be based on the Holland House set, who indulged in some gentle political sparring at Cheltenham that year. The instant success of the first two cantos of *Childe Harold*, which were published on 10 March, meant that Byron was a great catch for literary hostesses, but his political convictions endeared him to political hosts as well.

Byron cast Lord Holland, a middle-of-the-road Whig, in the role of his political mentor. He consulted him about how to frame his maiden speech about the Luddites. His tone was surprisingly diplomatic:

I believe your Lordship does not coincide with me entirely on this subject, & most cheerfully & sincerely shall I submit to your superior judgment & experience, & take some other line of argument against ye bill, or be silent altogether, should you deem it more adviseable.[5]

It is thus somewhat ironic that the Lord Amundeville–Lord Holland character should be criticized in *Don Juan* for being a political trimmer. He covers his options by being 'always a patriot, and sometimes a placeman'.[6] He also, incidentally, stages little shows, such as estate dinners, to further his political career. Holland was quite prepared to help Byron establish himself in the Lords, although he had two major criticisms of the aspiring orator. First, Byron was not a real party man, since he despised parliamentary procedure and diplomacy. He was not averse to likening such protocol to a mummers' show. Second, Holland considered Byron's style of delivery to be much too flamboyant for day-to-day parliamentary debating. This outrageousness may have caused some unintentional mirth during the second speech. It created bad feeling during the third. Byron went over the top too often with his verbal swagger-stick.

The apparent discrepancy between Byron's tactful approach to Holland and his later performances is an interesting one. The most familiar Byronic *persona* is probably that of the alienated outsider, who, even when he stands among the crowd, refuses to be one of them. Byron derived a certain amount of pleasure from the fact that, during his third speech, he stood almost alone against the rest of the House. Yet he may have only adopted this swaggering attitude after the failure of diplomatic overtures to open up the political main chance. Byron's public character, rather like Timon of Athens's perception of humanity, can only be understood in terms of extremes. He became, at one extreme, Lord Byron, who had been born and bred to be one of the natural leaders of society. His rightful place was in the Senate and his literary tastes were formal and classical. He might even get some deer for his park. Yet Byron was what might be described as an accidental aristocrat. He did not gain his title by lottery, but it might well have felt like that. The poor boy from Aberdeen woke up to find himself the heir to a title. This in itself was bound to create tensions, but these were in turn exaggerated by the fact that the Byrons were not very high up the aristocratic pecking order. When Byron took his seat in 1809, many were surprised to learn about the existence of this obscure peerage. It is customary to think of Byron as the great bedazzler, and yet he could also be bedazzled by aristocratic high fliers such as Caro Lamb. His sense of social unease was further exaggerated by physical deformity. The extreme measures became a way of escaping from these tensions. He became the aristocrat's aristocrat, but his obsession with crests, which he took with him to Italy, betrayed all the anxieties of the *parvenu*. Even his close friends such as Shelley felt that he overplayed the part. He might, alternatively, opt for the extreme of flash George Gordon, the very eighteenth-century writer of witty, satirical verse. He enjoyed playing fleshy George Gordon, whose loose living finally shocked the unshockable generation. He also pushed the Romantic outsider to geographical and psychological extremes in *Childe Harold's Pilgrimage* and later work. At one level, the Regency period may have got the literary hero it really deserved in Byron, the minor aristocrat who enjoyed a common touch or three. Yet Byron's public characters were as complex as Regency society was superficial. The projection of the alienated hero, the savage satirist and the loose liver may all have been, initially at least, masks which Byron wore in anticipation of the humiliation of his rejection as Lord Byron, peer without peer in the realms of statesmanship. The problem involved in studying his brief parliamentary career is that the evidence about it is tangled over with webs of camouflage. Defence mechanisms, which explode like landmines, obscure the view. Hector Berlioz's Byron, the so-called Byronic Byron, has become so familiar that there is a very real danger of forgetting that he may also have had, or wanted to have, more in common with the Lord Hollands of the political world than he was ever prepared to admit to consistently. *The Bride of Abydos* (1813) was, incidentally, dedicated to Holland. Byron may well have been parodying his own aspirations in the portrayal of Lord Amundeville in *Don Juan*.

Byron revelled in the fact that his style of public speaking was not particularly parliamentary. Politicians, then as now, could get away with camping it up outrageously at large public meetings, but such histrionics usually appeared faintly ridiculous in Parliament itself. Television directors often maintain that they are in the business of curing old hams. The theatre may afford opportunities for extravagant showmen, but television acting, like parliamentary acting, tends to thrive on understatement. William Hamilton's carefully rehearsed throwaway lines could be more effective than Byron's grand, hectoring manner. Sheridan, it will be remembered, made his reputation with comedies of manners rather than tragedies. Byron felt that his own delivery was loud enough. It may, perhaps, have been too loud. He also realized that it was rather theatrical: in other words that he had not mastered the particular conventions of understated parliamentary theatre. It is hard to tell whether he deliberately decided to ignore these conventions. He certainly believed that Parliament ought to be used as a platform from which to address the country at large. He perhaps felt an urge to put the newspapers out of business by delivering his message directly. *Manfred* (1817) contains one of the many interesting references in the later poetry back to the parliamentary career. The hero remembers his 'earthly visions' and 'noble aspirations' to make his own 'the mind of other men' and thus become 'The enlightener of nations'.[7] An orthodox interpretation might stress, then, that Byron deliberately flouted the rules of the parliamentary game because he wanted to play another one. This has much to recommend it. It may be worth bearing in mind, however, that Byron's objections might have been practical as well as theoretical. He refused to play the game for fear that he might fail rather conspicuously at it. His fear of failure bordered on the obsessive. Perhaps that was why, in certain fields, he achieved so much. Perhaps that was why all forms of theatre tended to resist his incredibly *gauche* advances.

Byron's maiden speech was, inevitably, too well researched and stylistically honed. Although he was a fast worker when it came, among other things, to writing poetry, he laboured long and hard at his parliamentary speeches. When a certain W. J. Baldwin asked him in 1813 to present a petition on the prison system, he replied that he did not have the

quickness of comprehension sufficient to enable me at a few hours notice to do justice to a subject which I regard as of too much importance to hazard the interests of the petitioners by a premature & precipitate pressure of the question upon the legislature . . . .[8]

He spoke many a true word in excuse as in jest. He asked Lord Holland to present the petition instead. This request was accompanied by an apology for the 'variety of impudencies'[9] Byron had uttered within the sacred portals of the House of Lords. Old Harrovians would have noticed that the maiden speech was tied to old school methods of construction and delivery. It opened with a reminder that it was based on personal experience. Newstead was in the heart of King Ludd's country. Byron then offered some reflections on the causes of the present discontents:

the real cause of these distresses and consequent disturbances lies deeper. When we are told that these men are leagued together not only for the destruction of their own comfort, but of their very means of subsistence, can we forget that it is the bitter policy, the destructive warfare of the last eighteen years, which had destroyed their comfort, your comfort, all men's comfort? That policy, which, originating with 'great statesmen now no more', has survived the dead to become a curse on the living, unto the third and fourth generation![10]

He then moved on to an attack on the forces of law and order. Such a theme was to become a familiar Byronic set-to-piece, yet, in this carefully constructed piece, he grasped the reins a little too tightly:

Such marchings and counter-marchings! from Nottingham to Bullwell, from Bullwell to Banford, from Banford to Mansfield! and when at length the detachments arrived at their destination, in all 'the pride, pomp and circumstance of glorious war', they came just in time to witness the mischief which had been done, and ascertain the escape of the perpetrators, to collect the '*spolia opima*' in the fragments of broken frames, and return to their quarters amidst the derision of old women, and the hootings of children.

Byron may have been trying to reach audiences outside Parliament, yet this kind of tag-rag Latin and knowing quotation would have limited his potential audience. Some parallels with nursery rhyme characters might have been more effective both inside and outside Parliament. There was a tendency for all patrician radicals to address themselves in rather a narcissistic way. The speech, unlike the military, did at least go in a straight line and gather momentum as it did so. Byron, who drew attention to gentlemanly mobs in 'Hints from Horace', lashed out here at those gentlemen who capitalized on the threat of mob rule:

It is the mob that labour in your fields and serve in your houses, – that man your navy, and recruit your army, – that have enabled you to defy all the world, and can also defy you when neglect and calamity have driven them to despair. You may call the people a mob; but do not forget, that a mob too often speaks the sentiments of the people.

It was a good debating point, but it is debatable just how much Byron picked up about 'the sentiments of the people' from Nottinghamshire Luddites, or indeed from the Lancashire coal-miners who provided him with most of his revenue. He knew about the *demi-monde,* for, like most self-disrespecting Regency rakes, he was not averse to its bruising charms. Rude mechanicals, both in poetry and life, were another matter entirely. Byron's attempt to authenticate the speech through personal experience was more successful when, towards the end, he claimed that England was more oppressive than anywhere he had been to on his recent travels. Show trials did not escape his attention. The proposed legislation against the Luddites would probably be administered, he suggested as a final flourish, by 'Twelve Butchers for a Jury, and a Jefferies for a Judge'. The speech, which illustrates the strengths and weaknesses of the patrician position, might have been more successful as a piece of platform oratory, but Byron was both too shy and too snobbish to consider moving out of the Senate.

Byron's second speech was concerned with the treatment of Roman Catholics in Ireland. He attacked the insolence of the English officers there. They were probably more effective than the fumbling, bumbling yeomanry in Nottinghamshire:

the Catholics are at the mercy of every 'pelting petty officer', who may choose to play his 'fantastic tricks before high heaven,' to insult his God, injure his fellow-creatures.

Both speeches show that Byron was at his best when savaging the ignoble savages, who actually enforced laws passed by Parliament. He could never really have become a law-maker himself, since he believed that the spirit as well as the letter of any law was bound to be broken. This second speech appears to have been a little bit more relaxed than the first one. This may have been because the first two cantos of *Childe Harold's Pilgrimage* had been published in the interim. Byron also began to experiment with a more anecdotal approach. He illustrated the fact that Protestants had a 'licence to kill Catholics' by dealing with 'a striking example' from 'the last Enniskillen assizes'. He also told a story about a particular military flogging. Byron used to fight off boredom at Newstead by getting one of his servants to line up a row of wine bottles for the young master to shoot at. He fired away at bottles, pumpkins, walking sticks and coins, not to mention members of Regency society, for the rest of his life. He hit more bottles in this second speech. He shattered the hypocrisy of the conspicuous philanthropy behind piecemeal grants to Catholic institutions. He also side-stepped the issue of his lack of direct experience with great rhetorical ease:

Should it be objected that I never was in Ireland, I beg leave to observe that it is as easy to know something of Ireland without having been there, as it appears with some to have been born, bred, and cherished there, and yet remain ignorant of its best interests.

His use of political imagery, although not original, was nevertheless more assured and effective:

If it must be called a Union, it is the union of the shark with his prey; the spoiler swallows up his victim, and thus they become one and indivisible. Thus has Great Britain swallowed up the parliament, the constitution, the independence of Ireland, and refuses to disgorge even a single privilege, although for the relief of her swollen and distempered body politic.

This image of 'spoiler' and 'victim' may also be related to Byron's brand of satire. Childe Harold was apparently rather a deft hand at what Byron described as 'the spoiler's art'.[11] He was destructive and oppositional for its own sake. The particular cause and person were rather immaterial. This was certainly true of Byron himself. He developed a certain sentimental attachment to Italian Roman Catholicism and had his daughter by Claire Clairmont, Allegra, brought up by the nuns. The antiquity and splendour of Catholic rituals appealed to his sense of theatre, yet he held no brief for institutionalized religion. He had been 'cudgelled to church'[12] when a lad. He became the satanic poet who raised Cain against Christianity. He was merely using the Irish religious situation in this particular speech as a means of attacking, or spoiling, the English political establishment. The 'spoiler' and 'victim' are, in this and other cases, 'one and indivisable'. Byron was the satiric 'shark', but he was also, more often than not, his own establishment 'prey'. Byron's satire is based on what Tom Wolfe would call 'double-track thinking'. He affected to despise the English political establishment, but felt that the House of Lords was the only place to make such criticisms in. Track one plays new wave radicalism, while track two plays more old-fashioned, established tunes. Byron was the great scourge of such double-tracking, or what he himself would call double-fronting, yet these attacks may need to be seen in terms of self-parody as well.

Byron was not the only aristocrat, or member of the 'genteel part of the reformers',[13] who liked to keep the radical fires burning inside the comfortable chamber of the House of Lords itself. He was, for instance, aided and abetted by 'red' Earl Stanhope, when he petitioned on behalf of Major Cartwright. Lofty ideals about patrician senators have a habit of degenerating into the reality of eccentric noblemen. Stanhope had at least courage and convictions, which was more than could be said for most of his contemporaries. Byron, the 'shark', caught young political noblemen for his 'prey' in Canto XI of *Don Juan*:

They are young, but know not youth – it is anticipated;
  Handsome but wasted, rich without a sou;
Their vigour in a thousand arms is dissipated;
  Their cash comes *from*, their wealth goes *to* a Jew;
Both senates see their nightly votes participated
  Between the tyrant's and the tribunes' crew;
And having voted, dined, drank, gamed, and whored,
The family vault receives another lord. (LXXV)

Byron catches himself in his own satiric jaws. *Don Juan* certainly gives the appearance of being discursive and digressive. The poet seems just to be slicing into slices of life almost at random, yet one of the interesting things about Byron's shooting gallery is that the same targets have a habit of reappearing with unmonotonous regularity. The parliamentary career he set his heart on was to elude his deceptively tentative grasp. Byron needed constant doses of adulation to overcome shyness of manner and slyness of purpose. English parliamentary life has never been famous for such praise. Backs are there to be stabbed not slapped. Byron might have followed in Sheridan's tipsy footsteps, if he had been both willing and able to follow party rules. Yet spoilers look for fights rather than for unholy political alliances. Byron employed the 'spoiler's art' against parliamentary life throughout *Don Juan*. It was one of the bottles he got most satisfaction out of shooting down. The satisfaction probably came from being able to pretend that the system was almost beneath his contempt. The dissatisfaction must have come from an inability to act on this belief.

Leaden Castlereagh

This failure to consummate senatorial desires provided the cutting edge to Byron's satirical thrusts against Castlereagh, who was a very dull and dogged speaker. Byron, in common with most self-respecting radicals, had a healthy dislike of Castlereagh's unhealthy policies in Ireland, Europe and, closer to the bone, at home. He also became obsessed by the eventual Leader of the House of Commons' pedestrian attempts to explain away such policies. Such an approach was by no means unique to Byron. *The Examiner*, for instance, was a great connoisseur of Castlereagh's lack of wit as well as lack of wisdom. Byron made the point more pointedly by keeping the witless politician in his sights throughout *Don Juan*. The Dedication contains a particularly good caricature impression of 'The Intellectual eunuch Castlereagh':

Cold-blooded, smooth-faced, placid miscreant!
   Dabbling its sleek young hands in Erin's gore,
And thus for wider carnage taught to pant,
   Transferr'd to gorge upon a sister shore,
The vulgarest tool that Tyranny could want,
   With just enough of talent, and no more,
To lengthen fetters by another fix'd,
And offer poison long already mix'd. (XII)

His satiric, satanic majesty followed this grotesque description with a swipe at Castlereagh's castrated oratory:

An orator of such set trash of phrase
   Ineffably – legitimately vile,
That even its grossest flatterers dare not praise,
   Nor foes – all nations – condescend to smile; (XIII)

Castlereagh abused figures of speech in the same way that he abused the figures, or persons, of his countrymen. He was, Byron suggested in a short satire entitled 'The Devil's Drive', the best cure for insomnia there was. He was a vile politician who would tax heartbeats if he could, but Byron was just as concerned about the way he taxed the patience of any audience. Some politicians may be able to disguise their corruption with linguistic and aesthetic plumages, but Castlereagh quite simply corrupted the English language. *The Preface* to Cantos VI, VII and VIII continued the good fight against political and linguistic corruption. Byron stressed that somebody did not automatically go out of satiric season just because he committed suicide. Castlereagh was still foul game:

As a minister, I, for one of millions, looked upon him as the most despotic in intention, and the weakest in intellect, that ever tyrannised over a country. It is the first time indeed since the Normans that England has been insulted by a *minister* (at least) who could not speak English, and that parliament permitted itself to be dictated to in the language of Mrs Malaprop.

The way in which the stage-managers of the state theatricals capitalized on Castlereagh's suicide provided an added urgency to Byron's need to publish about the damned man:

if a poor radical, such as Waddington or Watson, had cut his throat, he would have been buried in a cross-road, with the usual appurtenances of the stake and mallet. But the minister was an elegant lunatic – a sentimental suicide – he merely cut the 'carotid artery', (blessings on their learning!) and lo! the pageant, and the Abbey! (p. 730)

The pageantry of society was used to cover up its hypocrisy. It was, on this particular occasion, used to provide an elegant cloak to disguise the facts about a scandalously inelegant and unintelligent man.

Byron continued to blast away at the inarticulate, drawling Castlereagh in the rest of *Don Juan*. He attempted to bag his particular brand of diplomatically phrased nonsense in Canto IX:

Oh, gentle ladies! should you seek to know
    The import of this diplomatic phrase,
Bid Ireland's Londonderry's Marquess show
    His parts of speech; and in the strange displays
Of that odd string of words, all in a row,
    Which none divine, and every one obeys,
Perhaps you may pick out some queer *no* meaning,
Of that weak wordy harvest the sole gleaning.

I think I can explain myself without
    That sad inexplicable beast of prey –
That Sphinx, whose words would ever be a doubt,
    Did not his deeds unriddle them each day –
That monstrous hieroglyphic – that long spout
    Of blood and water, leaden Castlereagh!
And here I must an anecdote relate,
But luckily of no great length or weight. (XLIX–L)

The digression from the digression concerns the way in which ladies of repute refer diplomatically to their lovers. It is, like so much of *Don Juan*, not quite so discursive as it might appear. Byron, the lover's lover, is digging away at the fact that Castlereagh was childless. His sexual parts, Byron suggests, must be as confused and weak as his parts of speech. The accumulative effect of 'strange', 'odd' and 'queer' indicates that 'gentle ladies' would be in for a bit of a shock if a panting Castlereagh dropped his trousers. Legitimacy's crutch would not be a pretty sight. Byron, who was not immune to the charms of choirboys, male servants and girls dressed up as pages, implies that men would be repulsed by the sight as well. Castlereagh was odious, tasteless, colourless and sexless. He inhabited a grimly grey emotional world of 'queer *no* meaning'. He may even be, like the Sphinx, ambiguously self-sufficient. The image of the Sphinx may also connect with the presentation of 'smooth-faced, placid' Castlereagh in the Dedication. Castlereagh is then described as being 'leaden'. Byron's satire is particularly effective here. This description reinforces the point about the cold, metallic personality. It also strengthens the sexual argument. Those unfortunate enough to have witnessed the full horror of Castlereagh's sexual parts might, if really forced to, begin to describe them in terms of a leaden pipe, which stuttered and sputtered forth unpleasant trickles of 'blood and water'. Those subjected to Castlereagh's rhetorical impotence usually did describe it as heavily 'leaden'. Castlereagh was, in every sense of the word, dry.

Byron's satiric thrusts against Castlereagh were particularly sharp and cutting. There is an important sense, however, in which the satire is double-edged. Byron's obsession with the career of this great corrupter of the English language was not accidental. It provided private and public excuses for his own failure to leave his mark upon parliamentary history. If Castlereagh was the one who reached the top, then the reason for Byron's failure was plain and simple. He was just too talented to succeed. Yet, every time he wounded Castereagh, he was also wounding himself by admitting that such excuses were still necessary. His satire, here and elsewhere, may be seen as either savage or light-hearted jests at the scars of a wounded pride.

Pageanting the pageant

Another way of coming to terms with his failure was to suggest that political life was merely a poor pageant. The role of the poet was to pageant, or send-up, these proceedings. Byron told his sister, Augusta, in March 1813 that his political dreams were over. He would not ' "strut another hour" on that stage'.[14] His relationship to the theatre of politics was more ambiguous than this remark suggests. He was frightened of the stage, even though he affected to mock and despise it.[15] He wanted to be an insider who played his part to the full, yet he was also an outsider who perceived that such stages were crudely and cruelly manipulated. He was, above all, wounded by the fact that these political stages appeared to favour collections of mediocrities. Like Shelley, he came to present politics as masquerade or puppet show. He had wanted it to be grand opera with himself in the title role.

Byron complained in a letter dated 3 October 1810 that nobody loved him:

I have really no friends in the world, though all my old school companions are gone forth in the world, and walk about in monstrous disguises, in the garb of Guardsmen, lawyers, parsons, fine gentlemen, and such other masquerade dresses.[16]

The constant round of masked balls and masquerades in London high society must have obliterated still further traditional distinctions between the theatrical and the political and social. Byron was one of the many young gents who attended the masquerade at Burlington House on 1 July 1814 to celebrate the Duke of Wellington's victorious campaigns. Byron went as a monk. His masquerade wardrobe also included the costumes of Turkish and Albanian officers, as well as that of a wagoner. He hurled himself manically into such dizzy whirls both in London and later on in Italy, particularly when he was in Venice. His criticism of the English theatre of politics was not that it was theatre, but rather that it had no style. The fact that the stuttering Castlereagh was the leading strutter and fretter provided merely the most grotesque example of the state of the political play. English politics were parochial, sodden and unkind when compared with the colour and excitement of the Italian Carbonari. They paled into insignificance when set alongside the glamour of the European and South American independence movements. Don Juan pays a visit to Parliament during his stay in England. The debates were shadows of their former glory. There was no orator capable of catching the eye or the phrase. Juan also witnessed one of the important state theatricals in Canto XII:

He saw, however, at the closing session,
    That noble sight, when *really* free the nation,
A king in constitutional possession
    Of such a throne as is the proudest station,
Though despots know it not – till the progression

Of freedom shall complete their education.
'Tis not mere splendour makes the show august
To eye or heart – it is the people's thrust. (LXXXIII)

The dignity or 'splendour' of the 'show' was very much in the eye of
the beholder. The great British public may think that the state
dissolution of Parliament represented one of the ceremonial
wonders of the modern world, but that was only because they were
coerced into thinking it was. Byron, in his role as insider, could tell
them that it was a shabby little show which was put on for even
shabbier motives. He could suggest, in his role as cosmopolitan
outsider and exile, where the real political glamour and colour could
be found. His early poetry fired the imaginations of those
whose daily horizons consisted of the restrictions and burdens of a
wartime, siege economy. *The Corsair* (1814) sold 10,000 copies on
the first day of publication. Jane Austen apparently read it and then
went back to darning her petticoat. The majority read it to try to
forget petticoats and petty lives. Byron was played by 'glamrock
star', David Essex, in the Young Vic's 1981 production of Romulus
Linney's play *Childe Byron*. Some of the quibblers felt this piece of
casting was misguided, but that was because they knew even less
about Byron than they did about the theatre. The fact that the
audience consisted of adoring fans provided an important parallel
with Byron's early poetic career. His politics also took the form of
what might be described as 'glam romanticism'. This was the 'very
poetry of politics'.[17]

One of Byron's objections to Castlereagh was that, after
Waterloo, the understated, parochial brand of English political
theatre began to extend itself to Europe as well. The place of
Napoleon was taken by Castlereagh and his minions. Byron's
support for Napoleon was more ambiguous than, say, Hazlitt's. Yet,
even if the great man had enslaved those whom he freed, he was still
in a very different league to the petty men who eventually brought
down the colossus. He had, for a start, a gloriously powerful
political style. Byron tried to emulate this by having a replica
Napoleonic coach built for him before he left England in 1816. He
thundered around Europe in it for the next six years. It was covered
with the family crest, '*Crede Byron*'. Byron, as befitted a great
literary and social stylist, was prepared to forgive almost anything
provided the style was suitably impressive and imposing. He
contrasted the high tragedy of Napoleon's career with the mean

little productions that followed in his wake in *The Age of Bronze*.
The Congress of Verona, for instance, is presented as a farce:

Ay, shout! inscribe! rear monuments of shame,
To tell Oppression that the world is tame!
Crowd to the theatre with loyal rage,
The comedy is not upon the stage;
The show is rich in ribandry and stars,
Then gaze upon it through thy dungeon bars;
Clap thy permitted palms, kind Italy,
For thus much still thy fetter'd hands are free! (426–33)

Napoleon may have been coercive towards the end of his career, but
at least he was never reduced to relying solely on such tawdry stage
props as 'ribandry and stars'. He was also always his own man.
Byron suggested, later on in the poem, that these new European
theatricals were stage-managed by the mean and unscrupulous:

Strange sight this Congress! destined to unite
All that's incongruous, all that's opposite.
I speak not of the sovereigns – they're alike,
A common coin as ever mint could strike;
But those who sway the puppets, pull the strings,
Have more of motley than their heavy kings.
Jews, authors, generals, charlatans, combine,
While Europe wonders at the vast design: (704–11)

Byron may have affected to be uneasy about Napoleon's dynastic
ambitions, but in reality he was not averse to waving his own crest at
all and sundry. Napoleon marched at the head of events; he pulled
the strings and other people were his puppets. Byron had no
difficulty at all in identifying with such a hypnotically powerful man.
They had both, after all, been whipping boys for the Tory press at
about the same time. Byron was also fascinated by the ruthless
exercise of both political and personal power. When he went to
Jannina in 1809, he saw plenty of examples of Ali Pasha's sadistic
cruelty. His radicalism did not prevent him from admiring this
stylish dictator. Perhaps Hazlitt's assertion in *The Spirit of the
Age* (1825) that Byron's literary 'genius' was 'haughty and
aristocratic'[18] goes some way towards explaining this kind of
hero-worship. Dictators are usually talented and ostentatiously
stylish. Byron, a dandy in aspect, described the restoration of the
Bourbons as 'the triumph of tameness over talent'.[19] He felt himself

unable to identify at all with what he described in *The Age of Bronze* as the 'foreign follies' (765), which had replaced the truly theatrical storms and furies of the Napoleonic period. The stories about Byron's use and abuse of his own personal power are well known, although perhaps the most telling example of his hypnotic effect on people is the fact that even Shelley felt himself at times to be merely a moth to the bad Lord's conversational candle.

The Age of Bronze, although not one of Byron's best works, is nevertheless still of interest for the way in which it plays variations on Byronic obsessions. It contains a lament for the golden age of eloquence which should not be taken too ironically:

Reader! remember when thou wert a lad,
Then Pitt was all; or, if not all, so much,
His very rival almost deem'd him such.
We, we have seen the intellectual race
Of giants stand, like Titans, face to face –
Athos and Ida, with a dashing sea
Of eloquence between, which flow'd all free,
As the deep billows of the Aegean roar
Betwixt the Hellenic and the Phrygian shore. (11–19)

This 'sea of eloquence' is contrasted with the seedy inelegance of modern debaters in both France and England. Byron exempted George Canning from this general condemnation, as indeed he did in both *Don Juan* and *The Vision of Judgment* (1822). Napoleon may have been a king, but at least he did it with style. Canning may have been a Tory statesman, but he was a true orator because he was also a wit and a poet. Hazlitt noted in his *The Eloquence of the British Senate* (1807) that Canning's rhetorical style was sharp but rather brittle. He certainly used the rapier rather than the bludgeon, but was in danger of having it dashed from his hand. Canning's opposition to Castlereagh's foreign policy could only count in his favour, as far as Byron was concerned.

Byron dealt with aspects of the political puppet show in an earlier work, *Marino Faliero: Doge of Venice* (1821). It is tempting to try to relate this play about a Venetian conspiracy to the Cato Street conspiracy itself. Byron was certainly aware of how Thistlewood had taken Fleet Street, if not quite the country, by storm. He began writing about conspiracy Venetian style in April 1820. He had, however, been toying with the subject for some time before this, so the connection was not a direct one. It may be that events in

England helped him at least to clarify in his own mind the horns of the revolutionary dilemma. He told his old friend, John Cam Hobhouse, that butchers could never make ideal revolutionaries:

I know that revolutions are not to be made with rose-water, but though some blood may & must be shed on such occasions, there is no reason it should be *clotted* – in short the Radicals seem no better than Jack Cade, or Wat Tyler – and need to be dealt with accordingly.[20]

This famous declaration of patrician principle and position was as much a criticism of Hobhouse's political activities as it was of those of the Cato Street conspirators. Byron felt that 'Hobby' was letting the genteel side down by standing as a radical candidate for Westminster. His letters during the latter part of 1819 and the early part of 1820 are full of snide references to popular demagogues in general and Hobhouse in particular. He even circulated some scurrilous verses about the way in which Hobhouse demeaned himself by courting the common people. The edge to Byron's satire was provided, once again, by the consciousness of his own failure to make the parliamentary grade. He was worried that Hobhouse, who had been his faithful shadow, might actually succeed in the only place that really mattered, the Senate. This is why he was unable to congratulate him without making some reference to his own abortive parliamentary career:

your last Speech is at great length in Galignani – and so you were called to order – but I think that you had the best of it. – You have done your part very well in Parliament to my mind; it was just the place for you – keep it up and go on. – If ever I come home – I will make a speech too – though I doubt my extempore talents in that line – and then *our* house is not animating like the hounds of the commons – when in full cry. -Tis but cold hunting at best in the Lords. – I could never command my own attention to either side of their oratory – but either went away to a ball – or to a beefsteak at Bellamy's – and as there is no answering without listening – nor listening without patience – I doubt whether I should ever make a debater.[21]

Byron's compliments come out of the back of his hand. He starts by pulling rank on Hobhouse. Nobody, not even Neapolitan patriots or members of the Carbonari, was ever allowed to forget that Byron was a member of the House of Lords. The reference to his 'extempore talents' is there to remind poor Hobhouse of the bad Lord's achievements on the sheets and between them. He then proceeds to blame the system rather than himself. The House of

Lords was full of some very dull dogs, who did not appreciate real talent. Finally, Byron tries to undermine Hobhouse's achievements by playing the flip side. He preferred balls to Parliament, which was just a way of saying balls to Parliament. He channelled some of this political envy into *Marino Faliero.*

The play deals with tensions between patrician and plebeian concepts of revolution. Faliero, although Doge of Venice, feels that he merely has the show rather than the substance of power. He is a puppet of the patrician councillors. He ponders the situation, borrowing much too freely from Shakespeare's English History plays as he does so. He contemplates his ducal cap:

>   – Hollow bauble!
> Beset with all the thorns that line a crown,
> Without investing the insulted brow
> With the all-swaying majesty of kings;
> Thou idle, gilded, and degraded toy,
> Let me resume thee as I would a vizor.
> How my brain aches beneath thee! and my temples
> Throb feverish under thy dishonest weight.
> Could I not turn thee to a diadem?
> Could I not shatter the Briarean sceptre
> Which in this hundred-handed senate rules,
> Making the people nothing, and the prince
> A pageant? . . . (I.II. 259–71)

This bout of the moody Shakespearean blues is triggered off by the fact that a slander against the Doge and his wife has been allowed to go virtually unpunished. Faliero, a patrician to his stiff backbone, is particularly concerned that 'loose mechanics' will now laugh at him. He decides, however, to join the plebeian revolutionaries. He wants to cleanse the state of corruption, but he also wants a more personal vengeance for being treated as a 'poor puppet'. His problem is very similar to the patrician dilemma which Byron faced. He believes in the theory of revolution, but continues in practice to adopt a *de haut en bas* attitude towards revolutionaries. As they have no sentimental attachments to the old order, they can set about their work without too many qualms of queasy conscience:

> You *feel* not – *you* go to this butcher-work
> As if these high-born men were steers for shambles:

When all is over, you'll be free and merry,
And calmly wash those hands incarnadine; (III.II. 506–9)

Faliero, on the other hand, will be forced to kill his own friends and
thus his past. One of the many things that appalled Byron about the
Cato Street conspiracy was that, before his exile, he had been to
dinner a great many times at Lord Harrowby's. The conspiracy,
however, is betrayed and the leaders put on trial. Israel Bertuccio,
the prime mover among the plebeians, has no illusions about the
purpose of this trial. It is a 'public spectacle', which is being used to
'appal your slaves to further slavery' (V.I. 48–9). The show trials
and the show execution confirm Faliero's earlier soliloquies on the
nature of the political power. The people, as well as their Doge, are
merely exploitable puppets as far as the managers of the state
theatricals and pageants are concerned.

Byron obviously felt that both he and Faliero faced the same
problem. They were born into the political élite, but were borne
along by events to think about opposing it. Byron, like Faliero, had
his doubts about how to resolve the dilemma. The familiar political
stanzas in Canto IX of *Don Juan* are as evasive as anything Byron
ever wrote. He claims that he is going to conduct a war of words, and
possibly deeds as well, against all those who attempted to control
and police thought. His motives must be seen as disinterested rather
than party political:

It is not that I adulate the people:
    Without *me*, there are demagogues enough,
And infidels, to pull down every steeple,
    And set up in their stead some proper stuff.
Whether they may sow scepticism to reap hell,
    As is the Christian dogma rather rough,
I do not know; – I wish men to be free
As much from mobs as kings – from you as me. (XXV)

Such a detachment from the opposing factions, Byron suggests,
means that at least his sincerity will remain intact. He can never be
accused of being a member of the 'mercenary pack' of 'jackals'
(XXVII), which feeds off the carcasses of the party political
battlefield. Byron pins a patrician label on Marino Faliero, but
appears to be trying to avoid displaying one openly on himself. His
detached, disinterested and independent position was, of course,
nothing of the kind. Independence, in this particular case, means

independent means. The content of these important stanzas should not, however, be read quite as literally as this. Byron is parodying and mocking the evasive nature of his own particular brand of oppositional politics. He deliberately deflates his own war of words at the beginning of Stanza XXIV:

And I will war, at least in words (and – should
My chance so happen – deeds), with all who War
With Thought;

The sword may be mightier than the pen, but Byron doubts his own ability to take up arms. Martial opportunities, like sexual ones, will need to knock on his door. He certainly wanted a life of action. He told the insufferable Annabella Milbanke that he preferred

the talents of *action* – of war – or the Senate – or even of Science – to all the speculations of these mere dreamers of another existence.[22]

He was forever boasting about his swimming, boxing and shooting exploits, yet, by the time he came to write *Don Juan*, he could mock his own attempts to be a man of action. There is also a hint in Stanza XXV that, despite revolutionary affectations, he will remain attached to the political *status quo*. We, the rude readers, are the mobs, whereas Byron is the King. It is a playfully punchy line. Stanza XXVIII continues the parody of the writer with revolutionary leanings:

Raise but an arm! 'twill brush their web away,
    And without *that*, their poison and their claws
Are useless.

It is surely not going to be quite as easy as this. I wonder why Byron conveniently forgets to mention whether the raised arm holds a pen or a sword.

Byron affected to write off English politics as a dishonest and poor pageant. It was dishonest because it attempted to coerce all the people all the time and it was poor because it had no style. He opposed it with the craft of his satire. His relationship towards his subject matter, audience and himself was more ambivalent than he was prepared to admit openly. This ambivalence took the form of affecting to despise what he really wanted. This was one of the many reasons why his battle against the English establishment was destined to remain a war of words. He also opposed the aesthetic poverty of the political pageant by staging, in his life as well as in his poetry, glamorous and stylish alternatives. He was the patrician, cosmopolitan theatre of politics made flesh. He sent up poor pageants by out-pageanting them. The Greek Committee and others tried to squeeze the maximum propaganda advantage out of his death in Greece in 1824. The reality was, of course, rather different. The leeches were draining his blood almost as quickly and effectively as the Greeks were draining his financial and idealistic resources. He was also 'haughty and aristocratic' to the last. He revelled in the fact that he had been given the honorary title of Commander-in-Chief of Western Greece and was more interested in uniforms than in battle plans. It is still possible to see, however, why his satiric majesty became the inspiration behind European revolutionary movements in the nineteenth-century. He was his own best critic and thus the best critic of political establishments and aristocracies. His influence was not, however, just in this kind of negative and oppositional vein. When Annabella Milbanke was pestering him to declare his principles and convictions, he wrote back that

The great object of life is Sensation – to feel that we exist – even though in pain – it is this 'craving void' which drives us to Gaming – to Battle – to Travel – to intemperate but keenly felt pursuits of every description whose principal attraction is the agitation inseparable from their accomplishment.[23]

It was this pursuit of sensation which in turn drove him to Greece and to his death. He offered all those who were fed up with placemen and pensioners an alternative grammar of politics, in which style and sensation were more important than the graft of the possible and the craft of the plausible.

The pack of hacks

Byron had always equated the poverty of the political pageant with the poverty of literary and artistic expression in general. *English Bards and Scotch Reviewers* (1809) tried to scotch the rumour that literature was both an honourable and gentlemanly pursuit. Writers scribbled and critics quibbled to make dishonest livings. They were in the same shameless ship as dry orators. Byron drew attention to the lamentable standard of contemporary oratory:

Then, hapless Britain! by thy rulers blest,
The senate's oracles, the people's jest!

Still hear thy motley orators dispense
The flowers of rhetoric, though not of sense,
While Canning's colleagues hate him for his wit,
And old dame Portland fills the place of Pitt. (1011–16)

The implication of the passage is that Byron will restore political, as well as literary, life to its former glories. The satire is not as barbed as it is in later variations on the theme, although the image of politicians as court jesters who are in turn jested at by the people has some power.

Dry Bob Southey was one of the many great literary figures that the youthful Byron decided to shoot down in the poem. He was, after all, a particularly long-winded 'ballad-monger'. Byron does get on target with a description of Southey 'verseward' plodding his 'weary way' (230), but the satire in general lacks aim and real urgency. Byron improved with practice. *Don Juan* was dedicated, ironically, to the plodding Southey, whom Byron suggested was the Castlereagh of the literary world. When Juan and Haidée set up a household together in Canto III, it consisted of 'Dwarfs, dancing-girls, black eunuchs, and a poet' (LXXVIII). This poet, who is obviously meant to be seen as small and perfectly castrated, is none other than Southey. He had by now added political insult to the literary injuries caused by his dreary, weary verse. He had become Poet Laureate. This made him, in Byron's eyes, a 'turncoat' and a 'sad trimmer', for he had abandoned youthful radicalism for a government pension. He had become one of old corruption's many placemen. Such conduct was unbecoming. It is important to be attuned to the levels of self-parody in these descriptions. Byron had an idealistic conception of himself as a patrician Senator. He scourged himself as well as the political hacks and placemen when this ideal, like all ideals, eluded his grasp. He also felt that he was destined to be the one English bard to remain aloof from the sordid literary market-place. He only started accepting money for his poetry in 1814. Thus, when attacking Southey as Poet Laureate, he was also jesting at, and perhaps reopening, the scars of his wounded pride. He smacked Southey as hard as he could, because he realized that his own conduct had a smack of Southey's about it.

Byron's crusade against Southey provided the impetus behind *The Vision of Judgment,* which, together with *Don Juan*, represents the pinnacle of his satirical achievement. Southey, the court poet, had written *A Vision of Judgment* (1821) to mourn the death of

George III. Byron objected to it on all counts:

The gross flattery, the dull impudence, the renegado intolerance, and impious cant, of the poem by the author of 'Wat Tyler', are something so stupendous as to form the sublime of himself – containing the quintessence of his own attributes. (p. 156)

Byron twists and burlesques Southey with great bitterness and great skill. The poem opens with petulant St Peter sitting redundantly by the pearly gates. Business has been very slack recently. There is even a possibility that the angels might have to shut up shop altogether. The death of George III occurs in the nick of time and appears to offer some justification for their eternal existence. Byron describes the funeral of the farmer King as being 'a sepulchral melodrame'. Like the funeral of Castlereagh, it was a state theatrical, which coerced the people into accepting the dignity of the *status quo*:

He died! his death made no great stir on earth:
  His burial made some pomp; there was profusion
Of velvet, gilding, brass, and no great dearth
  Of aught but tears – save those shed by collusion.
For these things may be bought at their true worth;
  Of elegy there was the due infusion –
Bought also; and the torches, cloaks, and banners,
Heralds, and relics of old Gothic manners,

Form'd a sepulchral melodrame. Of all
  The fools who flock'd to swell or see the show,
Who cared about the corpse? The funeral
  Made the attraction, and the black the woe.
There throbb'd not there a thought which pierced the pall;
  And when the gorgeous coffin was laid low,
It seem'd the mockery of hell to fold
The rottenness of eighty years in gold. (IX–X)

Grief, like the poets who wallowed in it, had its price. Byron, like Paine, refused to be bemused by the ornate, old-fashioned plumage, which was got out of mothballs for these occasions. The image of the 'rottenness of eighty years' being rolled into gold is even more grotesque than Paine's image of the 'dying bird'. It is, indeed, the most memorable of all the images of old corruption. Byron could smash bottles with one shot when he wanted to.

  Saint Peter, who is coarse and rather sweaty, is woken up and told to expect the farmer King. Archangel Michael arrives to officiate at the traditional debate with Satan to find out whether a soul had been discreet or not. Peter may be a bit earthy and petty, but Michael is the very essence of suave diplomacy. If it was ever decided to close down heaven instead of universities, he could easily become the Vice-Chancellor of some provincial stool of learning. He would be particularly good at sherry parties:

> The Archangel bow'd, not like a modern beau,
>   But with a graceful Oriental bend,
> Pressing one radiant arm just where below
>   The heart in good men is supposed to tend;
> He turn'd as to an equal, not too low,
>   But kindly; Satan met his ancient friend
> With more hauteur, as might an old Castilian
> Poor noble meet a mushroom rich civilian. (XXXVI)

The devil, needless to say, advocates that George III would be more at home in hell. One should feel no sympathy for 'this old, blind, mad, helpless, weak, poor worm' (XLII). He had, after all, been a determined opponent of Catholic emancipation. Peter falls immediately for Satan's rhetoric, but Michael is concerned to see the formalities of debate are strictly adhered to:

> Here Michael interposed: 'Good saint! and devil!
>   Pray, not so fast; you both outrun discretion.
> Saint Peter! you were wont to be more civil!
>   Satan! excuse this warmth of his expression,
> And condescension to the vulgar's level:
>   Even saints sometimes forget themselves in session.
> Have you got more to say?' – 'No' – 'If you please,
> I'll trouble you to call your witnesses'. (LI)

It appears, at first sight, that Byron is parodying legal language and ceremony in this section of *The Vision of Judgment*. Parliamentary procedure also seems to be one of his targets. The angels, we learn, are all Tories, so Satan must represent the Whigs in opposition. His attack on George III bears more than a passing resemblance to Whig speeches in favour of the Prince Regent. This interpretation of the poem as political allegory is confirmed by Michael's response to Satan's desire to call witnesses unlimited:

Then he address'd himself to Satan: 'Why –
  My good old friend, for such I deem you, though
Our different parties make us fight so shy,
  I ne'er mistake you for a *personal* foe;
Our difference is *political*, and I
  Trust that, whatever may occur below,
You know my great respect for you: and this
Makes me regret whate'er you do amiss – (LXII)

Political was a dirty word for Byron, as indeed it was for Shakespeare. It represented everything that was despicable about policy-makers. *The Vision of Judgment* provides yet another example, then, of Byron's obsession with the failure of his own parliamentary career. Michael's speech to Satan is a brilliant pastiche of neatly trimmed and well-moderated parliamentary theatre. Byron twists the knife here with a delicate precision. Perhaps he did not want to wound himself too much on this particular occasion.

Satan, like the good Whig that he is, has more political mouth than heart. He has no real intention of rocking the boat and so agrees to limit his witnesses. The first one turns out to be John Wilkes. Byron offers a marvellous satire on his particular brand of platform pageantry:

The spirit look'd around upon the crowds
  Assembled, and exclaim'd. 'My friends of all
The spheres, we shall catch cold amongst these clouds;
  So let's to business: why this general call?
If those are freeholders I see in shrouds,
  And 'tis for an election that they bawl,
Behold a candidate with an unturn'd coat!
Saint Peter, may I count upon your vote?' (LXVII)

Peter obviously finds the brisk, no-nonsense Wilkes just as plausible as Satan. The satire is effective because Byron captures accurately and economically the flow of such platform oratory. Wilkes begins with a joke about the weather and then throws in a rhetorical question. He implies that he is merely the servant of the people. If they want an election, then he is quite prepared to let them persuade him to become a candidate. His declaration of political principle is followed by the Byronic punch line. All politicians are in the business of purchasing votes, despite strutting rhetoric to the contrary. The political pamphleteer, Junius, is next into the witness box and there are plans to call George Washington, Horne Tooke and Benjamin Franklin as well. The proceedings are disrupted, however, when Southey himself is dragged in by one of the Devil's disciples. Like Castlereagh, the poet is heavy and leaden. He is accused of being the corrupt historian of old corruption. I wonder if such tribunals still take place. He is grateful for any audience and prepares to defend his indefensible conduct. He takes more than a while, however, to get into his stride. The audience becomes restive; Southey is unable to manage even a dry run:

> The tumult grew; an universal cough
>   Convulsed the skies, as during a debate,
> When Castlereagh had been up long enough
>   (Before he was first minister of state,
> I mean – the *slaves hear now*); some cried 'Off, off!'
>   As at a farce; till, grown quite desperate,
> The bard Saint Peter pray'd to interpose
> (Himself an author) only for his prose. (XCIII)

Byron was quite right to suggest that the world could be divided into the bores and the bored. Southey and Castlereagh were the great bores of their time. Castlereagh confirmed this every time he stood up in Parliament, and Southey's ratings soared each time another leaden volume crashed from the press. Byron, the aristocrat, despised Southey, the tradesman, who had 'turn'd his coat – and would have turn'd his skin' (XCVII). Southey offers his dubious services as a biographer to both Satan and Michael. His is 'a pen of all work' (C), master of none. The self-parody is just beneath the surface. Byron, as already suggested, felt that he too had betrayed his literary ideals. There is also just a sense in which he too was quite prepared to write for the devils as well as the angels. The last straw comes when the boring Southey threatens to read out his *A Vision of Judgment*. The devils rush thankfully back to hell. Saint Peter puts everybody out of their misery by crudely clouting Southey with his keys. George III slips into heaven unnoticed.

The Vision of Judgment provides an appropriate and high point on which to end this study of the theatre of politics. It contains incisive commentary on state pageantry. It offers some excellent pastiches of political rhetoric and theatre. It reveals Byron's wounded pride at not being able to become a colourful political performer. If these are 'caricature impressions' of politics, they are still infinitely more valuable and instructive than the leaden weight of much recent historical scholarship. They are also a little bit more amusing. History, Byron suggested in Canto VIII of *Don Juan,* 'can only take things in the gross'. Quantitative political history can be grossly obscene, particularly when it is devoid of qualitative perception. The modern historical establishment, like Southey and Castlereagh, prefer place to perception. The pages of history which you purchase have already been purchased. Byron was not of course the independent observer he often pretended to be. He was snobbish and patrician. He could afford to be. Historians are mad, however, to overlook his political visions and judgements. They are not full of dangerously bad empirical information and they are surprisingly accurate. It may never be possible to send the hacks packing, but at least Byron suggests ways of giving them a run for their money and pensions. He also suggests ways of reconciling oneself to membership of such a pack. That's satire for you.

Notes and references

Chapter 1: The propaganda of the victors

1   See M. Balfour, *Propaganda in War 1939–1945: Organisations, Policies and Publics in Britain and Germany* (London, 1979), for more details.
2   British Museum Additional Manuscript 28, 268, fo. 17.
3   ibid., fo. 19. W. Hart's *Selections of the Correspondence of Robert Bloomfield* (London, 1870) edits out political comment.
4   ibid., fo. 351.
5   Quoted in R. Blunt (ed.), *Mrs Montagu . . .* (London, 1927), 2 vols., I, p. 163.
6   Quotations from W. Windham, *Speeches* (London, 1812), 3 vols., I, pp. 340–56. For a fuller account of the debate, see *Parliamentary History of England* (1801–3), XXXVI, pp. 829–54. The Bill was eventually defeated.
7   BM Add. MS. 27, 825, fo. 144.
8   *Report from His Majesty's Commissioners for Inquiring into the Administration and Practical Operation of the Poor Laws*, Appendix B 1, Answers to Rural Queries in Five Parts, Part III, XXXII, p. 462 c.
9   The Countess of Warwick (ed.), *Joseph Arch the Story of His Life Told by Himself* (London, 1898), p. 20.
10 J. W. Tibble and A. Tibble (eds.), *The Letters of John Clare* (London, 1951), p. 132.
11 Home Office HO/40/3, fo. 30. For more details on the Spencean's activities, see HO/40/7 and 8, Treasury Solicitor's Papers TS/11/871, BM Add. MS. 27, 808, *Report from the Committee of Secrecy* (1817), IV and *Howells State Trials*, XXXII. Secondary sources include D. Johnson, *Regency Revolution: The Case of Arthur Thistlewood* (Salisbury, 1974), O. D. Rudkin, *Thomas Spence and his Connections* (London, 1927), and E. P. Thompson, *The Making of the English Working Class* (Harmondsworth, 1968).
12 R. W. Chapman (ed.), *Jane Austen: Letters 1796–1817* (Oxford, 1955), p. 170.

Chapter 2: George Crabbe's reverence for realism

1   Quoted by J. Wilson, *Green Shadows: The Life of John Clare* (London, 1951), p. 146.

2   H. T. Moore (ed.), *The Collected Letters of D. H. Lawrence* (London, 1962), 2 vols., I, pp. 51–2.

3   All quotations from A. W. Ward (ed.), *Poems by George Crabbe* (Cambridge, 1905), 3 vols.

4   E. Blunden (ed.), *The Life of George Crabbe by His Son* (London, 1947 edn), p. 10.

5   Grimes appears to have broken almost every rule in Richard Burn's book. See I, pp. 45 and 51–3.

Chapter 3: William Wordsworth and the real estate

1   E. de Selincourt (ed.), *The Letters of William and Dorothy Wordsworth: The Middle Years* (Oxford, 1937), p. 784, from a letter to Daniel Stuart dated 7 April 1817. Wordsworth's conservatism is also apparent in another letter to Stuart dated 22 June 1817, pp. 791–4.

2   W. J. B. Owen and J. W. Smyser (eds.), *The Prose Works of William Wordsworth* (Oxford, 1973), 3 vols., III, p. 160. For further details about Wordsworth's activities, see letters to Lord Lonsdale in de Selincourt's *The Middle Years*.

3   E. de Selincourt (ed.), *The Early Letters of William and Dorothy Wordsworth 1787–1805* (Oxford, 1935), pp. 261–2.

4   All quotations from *Lyrical Ballads* (1800), 2 vols., II, pp. 199–225.

5   For more details on the economic and social structure of the Lake District, see E. Hughes, *North Country Life in the Eighteenth Century: Cumberland and Westmorland 1700–1830* (Oxford, 1965).

6   *The Early Letters*, p. 262.

7   Quotations from the 1805–6 version in J. C. Maxwell (ed.), *The Prelude: A Parallel Text* (Harmondsworth, 1971).

8   Quoted by M. Moorman, *William Wordsworth: The Early Years 1770–1803* (Oxford, 1957), p. 497.

9   *The Nineteenth Century*, XXV (1889), p. 42.

10   Quotations from *Lyrical Ballads*, I, pp. 67–82. For the interesting textual history of this poem, see S. Gill (ed.), *The Salisbury Plain Poems of William Wordsworth* (Hassocks, 1975), pp. 3–16 and 119–209.

11   From M. Moorman (ed.), *Journals of Dorothy Wordsworth* (Oxford, 1971), pp. 129–30.

12   ibid., p. 71.

13   *The Speeches of the Rt. Hon. George Canning During the Election in Liverpool* (London, 1820), p. 42.

Chapter 4: The unacceptable face of rural society

1   Details from HO/42/150, Hobhouse to Sidmouth dated 29 May 1816.

A. J. Peacock's *Bread or Blood: A Study of the Agrarian Riots in East Anglia in 1816* (London, 1965) provides a good account of the Littleport incident, as well as of the disturbances as a whole.

2   Details and quotations from HO/52/9, letter dated 7 December 1830.

3   I have drawn heavily, both here and throughout this chapter, on E. J. Hobsbawm and G. Rudé, *Captain Swing* (London, 1969). Other secondary accounts which have proved useful include E. P. Thompson, *The Making*, especially ch. 7, P. Horn, *The Rural World 1780–1850: Social Change in the English Countryside* (London, 1980), and R. Williams, *The Country and the City* (London, 1973). Primary sources include HO/42/149 and 150, HO/40/25 and 26, HO/52/9 and 14.

4   *Answers to Rural Queries* (1834), XXXI, p. 340 b.

5   ibid., p. 462 b.

6   ibid., p. 450 b.

7   *Report from His Majesty's Commissioners for Inquiring into the Administration and Practical Operation of the Poor Laws* (1834), XXVIII, Appendix A, Report of Assistant Commissioners, Part One, Report no. 14, p. 401 a.

8   *Letters,* p. 194.

9   E. Robinson and G. Summerfield (eds.), *Selected Poems and Prose of John Clare* (Oxford, 1967), p. 172.

Chapter 5: John Clare and the politics of pastoral

1   Northampton Clare Manuscript 43, letter to John Taylor dated 28 August 1819.

2   E. L. Griggs (ed.), *Collected Letters of Samuel Taylor Coleridge* (Oxford, 1966), V, p. 25.

3   Northampton 43, letter to Taylor dated 3 June 1819.

4   British Museum Egerton Manuscript 2250, fo. 121.

5   ibid., fo. 132.

6   Northampton 43, letter to Taylor dated 13 February 1820. For Clare's own description, see J. W. Tibble and A. Tibble (eds.), *The Prose of John Clare* (London, 1951), pp. 68–9.

7   Egerton 2245, fo. 35.

8   Quoted in M. Storey (ed.), *Clare the Critical Heritage* (London, 1973), p. 105.

9   *Letters*, pp. 72–3.

10   Egerton 2245, fo. 118.

11   ibid., fo. 40.

12   *Letters*, pp. 120–1.

13   Egerton 2245, fo. 139.

14   Egerton 2250, fo. 146.

15   *Letters*, p. 58.

16 Egerton 2245, fo. 172.

17 Egerton 2247, fo. 152.

18 Details in Egerton 2246, fo. 88.

19 E. Blunden (ed.), *Sketches in the Life of John Clare, Written by Himself* (London, 1931), p. 88.

20 *Prose*, p. 140.

21 Peterborough Clare Collection B5, fo. 85.

22 *Letters*, p. 243.

23 Quoted in J. W. Tibble and A. Tibble, *John Clare: A life* (London, 1972), p. 378.

24 Quotations from the version of the poem in E. Robinson and G. Summerfield (eds.), *The Later Poems of John Clare* (Manchester, 1964), pp. 83–93.

25 *Sketches*, p. 70.

26 *Letters*, p. 259.

27 Peterborough A40, facing fo. 1.

28 This was also published by *The Champion*, 30 November 1830.

29 Quoted in J. W. Tibble and A. Tibble, *John Clare: His Life and Poetry* (London, 1956), p. 84.

30 Egerton 2245, fo. 192.

31 All quotations from E. Robinson and G. Summerfield's 1973 Oxford University Press edition. This presents the poem as it was before Taylor took the pruning hook to it.

32 *Prose*, p. 82.

Chapter 6: The craft of the plausible

1 HO/40/8, fos. 5 and 140–1. Details about Jocelyn's activities from *The Bishop!! Particulars of the Charge Against the Hon. P. Jocelyn* (1822).

2 *The Seven Years of William IV: A Reign Cartooned by John Doyle* (London, 1952), p. 4.

3 It is difficult to deal with caricature without being able to refer in detail to particular examples. Those interested in following up some of my tentative suggestions ought to consult D. George, *English Political Caricature 1793–1832: A Study of Opinion and Propaganda* (Oxford, 1959). It might be worth making a point of paying special attention to representations of Cato Street and the Queen Caroline affair. James Gillray is dealt with in D. Hill (ed.), *Fashionable Contrasts: Caricatures by James Gillray* (London, 1966). Caricatures such as 'Uncorking Old Sherry' (1805), 'View of the Hustings in Covent Garden' (1806) and 'Election Candidates; or, the Republican Goose at the Top of the Poll' (1807) are particularly relevant to the theatre of politics theme. R. Paulson's *Rowlandson: A New Interpretation* (London, 1972) provides a good introduction to one of the other great caricaturists of this period. Rowlandson's 1784 political caricatures

are worth referring to. Some impressions of radical iconography can be gained from E. Rickwood's edition of *Radical Squibs and Loyal Ripostes: Satirical Pamphlets of the Regency Period, 1819–1821 Illustrated by George Cruikshank and others* (Bath, 1971).

4   R. S. Sylvester (ed.), *The Yale Edition of the Complete Works of St Thomas More* (New Haven, Conn., 1963), II, p. 81.

Chapter 7: Catogate

1   *The Times* offered a comparison between the Despard conspiracy and the Cato Street one on 25 February 1820. Thistlewood was not averse to letting people believe that he had been involved with Despard, although there is no evidence to support this story.

2   HO/40/8, fos. 101–2. Further details on these discussions may be found in HO/40/7.

3   HO/42/192, report dated 22 August 1819 of a meeting held at the White Lion.

4   HO/42/200, letter dated 8 December 1819. A coloured man called William Davidson carried the black flag on this occasion. He was one of the five Cato Street conspirators to be executed. TS/11/205–876 contains the examination of John Hacknett, who was another radical standard bearer.

5   For example, the reports of 'B.C.' dated 6 and 7 December 1819 in HO/42/200.

6   See HO/40/8, fos. 23 and 59 and HO/44/5, fo. 462.

7   HO/44/5, fos. 429–30.

8   G. T. Wilkinson's *An Authentic History of the Cato Street Conspiracy* (London, 1820) is just a compilation of newspaper reports. J. Stanhope's *The Cato Street Conspiracy* (London, 1962) does not make enough use of Home Office records, and so needs to be supplemented by D. Johnson's *Regency Revolution*. E. P. Thompson has an excellent summary of the conspiracy in *The Making*, pp. 769–79, which stresses links with the radical tradition as a whole.

9   Privy Council Papers PC/1/4192, the examination of Charles Cooper.

10 *Hansard*, XLI, pp. 1643–4. The speech was read before the Lords on 28 February 1820 by the Lord Chancellor.

11 HO/44/6 contains most of the details about Edward's movements after 23 February. Additional particulars may be found in TS/11/203 and 204.

12 *Howells State Trials (ST)*, XXXII, p. 915.

13 Castle's activities can be traced in TS/11/202–87. Johnson's *Regency Revolution*, especially ch. 4, is particularly good at turning over this worm's movements.

14 HO/40/9, fos. 77–124.

15 My interpretation of HO/44/4, fos. 280–1.

16   *ST*, p. 1546. Edwards was probably surpassed as a master of disguise by Sergeant Popay, who was twisted into the radical movement at the beginning of the 1830s.

17   Details and quotations from *ST*, pp. 809–10. Additional particulars in PC/I/4192 and TS/II/202–871. Ruthven's evidence at the inquest on the Bow Street runner who was killed on 23 February was reported in *The Times* on 26 February. It must have been something of an old enemies' reunion at Cato Street, since Westcoatt, another member of the patrol, had been in charge of 'looking after' Thistlewood when he was accused of High Treason in 1817.

18   HO/44/5, fo. 370.

19   For the influence of the French Revolution on Thistlewood, see PC/I/4192, TS/II/205–876, HO/40/8, fo. 36, HO/44/4, fos. 434–4 and HO/44/5, fos. 19, 260 and 282. *Report from the Committee of Secrecy* (1817), IV, was not just being alarmist when it noticed similarities between the Spenceans and French revolutionaries.

20   *ST*, p. 759.

21   HO/42/201, reported dated 23 December 1819. For another example of this kind of self-conscious disguise, see HO/44/5, fos. 701–6.

22   HO/40/8, fos. 75–8 contains a good description of the oaths and initiation ceremonies. There is, incidentally, an interesting account of the rites of passage into the Crofter's Union in HO/40/30, fo. 276. HO/42/192 and 193 contain a number of reports relating to flags. Passwords were discussed at the trials, *ST*, p. 753. *The Times* tried to deal with aspects of this society within society on 26 February.

23   Most of the evidence is in HO/44/5, for instance, fos. 27, 45, 68, 202–339 and 477–91. The crucial sentence is probably 'The following is what I wish to take place at the close of my cross examination' (fo. 477).

24   The evidence is again in HO/44/5, especially fos. 45, 61, 68, 116 and 132–97.

25   *The Times* reported on aspects of Thistlewood's confinement on 4 and 13 March. Further details are in HO/44/5, fo. 466.

26   Quoted in E. Henderson, *Recollections of the Public career and Private Life of the Late John Adolphus* (London, 1871), p. 111.

27   ibid., pp. 97–8. Adolphus, needless to say, went out of his way to deny that he had any party political convictions.

28   HO/44/6, fo. 35. Additional details in TS/II/203 and 204.

29   *ST*, p. 836.

30   Quoted in J. Stanhope, *The Cato Street Conspiracy*, p. 12.

31   *ST*, pp. 1547–8. Thistlewood was, incidentally, in double leg irons when he delivered this speech.

32   HO/44/6, fos. 135–6. *The Morning Chronicle* carried a very detailed description of the execution on 2 May.

33   *ST*, p. 1110.

Chapter 8: Carnival turns 1820

1   HO/40/30, fo. 200.
2   HO/42/200, enclosed in a letter dated 2 December 1819.
3   *The Diary of a Country Parson 1758–1802* (Oxford, 1978 edn), p. 224. *The Times* carried a good summary of electoral behaviour and practices on 1 April 1820.
4   J. Brewer's *Party Ideology and Popular Politics at the Accession of George III* (Cambridge, 1976), esp. ch. 9, ought to be consulted as an example of how to blend the study of both form and content.
5   Electioneering Bills, Sheffield City Library, fo. 108 a.
6   Quotations from HO/40/11, fos. 198–200. I have taken most of the details from documents in this file (fos. 167–201). HO/40/13 and HO/41/6 contain details on the aftermath of the riot. Additional details are from the *Oxford University and City Herald* and *Jenkinson's Oxford Journal*, both for 18 March 1820.
7   Details from T. W. Whitley, *Parliamentary Representation of the City of Coventry* (Coventry, 1894), as well as from the various newspaper accounts referred to.
8   V., pp. 870–1.
9   These activities are described in more detail in HO/42/200, report by B dated 1 December 1819 and in a letter of the same date from Robert Bevin.
10 HO/40/15, fo. 22.
11 ibid., fo. 37. The fact that the various departmental files are rather thin when it comes to the trial of Queen Caroline indicates that there is probably a secret file, which is still not thought to be fit for public consumption.
12 Quoted in R. Fulford, *The Trial of Queen Caroline* (London, 1967), p. 206. I have drawn quite heavily on this particular account of the trial.
13 HO/40/14, fo. 273.
14 ibid., fos. 277–8 and 319.
15 HO/40/15/, fos. 106–7.

Chapter 9: Shelley's theatre of politics

1   F. L. Jones (ed.), *The Letters of Percy Bysshe Shelley* (Oxford, 1964), 2 vols., II, p. 207.
2   ibid., p. 213.
3   It has generally been assumed that the vigilantes in question were members of the Society for the Suppression of Vice. Paul Dawson is probably right, however, to suggest in his *The Unacknowledged Legislator: Shelley and Politics* (Oxford, 1980), that they might have in fact been members of 'Dr Slop's' Constitutional Association (pp. 179–80).

4 For instance, N. I. White, 'Shelley's Swellfoot the Tyrant in relation to contemporary political satire', *Publications of the Modern Language Association* (1921), 26, pp. 332–46.

5 All quotations from Shelley's poetry are from G. M. Matthews (ed.), *Shelley: Poetical Works* (Oxford, 1970).

6 *Shelley: The Pursuit* (London, 1976 edn), p. 532. I am deeply indebted to this superb biography.

7 R. Ingpen and W. E. Peck (eds.), *The Complete Works of Percy Bysshe Shelley* (London, 1965 edn), 10 vols., VI, p. 63.

8 ibid., VII, p. 20.

9 E. Rickwood (ed.), *Radical Squibs*, p. 289.

10 George Cruikshank's caricature 'Death or Liberty! or Britannia & the Virtues of the Constitution in Danger' (1819) offers an interesting contrast to Shelley's portrayal of the politics of Peterloo. Cruikshank depicts radicalism as a masked skeleton who is trying to rape Britannia.

11 HO/41/41. Sidmouth wrote to congratulate Hay on 18 August: 'I am gratified equally by the deliberate & spirited manner in which the magistrates discharged their arduous and important duty on that occasion & have had great pleasure in representing their meritorious conduct to his Royal Highness the Prince Regent – I do not fail to appreciate most highly the merits of the two corps of yeomanry cavalry, and the other troops employed on this service, but a more appropriate season will arrive for expressing my sentiments upon that part of the subject.'

Chapter 10: Lord Byron's speaking part

1 Quotations from edition by C. S. Kenny (Cambridge, 1927), pp. 9, 14, 75 and 38.

2 For more details, see L. Gibbs, *Sheridan* (London, 1947) and two articles by J. Landfield, 'The triumph and failure of Sheridan's speeches against Hastings', *Speech Monographs* (1961) XXVIII, pp. 143–56 and 'Sheridan's maiden speech: indictment by anecdote', *Quarterly Journal of Speech* (1957), 43, pp. 137–42. L. D. Reid's *C. J. Fox: A Study of the Effectiveness of an Eighteenth Century Parliamentary Speaker* (Iowa, 1932), provides a useful account of the theory and practice of parliamentary rhetoric at the beginning of this period.

3 All quotations from the Oxford Standard Authors (Oxford, 1970 edn) of Byron's *Poetical Works*.

4 For more details on Byron's parliamentary career, see D. N. Raymond, *The Political Career of Lord Byron* (London, 1925), D. V. Erdman, 'Lord Byron and the genteel reformers', *PMLA* (1941), 56,

pp. 1065–94, and 'Lord Byron as Rinaldo', *PMLA* (1942), 57, pp. 189–231.

5   L. A. Marchand (ed.), *Byron's Letters and Journals* (London, 1973–81), 11 vols. II, p. 166. Subsequently referred to as *LJ*.
6   Canto XIII, stanza XXI.
7   Act III, Scene I, from Manfred's speech, lines 104–14.
8   *LJ*, III, p. 165.
9   ibid., p. 193. Byron reflected on his decision to turn down Baldwin's petition in his journal for 1813 as well. He claimed that he had not set to parliamentary oratory '*con amore*; – one must have some excuse to oneself for laziness, or inability, or both, and this is mine' (p. 206). He needed to make excuses to himself as well as to others.
10   All quotations from *The Parliamentary Speeches of Lord Byron Printed from the copies Prepared by his Lordship for Publiation* (London, 1824).
11   Canto II, stanza XXXIII.
12   *LJ*, III, p. 64.
13   *LJ,* VII, p. 44.
14   *LJ,* III, p. 32.
15   See D. V. Erdman's excellent article on 'Byron's stage fright: the history of his ambition and fear of writing for the stage', *English Literary History* (1939), 6, pp. 219–43.
16   *LJ*, II, p. 19.
17   *LJ*, VIII, p. 47.
18   World's Classics Edition (Oxford, 1970), p. 106.
19   *LJ*, IV, p. 101.
20   *LJ*, VII, p. 63.
21   ibid., p. 205.
22   *LJ*, III, p. 179.
23   ibid., p. 109.

Index